AF787444

Max Planck Institute for Intellectual Property and Competition Law

For further volumes/weitere Bände:
http://www.springer.com/series/7760

MPI Studies on Intellectual Property and Competition Law

Volume 19

Edited by

Josef Drexl
Reto M. Hilty
Joseph Straus

Wolfgang Fikentscher • Philipp Hacker
Rupprecht Podszun

FairEconomy

Crises, Culture, Competition and the Role of Law

Springer

Wolfgang Fikentscher
Max Planck Institute for Intellectual
Property and Competition Law
Munich
Germany

Philipp Hacker
Humboldt University Berlin
Berlin
Germany

Rupprecht Podszun
Max Planck Institute for Intellectual
Property and Competition Law
Munich
Germany

ISSN 2191-5822 ISSN 2191-5830 (electronic)
ISBN 978-3-642-36106-7 ISBN 978-3-642-36107-4 (eBook)
DOI 10.1007/978-3-642-36107-4
Springer Heidelberg New York Dordrecht London

Library of Congress Control Number: 2013933135

© Springer-Verlag Berlin Heidelberg 2013
This work is subject to copyright. All rights are reserved by the Publisher, whether the whole or part of the material is concerned, specifically the rights of translation, reprinting, reuse of illustrations, recitation, broadcasting, reproduction on microfilms or in any other physical way, and transmission or information storage and retrieval, electronic adaptation, computer software, or by similar or dissimilar methodology now known or hereafter developed. Exempted from this legal reservation are brief excerpts in connection with reviews or scholarly analysis or material supplied specifically for the purpose of being entered and executed on a computer system, for exclusive use by the purchaser of the work. Duplication of this publication or parts thereof is permitted only under the provisions of the Copyright Law of the Publisher's location, in its current version, and permission for use must always be obtained from Springer. Permissions for use may be obtained through RightsLink at the Copyright Clearance Center. Violations are liable to prosecution under the respective Copyright Law.
The use of general descriptive names, registered names, trademarks, service marks, etc. in this publication does not imply, even in the absence of a specific statement, that such names are exempt from the relevant protective laws and regulations and therefore free for general use.
While the advice and information in this book are believed to be true and accurate at the date of publication, neither the authors nor the editors nor the publisher can accept any legal responsibility for any errors or omissions that may be made. The publisher makes no warranty, express or implied, with respect to the material contained herein.

Printed on acid-free paper

Springer is part of Springer Science+Business Media (www.springer.com)

Foreword

This book aims to show that imminent economic crises can be discovered earlier, ongoing crises better controlled, and past crises healed more efficiently if certain economic laws of freedom and fairness, of risk-taking and liability are observed. Its three co-authors submit their ideas about what free and fair competitive economy and adjacent social cost economy may contribute to foresee, mitigate and overcome crises in national, regional and world economies.

At the core of this concept is a functioning market economy with competition at its center. This economy, however, is also workable in a culturally freedom- and justice-oriented society where competition is absent or of no interest. The central economic value under scrutiny in this investigation is contained in a principle of a merchant's ordinary, recognized behavior and engagement in trade and commerce. Part of this behavior and engagement is an adequate involvement in taking economic risks and carrying certain legal responsibilities if those risks become reality.

To initiate a market, to keep it going, to protect it against disturbances and in case of emergency to imitate it (by "as-if-competition"), rules concerning economic freedom of competition are required. Free competitive bargaining includes entering into economic risks and someone to be held liable if they hit. Therefore, competition involves a decision of whether to keep a risk concealed or having to bring the business partner up-to-date. Whether the one or the other is recommendable or even due, is judged by legal rules regulating fair competition. Thus free competition has to be fair and fair competition concerns, among other circumstances of the deal, the relation between risk and liability. The offer to sell a toxic derivative as well as the incitement to acquire one serve as an example.

The title "FairEconomy – Crises, Culture, Competition and the Role of Law" aims at indicating this program.[1]

The book consists of five chapters, on the anthropological and economic foundations of FairEconomy as a free market system (drafted by Wolfgang Fikentscher), on Rules of Freedom and Fairness (drafted by Rupprecht Podszun), on Risk and Liability (drafted by Philipp Hacker), and on possible Sanctions and some

[1] The unusual word combination "FairEconomy" is to distinguish between the authors' intent to concentrate on a study on reasons and dealings with economic crises from the point of view of competitive economies and social cost economies on the one hand, and the so-called Fair Trade movement that propagates and organizes procurement and supply of food and merchandise from developing countries, produced there under humane conditions such as minimum wages, ILO conforming labor conditions, exclusion or reduction of child labor, protection of environment, sustainability of harvesting, etc., on the other. Surveys on Fair Trade in this sense: www.fairtradefederation.org; Raschke, Fairer Handel. Engagement für eine gerechte Weltwirtschaft, 2009; Kuhn, Fairer Handel und Kalter Krieg, 2005; Stiglitz/Charlton, Fair trade for all, 2005; Warrier, The politics of fair trade, 2011. FairEconomy, by contrast, focuses on the engagement in markets, under fair conditions, in the broad sense of an economic system.

Procedural Aspects (drafted by Wolfgang Fikentscher). Rupprecht Podszun provided the draft of the summary. The contributors joined in working on all texts so that the scientific responsibility remains with all three co-authors alike. The links between the concepts of a free market system (Chapter 1), economic freedom and fairness (Chapter 2), risk and liability (Chapter 3) and sanctions (4) are discussed in Subchapter 1.5 below.

The three authors are affiliated with the Max Planck Institute for Intellectual Property and Competition Law, Munich. Josef Drexl, one of the Institute's directors, encouraged the authors from the beginning and offered many valuable comments. The authors are very grateful to him. They also wish to thank the editors of this series and Dr. Brigitte Reschke from Springer for their support to publishing "Fair Economy".In the Max Planck Institute, a politically and economically independent research institution, fundamental aspects of free and fair competition form part of its daily agenda. In 1993, the presentation of a Draft International Antitrust Code and, in recent years, proposals for the reform of the law of unfair competition to European Union authorities and the World Intellectual Property Organization, Geneva, reflected activities within the framework of said agenda. The present series of economic crises gave rise to resuming the idea to contribute old and new thoughts to the field of national, regional and international market and competition issues and to submit them to the interested public. Of interest are not the histories of these crises as such that began to attract public attention in 2006 with the real estate crisis in the U.S.A., and were followed by the international banking crisis in 2007 and the general economic crisis of 2009, which in turn triggered the debt and financing crisis of 2010 including the Euro crisis of 2011. Instead of focusing on particular facets and singular acts of this drama, the focus is on the underlying story, that is, on what might have gone wrong with regard to the driving forces of contemporary economy: competitive market behavior in a globally interconnected world. Thus, our suggestions do not contain blueprints for formalized legal provisions. They are meant as a stimulus for further thought.

Looking for a general trend underlying the unrest and upheavals not only in the economic sphere – which of itself is broad enough – but also with respect to political, cultural and societal longings, one concern or drive seems to be evident: the longing for individual participation in matters that affect oneself. In politics, the plea goes for democratization, as in Arabia; in environmental affairs, for individual protection, such as against the consequences of oil spills and global warming; in health, for vaccination campaigns, personal inoculations and the availability of pharmaceuticals; in economics, for private law suits against merger and monopoly power. There is a global mistrust in all existent powers. Private litigation in economic matters is a recurrent theme in these deliberations.

In economic matters private enforcement exists in many variations in a number of countries. EU law favors customers' rights, common law countries use tort actions, the U.S.A know class actions and treble damage claims. Younger antitrust and unfair trade practices systems often prefer a public law administrative approach over private claims raised by individual victims of restraints of competition and unfair trade practices. The PR of China, China RoC and Indonesia are examples.

Yet, these jurisdictions also have private enforcement mechanisms in place. India's collective claims use a middle road by rallying economically underprivileged victims around a more powerful and politically respected leader as their authorized plaintiff. Whether to go one way or the other depends on the prevailing social and economic culture and tradition, including the aims a government seeks to achieve by using economy-related litigation. The PR of China, for example, presently opts for government regulated control of economic relations.[2] As is common for younger self-industrializing nations, the PR of China partly uses its economic law to protect business at home in a mercantilist way in order to catch up with competing nations.[3] Under this ideology, the wealth of nations is seen as the wealth of one's own nation, and it takes a while until it is seen as a matter of competing individuals of several nations. While the PR of China understandably took a rather self-absorbed path in the past, it now seems to seek at least minimal cooperation. This is the background for the attempt, repeated in 2011 after a long period of limited activity, to reinforce and expand ASEAN, the Association of Southeast Asian Nations. Now PR China, Japan, Australia, New Zealand and U.S.A. show, if reluctantly, interest in acceding ASEAN as a free trade agreement in one way or another. If successful, ASEAN's legal impact – administrative measures and/or private claims – will be of interest.

One of the major characteristics in today's economic-political world is the desire to turn to democratic individual participation in daily political and economic life, as against the dictatorship of a one-party system, an aggressive theocracy, a militant junta or a charismatic leader. Those countries in the world that want to pursue cultural diversity and tolerant value assessment could be called – for lack of a name – the "Free Nations". Amazingly, freedom seeking nations proceeded collectively, but not under this or any other name, in 2010 and 2011 on issues concerning Libya, Syria and Iran. They acted as nations that wanted to resist cross-border human right abuses and expansionist trouble-making.[4] Would Free Nations settle on rules of economic law and good performance intended to establish and maintain social and economic justice and fairness, and would they do so by assigning standing to the individual victim?

---

2 Hertz, The Trading Crowd: An Ethnography of the Shanghai Stock Market, 1998; Fikentscher, Die Rolle von Markt und Wettbewerb in der Sozialistischen Marktwirtschaft der Volksrepublik China: Kulturspezifisches Wirtschaftsrecht, GRUR Int. 1993, 901 – 909; Chinese translation by Shao Jiandong in: Jahrbuch des Deutsch-Chinesischen Instituts für Wirtschaftsrecht der Universitäten Nanjing und Göttingen 4 (1993) 17 – 37.

3 Masseli, The Application of Chinese Competition Law to Foreign Mergers: Lessons from the Draft on New Guidelines, Journal of European Competition Law & Practice (2012) 3 (1): 102-109.

4 An early proposal: W. Fikentscher, Blöcke und Monopole in der Weltpolitik: Die Herausforderung der Freien Nationen, 1979 ; Chinese translation by Yeong-chin Su, 1985.

Contents

Authors

Wolfgang Fikentscher is an emeritus professor of law for civil, commercial, intellectual property and comparative law at the LMU University of Munich and an External Scientific Member of the Max Planck Institute for Intellectual Property and Competition Law in Munich. He holds course on anthropology and methods of law; his main fields of research are competition law and comparative legal-economic cultures. His ethnographic fieldwork covers pueblo and tribal laws in the USA and Taiwan. Prof. Fikentscher has also served as a guest professor at universities and institutions in Ann Arbor, Georgetown, Yale, Berkeley, Nanjing, Wassenaar (NIAS), Santa Fe and Portola Valley (Gruter Institute). He has published on civil and comparative economic law, methods and cultures of law.

Philipp Hacker studied law in Munich and Salamanca with a focus on competition and intellectual property law. After a foray into the fields of literary studies and philosophy, he recently completed his legal traineeship in Berlin. Currently, he is preparing his Ph.D. thesis on the influence of behavioral economics on European private law.

Rupprecht Podszun is a Senior Research Fellow at the Max Planck Institute for Intellectual Property and Competition Law in Munich. In the winter semester 2012/2013 he served as Acting Chair of Civil Law and Economic Law at the University of Bayreuth. He is a member of the Asian Competition Law and Economics Centre, Hong Kong, and was a Visiting Scholar at National Tsing Hua University, Taiwan, in 2009. He has also worked as a case handler at the Bundeskartellamt, the German competition authority. His main fields of research are competition law, law of civil procedure and institutional questions on legal regimes.

1 Anthropological and Economic Foundations of FairEconomy as a Free Market System

The main task of every economy is to enable humans to meet their needs. An economy is to satisfy hunger, not to create it; to quench thirst, not to make thirsty. To have an economy serve this goal, social norms have to be in place and be applied.[1] These norms may have legal, moral, religious, political (or other) character.[2] They have to be ready to deal with human needs, which in turn represent the data to be judged by them. Human needs may be culturally universal or culture-specific.[3] They may refer to tangibles such as food and clothing, or to intangibles such as music, dance and travelling. Thus, the data to be subjected to social norms for evaluation are of an anthropological nature. The science of economics reflects social norms, and therefore is arguably dependent on an anthropological input. Chapter 1 describes this contingency of economics upon cultural anthropology.

1.1 Cultural premises

1.1.1 The meaning of economy. The fund theory

Since hunger, thirst and scarcity are part of this world, it follows that economy does not do what it is meant to do. The social norms that regulate economy do not seem to work, either because they are missing, or because they are there but ill-employed. Therefore, economic anthropology asks for the proper social norms and their proper employment. The following pages on the anthropological meaning of economy are concerned with this question.

A brief and necessarily incomplete remark will sketch what humans understand by engaging in what in Western terms is called economy. In anthropology, the ques-

---

1 Kottak, Cultural Anthropology, 4th ed. New York 1987, 182 ff., 185 f., 1st ed. 1974/75, in later editions condensed or omitted, see for example 9th ed. 2003, 178 ff.; Fine, Enacting Norms: Mushrooming and the Culture of Expectations and Explanations, in: Social Norms, Hechter & Opp (eds.), 2001, 139 – 164; Joas (ed.), Lehrbuch der Soziologie. 3rd ed., 2007; Rehberg, Artikel: Kultur, in: Jonas, op. cit. Social norms may be defined as rules – explicit or implicit – that a group uses for appropriate and inappropriate values, beliefs, preferences, attitudes or behaviors, cf. Fikentscher, Law and Anthropology: Outlines, Issues, Suggestions, Abhandlungen N.F. Heft 132, 2009, 57, 129 – 140, and authorities cited there.

2 Fora (or forums) are platforms established by social norms that underlie group evaluations. Heeschen, Humanethologische Aspekte der Sprachevolution, in: Gessinger/von Rahden, Theorien vom Ursprung der Sprache, vol. 2, 1988, 121. 232; on kinds of fora Fikentscher (Fn. 1), 130 ff.

3 A list of authorities on universals and a discussion of some related theories, also with regard to economics, in: Fikentscher, Intellectual Property and Competition - Human Economic Universals or Cultural Specificities?, International Review of Industrial Property and Copyright (IIC) 2/2007, 137, 149 ff., 154 f.

tion is answered by cultural-economic fund theory.[4] Fund theory may be said to be at the hub of basic economic anthropology. It can be found, e.g., in the writings of Karl Polanyi, George Dalton, Paul Bohannan, Conrad Phillip Kottak, and Marvin Harris.[5] *Fund theory* and its implications, as developed chiefly by Kottak, divides the activity of economizing (in a wide sense) into five "funds": Economizing may contribute to (1) subsistence, (2) replacement (such as filling up depleted stocks, watering plants or reseeding wild rice), (3) a "social fund", (4) a "ceremonial fund", (5) or making a surplus, a rent, be it for a superior who collects taxes, or for private ends ("rent fund"). Rent-seeking, according to Kottak, leads to unequal distribution of means of production (p. 186), thus to stratification of society, divided labor, urbanization, and finally to formation of states (p. 182 ff.). From rent-seeking also follows what in economic theory is called scarcity (p. 185). In a stable subsistence or replacement oriented society, whether or not enriched by a social or ceremonial fund, people may say: "We have all we need." In a society with divided labor, (that is, after what V. Gordon Childe called the urban revolution around 8000 B.C.E.[6]) scarcity becomes synonymous with a lack of resources in the rent fund.

Apparently only the rent fund, with its specific concept of scarcity in a society of divided labor, brings about economic alternatives and, hence, rivalry. This is important for the concept of the individual (or subjective) market, which should be distinguished from the objective market that may also be found in subsistence, replace-

---

4 As such, fund theory is little developed. "Fund" in this context is the mere name of the reason why a culture engages in what the Western mind would call economic activity. See Kottak (Fn. 1 and 5).

5 Polanyi, The Economy as an Instituted Process, in: Polani/Arensburg/Pearson (eds.), Trade and Markets in the Early Empires, Ill 1957, 243, reprinted in E.E. LeClair/H. K. Schneider (eds.), Economic Anthropology: Readings in Theory and Analysis, 1968 (orig. 1961), 122, sees economy as a bundle of exchanges, the three types of exchanges being market, redistribution, and reciprocity. Dalton, Economic Theory and Primitive Society, 63 American Anthropologist 1961, 1 – 25; idem, Primitive, Archaic and Modern Economies: Karl Polanyi's Contribution to Economic Anthropology, in: Helm (ed.), Essays in Economic Anthropology, 1965, 1; cf., idem, Tribal and Peasant Economics, 1957. Dalton and the Bohannans (Paul Bohannan/Laura Bohannen, Tiv Economy, Ill. 1968) distinguish marketless societies, societies for which markets have only limited importance, and modern markets, starting thus from a uniform type of human economic activity and neglecting the possibility of different kinds of economic engagement in general, for example such as the fund theory does. The essence of economy according to anthropologists Kottak (Fn. 1, above) and Marvin Harris, Cultural Anthropology, 4th ed. 1995, 98 (1st ed. 1983, 6th ed. 2003, with Orna Johnson) consists in a series of attributes: For Kottak, economy is a population's production, distribution, and consumption of resources. For Harris economy is a set of institutions that combine technology, labor, and natural resources to produce and distribute goods and services. According to Kottak economy has several possible motivations, not just maximization of profits. Harris distinguishes, what he calls economizing, in a wider sense as an activity that varies between cultures as to its premises and consequences, from economizing in a narrower sense that is maximizing benefits while minimizing cost such as collecting food for survival; see also Plattner, Economic Anthropologgy, 1989, 13; and Fikentscher, Culture, Law and Economics, 2004, 25 f.; idem (Fn. 3) 140 – 142; idem (Fn. 1) Chap. 10 II. 1.).

6 Childe, The Dawn of European Civilisation, 1925; idem, The Urban Revolution, Town Planning Review 21, 1950, 3.

ment, social and ceremonial fund societies. It is this rivalry which is essential for having competition, defining the market in the individual, subjective sense (see Subchapter 1.4.4., below). The (sometimes romantic) theories on "non-competitive societies" established to explain their economies and social structure by Cushing, Benedict, Kramer & Sigrist and others disregard this aspect of the fund theory.[7]

In the absence of rent-seeking, economizing (in Harris' wide sense) promotes subsistence, replacement, social, or ceremonial goals, or several of these at once. Kottak adds another goal without giving it fund character: peace. To the tribes it is adaptive to specialize for exchange in trading with other villages for peace-making.[8] This kind of trade does not have in mind the exchange of goods and services for getting materials or useful items, nor was urbanization intended. Instead, regional exchange networks for clay pots, hammock, or shells (as in Malinowki's description of the Kula trade of the Trobrianders)[9] serves to make or keep peace. Specialization sometimes takes care of local identities as assets in this peace-seeking. One aspect of this desired peace may be to obtain marriage partners from neighbor villages, a practice which may lead to veritable "rings" of exchange.[10] Thus, trade is done for peace, not to fight scarcity. Or, it is peace which is scarce. Kottak calls the aforementioned combinations of social aims and economic strategies the embedding of economy in society.[11]

In sum, the social norms needed in economic anthropology to ensure that economy does its job originate in up to five "funds" only one of which is rent-oriented

---

7 F. Cushing, My Adventures in Zuni, Palmer Lake, 1967 (orig. 1882); Benedict, Patterns of Culture, 1934; Kramer/Sigrist, Gesellschaften ohne Staat: Gleichheit und Gegenseitigkeit (Societies without State: Egality and Reciprocity), 1978; for a treatment of theories of non-competitive societies, see Fikentscher, Modes of Thought, 1995/2004, 263.

8 Kottak (Fn. 1) 187, quoting Chagnon, Yanomamo: The Fierce People, 4th ed. 1992; 1st ed. 1983; and Malinowski, Argonauts of the Western Pacific: An Account of Native Enterprise and Adventure in the Archipelagoes of Melanesian New Guinea, 1922, reprinted 1961. See also Malinowski, Kula: The Circulating Exchange of Valuables in the Archipelagoes of Eastern New Guinea, Man 20, 1920, 97 – 105.

9 See preceding footnote.

10 Bischof, Das Rätsel Ödipus (*The Riddle Oedipus*), 1985.

11 Kottak (Fn. 1) 188; Examples: Economically, big man societies such the San of Botswana and Namibia belong to subsistence fund societies and typically use hunting, gathering or fishing as means of subsistence. Social and ceremonial funds are thinkable and have been observed, see Kottak's (Fn. 1) remarks on social activities of big men, referring also to Pospíšil's reports (Pospíšil, Kapauku Papuan Economy, 1963 in Anthropology No. 67). Replacement funds exist at Kapauku who store harvest and animals (pigs). In addition to their hunting and gathering activities, Kapauku are horticulturalists and as such know the property of storable goods. According to the theory on cultural correlates (Fikentscher (Fn. 5), Ch. 9 IV.), Kapauku society as an increasingly reproducing society should have changed from big man type of societal leadership to chieftaincy because stored property invites envy and, as a rule, defense against theft and robbery asks for a police under an institutionalized command. Since this change did not take place as an obvious case of social inertia, Kapauku economic "individualism" (Leopold Pospíšil) including "Kapauku capitalism" (an expression attributed to Marvin Harris) are inevitable consequences. In Kapauku society, trust relations seem to exist but only at short-range (cf. Pospíšil loc. cit.).

and rivalry-defined. It is the rent fund to which modern economic anthropology turns for information in the first place.

1.1.2 Culture and environment

According to the still most frequently quoted definition by Edward B. Tylor (1881), "culture is that complex whole which includes knowledge, belief, arts, morals, law, custom and other capabilities and habits acquired by man as a member of society." A cautiously modernized version would be more precise with respect to the relationship of culture and society, and include additional attributes than those listed by Tylor, for example, reflect time, and try to integrate biological patterns of regularity. The definition would then read as follows: "Culture is the attribute of a society that refers to the patterns of conduct of its participants – traditional but open to change – in situations concerning knowledge, belief, art, morals, law, custom or other mentally reflected themes."[12]

Both definitions are broad enough to include economy. Hence, in economy culture counts. Culture is in what a human being is at home. Engaging in economy does not mean to leave cultural traits and conditions behind. Whether a handshake is binding is just as culture-specific as the meaning of nodding or shaking one's head.

Part of one's culture is the environment where a person feels "at home," or what it would like to share. The two Germanys' reunification in 1990 was facilitated by Russia's Secretary General Michail Gorbachov's visit to West Germany in July 1989 during which he was invited to see several industrial installations. An anecdote goes that Gorbachov was impressed by the fact that the factory floors were so "clean that one could eat on the floor" that he envisaged a joint system of economic and political "Ordnung" (under this term) for Russia and Germany.[13] It was never realized. But reunification happened. The example illustrates that economic anthropology works culture-and-environment-specific. The social norms that work as basis of an economy and keep it running reflect human cultures and environments. For a discussion of economic universals (that cannot be offered here) this result would be to be kept in mind.[14]

1.2 Societal premises

The foreword identified individual claims and personal rights as vehicles of economic justice. In the context of legal protection against violation of such rights, private or public, more precision than usually dispensed is in order. These rights may be designed to protect free and fair economic behavior. They may also be designed to protect individuals or collectives in those sub-elasticity areas where inelasticity, for social or other reasons, prevents competition from being the most efficient pro-

---

[12] Fikentscher (Fn. 1), Ch. 3, before 1.

[13] The anecdote is reported in: Teltschik, Als die Mauer fiel..., 40 Zur Debatte: Themen der Katholischen Akademie in Bayern 1/2010, 4, 5.

[14] More in Fikentscher, (Fn. 3), 137ff.

duction or distribution enhancing economic factor. It may be unavoidable to direct the claim to participate as supplier or buyer in a free and fair economy, or the right to participate in sub-elasticity markets (social cost and collective goods economy, coupon economy (*Bewirtschaftung*), economic development ("affirmative action economy", *Entwicklungswirtschaft*), and economic control), not only against a private person, but also against a government.

At this point, what elsewhere has been called the Frankish and the Normannic democracy for centuries have gone different paths.[15] A brief digression into European history may be permitted. The Franks, a Germanic tribe from the lower Rhine, were a confederation of smaller tribes (Ingvaeonians, Istvaeonians, etc.) based on a pledge-of-faith system that provided for peace-keeping within the inside, mutual assistance directed towards the outside, and election of a "kuning" or "king" by a regularly convened assembly called "thing" or "Ding". In this manner, the unwritten Frankish federal constitution combines a horizontal element similar to the "*isegoria*" right of the classical Attic city state (i.e. the right to speak up in the assembly regardless of family descent, social status and education) and a vertical element, the election of a governor or governors (Greek: *archontes*, i.e. elders) for a period of time. Another similarity exists with the Japanese duality of Samurai verticality and rice farmers' cooperative horizontality, a combination that after the Meiji Revolution enabled Japanese businesses almost immediately to internalize the principles of the stock corporation. Again, similarities exist with the Iroquois League of Nations (peace inside and common tasks outside), and the separation of person and office (caciques) among the Tewa speaking Pueblos of New Mexico.[16] These seemingly disparate windows of history are important for understanding cultural differences between what today is called judicial review of norms and/or of administrative acts, as parts of the rule of law.

The Franks were first mentioned in the year 252 A.D. The *wergeld*, the indemnification to be paid for unlawful killing, was the same for every Frank. From this the experts derive that there was no Frankish nobility, and therefore no duke as military or born political leader. Instead of noblemen, Frankish kings used intellectuals who could read, write (Greek: graphein, hence *Grafen*) and engage in accounting (hence *Counts*) for solving administrative tasks. "Franks" is not a tribal name such

---

[15] For this distinction and the following text see Fikentscher, Staat vs. Government – eine Beobachtung zum Thema Kulturpersönlichkeit, in: Ziemske and others (eds.), Festschrift für M. Kriele, 1997, 1407 – 1416; more examples in idem (Fn. 1), Chap. 9 II, III. English dictionaries identify the member of one of the historical Frankish tribes as „Frank", the corresponding adjective is "Frankish" or "Frankonian". The modern name for an area (composed of three provinces) of Northern Bavaria is in German Franken (adjective: fränkisch).

[16] Etymologists relate "kuning" to Old High German: "kun" = respectable family. Note the inclusion of the elements of time and periodicity into the structure of Frankish leadership and government. Here the parallels to the ancient Greek city state, the League of Iroquois and the Tewa pueblos are significantly visible; Fikentscher, Zur Anthropologie der Körperschaft – Polis, Genossenschaft, Tewa-Pueblo – (ein Feldforschungsbericht), Bayerische Akademie der Wissenschaften, Phil.-Hist. Klasse, Sitzungsberichte Heft 2/1995, 1995. In history and contemporary times there are not many more examples of early corporate structures of human society.

as Thuringians, Cheruskers, Suebians and Saxons, but a legal status, meaning "free", "outspoken", "brave", "trustworthy", "independent". By using the instruments of pledge-of-faith (to other members *and* to the king), majority-voted warfare, pledge-of-faith sworn accessions of tribes as new members, and value-oriented politics on the basis of Athanasian Christianity since 496 A.D., the "Franks" enlarged their "empire" until 850 A.D. extending from Denmark to Sicily, and from the Channel to Croatia. In the Mediterranean world, "Frank" became the designation for somebody from Western or Central Europe.

"Franconia", the Latin term of said horizontal and vertical pledge-of-faith system of governance, in German: "*Fränkischer Kreis*", officially lasted until 1806 A.D. when it was allegedly ended as a consequence to Napoleon's victories. After Napoleon's defeat, as a result of the Vienna Congress 1812 – 1815, the Frankish constitution was actually continued by Austria's presidential prerogative in the German Confederation from 1815 to 1871. In this year, the Second German ("Bismarck") *Reich* was founded. The confederate structure was downgraded to be upgraded again in 1945 and in 1990.[17] From this structure consisting of equal participants under a leadership to-be-held accountable, an individual's, directly claimable and thus *Rechtsstaat*-conforming right against the entity can logically be derived (*terminus technicus*: "general clause principle").[18]

Although militarily superior, the Norman Vikings of Denmark and Norway under Duke Rollo in 911 A.D. joined the Frankish pledge-of-faith system as vassals and borrowed the Frankish both horizontal and vertical system of government from the Franks. In 1066 A.D. under William the Conqueror, the Normans carried the Frankish pledge-of-faith to England. However, the traditional (and personalized) Norman ducal structure of government (from Latin *dux* = Duke, *Herzog*) never wholly disappeared. Rudimentary Normannic democracy therefore became, in comparison to the Frankish, a system mixed of Frankish *isegoria* elements and Normannic ducal leadership. This made the English conception of societal structure on the one hand more efficient and, correspondingly, less legitimate and therefore more contestable on the other. No Frankish or German king, until 1806, was ever assassinated because you cannot kill an office. Under the Norman tradition, in principle, the liability for governmental debts and wrongdoings is still based on the adage "the king can do no wrong" and not on a breach of a (vertical) pledge of faith. By consequence, state liability in common law countries must be based upon parliamentary act. In the Frankish system, this liability follows from the original con-

---

17 Willoweit, Deutsche Verfassungsgeschichte, 4th ed. 2005; Seif (ed.), Europäische Verfassungsgeschichte, 2003.

18 Art. 19 (4) German Constitution, applied also, e.g., in Art. 17 (3) and Art. 19 (2) DIAC. *Rechtsstaat* and rule of law are not quite identical. Rule of law includes, in form of a general clause, judicial review of norms but not necessarily of individual administrative acts. *Rechtsstaat* offers, in form of a general clause, both judicial review of norms *and* of their administrative implementation (see Art. 19 (4) German Constitution). In short: *Rechtsstaat* is rule of law plus rule of implementation of law. – Therefore, what will be said in 4 below (p. 131 ff.) about an *individual's* right to participate in a free and fair economy and to be protected accordingly is obviously in line with a long historical tradition.

stitutional act of confederation. This means that for common law countries, liabilities in connection with national and international rules for the protection of participation in a free and fair economy, as well as participation in sub-elasticity market situations, need to be expressly provided for. In technical language, this is called the "enumeration principle".[19]

It follows that European and German philosophy and theory of competition law concerning free and fair competition differ from U.S.-American philosophy and ideology. Expressed in catchwords, the European and German tradition builds upon a trilateral system of society, state and government, while U.S.-American tradition starts from a bilateral system of society and government. The historical background of this difference is – as described above – one between the horizontal-vertical construction of Frankish pledge-of-faith organized society on the one hand, and the retained ducal, more centralized tradition as part of the Normannic version of the borrowed Franconian pledge-of-faith on the other. In competition law, on the European continent in countries with Frankish constitutional history this favors an understanding of antitrust as a means of stabilization and reinforcement of the horizontal-vertical structure of organized society and of fair trade law as a means of a general control of unjustified getting ahead by one over the other, also in business. By contrast, in U.S.A. antitrust is an instrument of governmental use in the incessant conflict of power between government and business, a general fair trade law comparable to the continental one and in the broad meaning of Art. 10bis Paris Convention and Art. 2(2) TRIPs being near to non-existent (for details such as the "Mogul Steamship principle" and the "House of Lords' trilogy", see 1.4.5. below).

Sec. 5 of the Federal Trade Commission Act, Act of Sept 26, 1914, c. 311, 38 Stat. 717, as amended by Act of March 21, 1938, c. 49, 52, Stat. 111; 15 U.S.C.A. § 41 et seq., seems to point to a different legal situation in the U.S.A. The Act provides for the establishment of the Federal Trade Commission. Sec. 5

---

[19] Normannic ducal influence in common-law countries – along with Frankish pledge-of-faith horizontalism-verticalism of organized society – still holds sway in the constitutional position of the President of the U.S. The President of the U.S. has no cabinet of ministers, only secretaries of state without a "cabinet" as deliberating body. The U.S.-President may consult with single or several secretaries or with additional advisers, having the choice to consult with either one of them, with others, or with nobody. Although limited by the constitutional powers of Congress and Supreme Court as well as by certain laws, the decision is the President's alone. When Abraham Lincoln one day encountered the disagreement of all of his secretaries, he said. "Seven nays and one aye – the ayes have it." Hans Maier has pointed to this similarity of preponderance of decisionary power and lack of constitutional structure for opinion-forming in the U.S. government and in the position of the Pope who – for quite different reasons of canonical-theological nature – also prefers working without a cabinet and an organized consulting mechanism, Maier, Braucht Rom eine Regierung?, 219 Stimmen der Zeit 147 – 160 (2001/3); for the Abraham-Lincoln anecdote, Maier quotes Hübner, Das politische System der U.S.A., 3rd ed. 2003, 127. – An opposite tendency – German hierarchialism as against Roman, and especially French brotherliness – is alleged by Todd, Frei! Der Arabische Frühling und was er für die Welt bedeutet, 2011, 74 f.; Todds book is based on Todd & Courbage, Die unaufhaltsame Revolution: Wie die Werte der Moderne die islamische Welt verändern, 2008, from the French original "Le rendez-vous des civilisations", 2007, translated by Heinemann.

FTC Act takes the form of a general clause prohibiting unfair competition and subjecting it to broad administrative and judicial control. Sec. 5 FTC (a) Act reads: "Unfair methods of competition in commerce, and unfair or deceptive acts or practices in commerce, are hereby declared unlawful". Thus, Section 5 of the FTC Act prohibits firms engaged in competition from committing unfair or deceptive acts or practices in interstate commerce. Under FTC administrative practice an act is deemed *unfair* and therefore in violation of the FTC Act, if it causes *substantial* injury to *consumers* not outweighed by *countervailing benefits* to consumers, or damage done to competition or consumers could have reasonably been avoided. An act is *deceptive* if it involves a "material" representation, omission, or practice that is likely to mislead consumers acting reasonably under the circumstances. This shows that FTC administrative practice has diluted the unfairness test to mere consumer protection, and confined the deception test to quite severe cases of misrepresentation. This is far from the Paris Convention's and TRIPs' broad standards of a general inhibition of unfair competition. Written U.S. law comes close to the reluctant British approach.

1.3 Methodological premises

1.3.1 The Martin-Rössler-Problem. Formalism or substantivism? Two determinisms and the role of empiricism

The anthropology of economics borders on the anthropologies of religion, law and politics.[20] Interdisciplinary work in these four fields is essential. An anthropologist who is active in one of these four fields is used to look over the fences between the categories and to distinguish between the particularities of either field and the holistic-comparative approach of cultural anthropology as such that results from this interdisciplinary work. Thus, many anthropological issues can be tackled either from the side of those field-specific particularities or from the broader spectrum of interdisciplinary anthropology. Of course, both approaches may meet in the middle, creating an overlapping area of working possibilities. In the anthropology of economics, for instance, this raises the issue whether to approach the overlapping area

[20] The following lines in the text above are condensed from Fikentscher (Fn. 1), Chapter 10 I and II, and from earlier versions based on a series of conference lectures: Conference "Intellectual Property and Behavioral Science", co-sponsored by Gruter Institute for Law and Behavioral Research, Portola Valley, California/U.S.A., and Max Planck Institute for Intellectual Property, Competition, and Tax Law, Munich, August 28/29, 2006, http://www.bepress.com/giwp/default/vol4/iss1/art1; with shifting focuses, the lecture was also given at Arbeitsgemeinschaft Humanethologie, Max-Planck-Institut für Verhaltensphysiologie (i.L.) and Max-Planck-Institut für Ornithologie, Andechs, 17. – 18. September 2006 ("Eigentum und Wettbewerb: Ethnologische Universalien oder kulturelle Besonderheiten?"); at Ramapo College of New Jersey, Mahwah, New Jersey/U.S.A., School of Contemporary Arts, 28 November 2006 ("Intellectual Property and Competition: Indigenous Law Between Universal Norms and Cultural Relativism"; and at a workshop on Visions for Applied Knowledge, Andechs, organized by the Center for Human Sciences (HWZ), University of Munich, 5. December 2006 ("Empiricism and Models").

from the economic or from the anthropological side. This subchapter argues in favor of the latter, reporting on an overview of the mainstream theories involved, and because of their special importance for modern economical-political tasks, some essentials of the anthropology of market and competition.

The approach favored below is neither psychological, nor sociological, nor sociopolitical. Instead, it uses of the tools of micro-economical and (to a lesser degree) legal-empirical anthropology. Empirical anthropology in contrast to philosophical anthropology is a social science, divided into cultural and biological anthropology. Both these branches examine and define the conditions of the human being in a comparative way, and in their mutual interdependence.[21] For example, regarding intellectual property and competition, the biological branch researches possible innate predispositions, and the cultural branch the various cultural forms which intellectual property and competition may take on. There are two general, underlying human themes: the liberty to decide what to do with one's life (= the freedom *to*; for instance, but not only, in the economic sphere), and – when this liberty has produced retainable results – the liberty to own (= the freedom *from* interferences).[22]

The micro-economic and legal approach raises preceding issues: (1) are there economic laws and other generalities that apply to all cultures, and therefore claim to be observed in the first line, such as the laws of supply and demand, limited resources, unlimited needs, rational decision, utility maximizing, marginal utility, cost, perfect competition and market, property rights, and acting under risk and uncertainty, before there can be a cultural specification; or, (2) do we better start ascertaining the cultural variations of doing business (including the handling of material and intellectual property and of competition) before one can arrive at economic and legal generalities? This issue is a main methodological topic in economic anthropology.[23] In this discourse, the former position, moving from transcultural economic generalities (such as the doctrine of marginal utility) to cultural variations, received the name "formalism", and – after a careful evaluation of the two possibilities – Martin Rössler has come to share this view.[24] The latter position,

---

[21] Fikentscher (Fn. 7), 77, 91; Léopold Pospíšil, Le droit comme concept opérationnel fondé empiriquement, 13 Droit et cultures, Revue semestrielle d'anthropologie et d'histoire 5 – 23 (1987), 17.

[22] On the tensional relationship of these two basic economic interests: Fikentscher, Wettbewerb und gewerblicher Rechtsschutz, 1958.

[23] Rössler, Wirtschaftsethnologie, 2nd ed. 2005; Schumann, Grundzüge der mikroökonomischen Theorie, 1992; cf. Schneider, Economic Man: The Anthropology of Economics, 1974; Hertz, The Trading Crowd : An Ethnography of the Shanghai Stock Market, 1998, 21 f.

[24] Chief protagonists: Firth, Primitive Polynesian Economy, 1939; idem, Elements of Social Organisation, 1952; idem, Themes in Economic Anthropology: A General Comment, 1967, 1 – 28; Herskovits, Economic Anthropology: A Study in Comparative Economics, 1952; Schneider (Fn. 23); the leading German economic ethnologist Rössler shares the formalist view because "economy follows always and everywhere certain inherent patterns of regularity". However, Rössler also stresses the frequent shortcomings of neoclassic economic theory to do justice to the economic specificities of many preindustrial ethnic groups. Nonetheless, Rössler holds the basic ideas and laws of neoclassicism in principle applicable to all economies in the world.

starting from the wealth of cultural variations and empirically looking for common points of view and points of contact for comparisons, has been called "substantivism".[25]

The strength of the *formalist* argument rests upon the success of *neo*classic economic theory in the second half of the 19th century. Neoclassics were preceded by classical economics (Adam Smith (1776), David Ricardo (1817), Th. R. Malthus, N. W. Senior, J. Mill, J. St. Mill, J. B. Say, etc.), a theory that explains *observed* economic behavior by researchable inherent rules of general application. After 1870, the writings of Gossen (1854), W. S. Jevons, L. Walras , C. Menger, A. Marshall, F. Y. Edgeworth, J. B. Clark, V. Pareto) and others turned economics into a science that *postulated* economic behavior under certain preconceived fixed theoretical requirements.[26] Such requirements are marginal utility, rational choice, perfect competition, perfect market, property rights, and other models or "generalities".[27] The formalist camp finds the neoclassic economic concepts and laws to be so strong and convincing that it applies them to preindustrial societies as well.

On the other hand, the *substantivists* refer to the many forms of economic behavior which, in terms of Western economic science, can mainly be labeled ineffective and irrational, such as potlatching or circular gift-giving in the Kula style.[28] To quote one voice: "Western economists assume that scarcity is universal, which it isn't, and that in making choices, individuals try to maximize personal profit. However, in non-industrial societies people may maximize values other than individual profit. Furthermore, people often lack free choice in allocating their resources".[29] Other neoclassic tenets show significant flaws when applied to the wealth of eco-

---

[25] Chief protagonists: Malinowski, Kula: The Ciculating Exchange of Valuables in the Archipelagoes of Eastern New Guinea, 20 Man 1920, 97 - 105; idem, Argonauts of the Western Pacific, 1922; Polanyi (Fn. 5); Dalton (Fn. 5); Sahlins. Economic Anthropology and Anthropological Economics, 8 (5) Social Science Information/Informations sur les sciences sociales 1969, 13 - 33; idem, Stone Age Economics, 1974.

Why the opposing doctrines received these labels cannot be discussed here, see, e.g., Rössler (Fn. 23), 33 ff.)

[26] Rössler (Fn. 23), 34 ff.; Gregory, Gifts and Commodities, 1982; idem, Savage Money: The Anthropology and Politics of Commodity Exchanges, 1997; Appadurai, Introduction: Commodities and the Politics of Value, in: Appadurai (ed.), The Social Life of Things: Commodities in Cultural Perspective, 1986, 3 - 63; Schneider (Fn. 23).

[27] This change of paradigms is also called the „marginalistic revolution", for details see, e.g., M. Blaug, Economic Theory in Retrospect, 1985; Boland, Neoclassical Economics, in: Kuper/Kuper, The Social Science Encyclopaedia, 1985, 554 – 555; Rössler (Fn. 23), 35 – 45, 128 – 131.

[28] Malinowski, Kula: The Circulating Exchange of Valuables in the Archipelagoes of Eastern New Guinea, 20 Man 97 – 105 (1920); Ziegler, The Kula Ring of Bronislaw Malinowski: A Simulation Model of the Co.Evolution of an Economic and Ceremonial Exchange System, Bavarian Academy of Sciences, Philos.-Historical Class, Proceedings (*Berichte*) 1/2007, 2007.

[29] Kottak (see Fn. 5) 4th ed. 1987, 144. For other substantivists see Fn. 25. My own position in Culture, Law and Economics (Fn. 5) is substantivist because since anthropology works empirically, economic anthropology should work empirically, too. For literary attempts – none of them convincing – at bridging the opposing views, see e.g. Rössler (Fn. 23), 128 – 131.

nomic realities, even beyond Rössler's doubts: The laws of supply and demand do not work in moneyless societies. As Kottak remarks, resources are often unlimited. Needs, always unlimited in neoclassics, are often limited. Rational decisions are lacking in ceremonial exchanges. In turn, utility maximizing and the concept of marginal utility often yield to what appears as irrationality. Cost calculation is missing or suppressed, whenever ideologies prevail. For both pre-industrial and industrial societies perfect competition and perfect market exclude rivalry and are therefore opposites of competition and market.[30] Property rights may take very different shapes and lack a coherent theory of cost and participation.[31] This also holds true for pre- and industrial societies. Acting under risk and uncertainty is just as culture-specific as are societal structures.[32] All this speaks in favor of substantivism.

Regarding the interface of economics and anthropology, the alternative between the formalist and the substantivist position does not only affect a basic approach to economic anthropology. The alternative touches upon a general societal and science-theoretical attitude towards the social science of economics as such. This is also reflected by the policy of selecting the Nobel laureates in economics during the last decades. Followers of the "Chicago School", a version of a Hayekian paradox-free unfettered "discovery liberalism", contrasting with the Böhmian freedom-paradox-avoiding "sustainable liberalism", have received several prizes. Only later, side fields of economics were acknowledged (history, psychology) but also here deductive *model* thinking dominates. A "substantivist" researcher, whose "lab" is real economic life to be empirically observed and cautiously generalized, can hardly be found. A return to economic empiricism seems appropriate. It is time to shift to economic realities including cultural-economic realities, to be researched empirically. Instead of fittingness of models, appropriateness for humans is the core issue of today's economic science.

The main incongruence between economic neoclassic formalism and substantivist economic ethnology lies in the clash of two determinisms: Neoclassic economy does not aim at explaining observations of economic occurrences, but at establishing a *model* for a given economic behavior, for example: rational, utility maximizing, cost conscious, perfect, etc.[33] Thus, neoclassics deductively and normatively postulate and study, among other topics, model-conformity of actions of an ideal type of economic agent called *homo economicus* with general rules. Whereas neoclassics check reality against preconceived models, its opposite – a free and fair economy in the sense of FairEconomy – check generalizations against empirically observed reality. Defying empiricism, neoclassics are not relevant for reality, and vice versa.[34] Economy-oriented ethnology, on the other hand, is determined culturally by observable economic behavioral specificities, and has no *raison d'être* but

[30] Fikentscher (Fn. 5), 119 – 178, with references.
[31] See, e.g., Rössler (Fn. 23), 97 f. on the one hand, and Fikentscher (Fn. 5), 37, 185, on the other.
[32] Fikentscher, 1995/2004 (Fn. 7), 183, and at the different modes of thought.
[33] Rössler (Fn. 23), 36 f., 39, 71. Obviously and as a matter of fact, not of theoretical conclusion, globalization tends to foster neoclassics.
[34] Rössler (Fn. 23), 37 f.

empiricism. These two determinisms oppose and conceptually exclude one another. This may be a reason why conciliatory theories are so difficult to find. A decision between these two determinisms depends on the role assigned to empiricism.

1.3.2 The Jerry-Moore Problem. Inherent structures or open, but cautious generalizations?

The Martin-Rössler problem of formalism vs. substantivism is part of a larger problem that might by want of another name be called the Jerry-Moore problem because Moore's survey of cultural anthropology succeeds in sharpening it for the reader. The problem dates back to Emile Durkheim, the "founder" of sociology. It also emphasizes the difference between sociology and anthropology as they are taught today. For those who prefer personal names to pale concepts, it relates to the conflicting methodologies of Emile Durkheim and Franz Boas. Jerry D. Moore's "Visions of Culture" was written for students of cultural anthropology and not intended to discuss a major epistemological anthropological issue. Still, the book helps a lot to understand the conflicting positions of Durkheim and Boas.[35]

By lucidly comparing anthropological theories and theorists the author points to a recurring theme: Does anthropology as a social science concerned with cultures attempt a discovery of inherent models, rules and structures of those cultures in order to identify them and hereby explain their identities, or does anthropology deal with observable phenomena, overt or covert, that first of all defy models, rules and structures, inherent or otherwise? If the former is true, anthropology's task would be to check whether known inherent structures are mirrored in reality; if the latter applies, then anthropologists circumspectly may give fitting names to the researched objects, form them to communicable concepts and values, and piece them together to reluctantly proposed generalities. In Moore's words: do human societies and human individuals live according to "preordained patterns" or to individual "unfettered creations" of behavior that ask for "humanistic interpretation"?

These are indeed two different approaches in the social sciences, and it is interesting to see how every theorist presented in J. D. Moore's book goes one or the other way, often without giving account why she or he chooses it. As representatives of the first structure-and patterns-checking type, Emile Durkheim and Ruth Benedict serve as examples, while Franz Boas and Leopold Pospíšil (the latter not being mentioned by Moore) stand for the second observation-oriented approach. It is obvious that the formalism vs. substantivism debate discussed above mirrors the pattern vs. observation debate. The first – formalism vs. substantivism – may even be regarded as a part of the latter which is of general epistemological caliber.

Thus, in cultural anthropology, not only the Rössler but also the Moore problem deserves attention. When "appropriateness for humans" is the goal set in modern economic anthropology, the scales tip to the side of pattern-critical observation and "humanistic" creative activities, to use Moore's words again. The Durkheimian approach of looking at reality in order to examine its consistency with formerly

[35] J. Moore, Visions of Culture: An Introduction to Anthropological Theories and Theorists, 2nd ed. 2004. For the following see J. M. at IX f., 49 ff., 78 ff., 195 f., 367 f.

found structures runs the risk of overlooking reality that has never been observed before and therefore does not fit into established structures. Every fieldworker knows this challenge of professional investigation, of overlooking the green swan because biologists (and Tchaikovsky) know only white and black swans. Giving preference to pattern-critical observation and "simple asking" may also work the other way, reducing instead of expanding generalities. For example, according to a widespread opinion, homosexuality can be found in every human society, even at a comparable percentage. When Pospíšil raised the subject in discussions with members of the Kapauku nation in the Kamu Valley in New Guinea with whom he lived for more than a year, his conversation partners reacted with amused disbelief. The pattern may have proved to be incomplete.

1.4 Dogmatic contours

1.4.1 On reading and misquoting Adam Smith's theoretical propositions

John Holland calls it a mystery, a magic, that in a big city like New York everyone gets his breakfast. He sees no system that takes care of the supply.[36] The reason for his perceived lack of system may be that Holland reduces the use of the concept of system to the sciences, and that the sciences, in the Anglo-American philosophical world and academic tradition, do not deal with value judgments, but with facts alone. Adam Smith, a Scotsman, deals with value judgments, systematically.

Holland's mystery unravels when the observer turns from the system in the context of the natural sciences to the system as a methodological concept in the humanities and the social sciences. The latter concept works, in a scientific way, with values, and value judgments. Of course, in the first place one has to accept that working with values in a scientific sense is possible. David Hume denies this, Immanuel Kant affirms it, and here we follow Kant. The fact that social sciences are *sciences* in the U.S., but *humanities* in Europe, says something about the Kant (non-)reception in the U.S. The non-acceptance of a concept such as "fairness" in law as found in many writings of Anglo-American legal publications finds its justification here.[37]

The *values* that regulate the availability of breakfast in New York City are technically often called preferences.[38] Economic value judgments within a market

---

[36] Holland, Hidden Order; How Adaptation Builds Complexity, 1995, 1.

[37] The subject cannot be expanded here; for more details, see Fikentscher, Ein juristisches Jahrhundert, 19 Rechtshistorisches Journal 560 – 567, 2000, 561 f.; idem, 1995/2004, 39 f.; idem 2004, 14, 43, 55 ff.; issues concisely stated by Hahlbrock, Thematische Innovation – eingeschränkt durch ein Vorurteil über `soft science`, MPG-Spiegel 3/1995, 2-3. 1995.

[38] Raiffa, Decision Analysis: Introductury Lectures on Choices under Uncertainties, 1968, repr. 1997; Raiffa/Schlaifer, Applied Statistical Decision Theory, 1961 (student edition 1968): Tietz, Wert- und Präferenzprobleme in den Sozialwissenschaften, Schriften des Vereins für Socialpolitik, N. F., Bd. 122, 1981; Fikentscher, Zum Stand der Werte-Diskussion in der heutigen deutschen Jurisprudenz und eine juristische Theorie der Meta-Werte, Schriften des Vereins für Socialpolitik, Gesellschaft für Wirtschafts- und Sozialwissenschaften, Neue Folge Bd. 22, Wert- und Präferenzprobleme in den Sozialwissenschaften, 1981, 43-78.

defined by alternatives lead, to a system of competing offers at diminishing return, at least in the bulk markets.[39] Such a market attracts suppliers of breakfast wherever there is a demand, at prices near cost, as long as there is enough rivalry, that is, competition. Competitive markets follow what Adam Smith has called the "invisible hand". The following figure attempts to make the invisible hand visible:

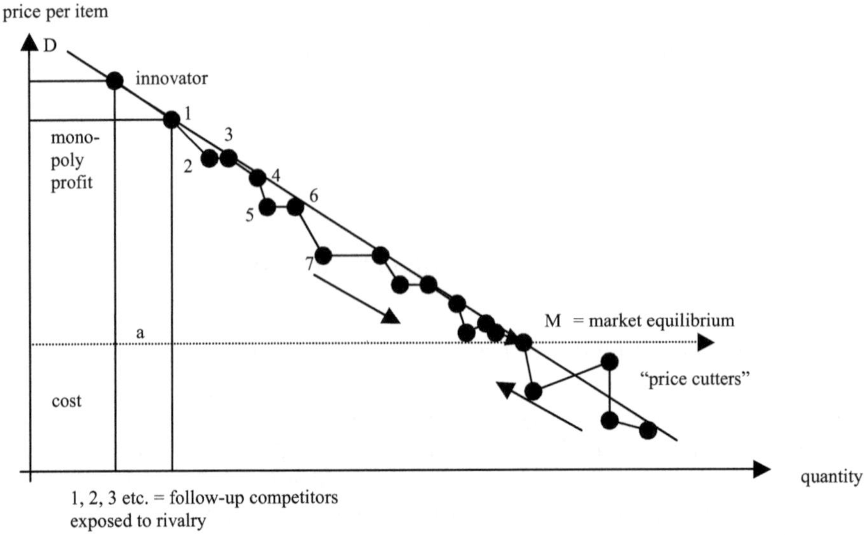

Fig. 1: Curve of the invisible hand made visible (prior publications of the "curve of the invisible hand made visible" and related discussions in: Wolfgang Fikentscher, Culture. Law and Economics: Three Berkeley Lectures, Berne & Durham 2004: Stämpfli Publishers & Carolina Academic Press, p. 129; idem, Law and Anthropology: Outlines, Issues, and Suggestions, Munich: Bavarian Academy of Sciences & C.H. Beck 2009, p. 391).

Every offeror, and every customer finds her place along this curve, because it represents a system, the system of a market in an individual (= "subjective"), perceived sense.[40]

Through its constituent parts, the rule, and the items brought under the rule, a system brings order into a disorderly, motley world, and – in theory – breakfast to every New Yorker.[41] The fact that there are New Yorkers who stay hungry in the

---

[39] Arthur (ed., with Durlauf and Lane), Increasing Returns and Path Dependence in the Economy, 1994; idem, The Economy as an Evolving Complex System, 2nd ed. 1997; Waldrop, Complexity: The Emerging Science of Order and Chaos, 1992, 252.

[40] See Fikentscher 2004 (Fn. 5), 107 – 178.

[41] Of course, there are more ways to order things, besides by a system. The system is an invention of the ancient Greek mind. Herodotus wondered why the Persians and the Egyptians did not know the system, and accordingly distinguished the Greek, the Persian and the Egyptian mind (logos). In cultural anthropology, it appears that the system is a culture-specific trait; for details see Fikentscher, Methoden des Rechts, 1975-77: Vol. IV (1977), 108 ff.; idem 1995/2004 (Fn. 7), 157 ff., 183, 351, 465.

morning because they do not own a breakfast table or enough money to buy some rolls, follows from what has been called scarcity above. It causes the issues of unsatisfied hunger and unquenched thirst mentioned before, and – in economic theory – the issues of social cost, scarcity, need and poverty, development and economic control that will be discussed in this introductory survey below.

Because of his alleged discovery of the invisible hand – general welfare growing from individual egoisms –, Adam Smith happens to be credited with being the first leading liberalist economist. However, ever since Bernard de Mandeville's fable of the bees (1705) had asserted that private vice could result in public virtue, this topic of moral science was broadly discussed during the 18th century.[42] Obviously, the issue was familiar. Adam Smith rejected Mandeville's ironic juxtaposition of vice and virtue by positing the issue into the context of a wider range of societal morality. This range is developed in Smith's "Theory of Moral Sentiments", a work designed for drafting a general societal moral theory.[43] The observation that an aggregate of individual economic egoisms may constitute – as if guided by an invisible hand – a market for general usage and utility is published in Smith's treaty "An Inquiry into the Nature and Causes of the Wealth of Nations."[44] It belongs into the context of the "Moral Sentiments" and shares their preconditions.[45] Other preconditions are stressed in his "Wealth of Nations". Therefore, it is accurate that the discovery of the invisible hand as an economic law is Smith's. But it is also true that the validity of this law depends on a series of requirements which are listed and discussed in the treatise on Moral Sentiments. If only one of these requirements is missing, the invisible hand does not work and its liberal-economic result fails to be predictable, desirable, or justified. This is a far-reaching premise. Economic liberty, both as descriptive result and as an economic policy goal depends on preconditions. Liberty is no product of nature, but of morals, law, and other caveats. As a consequence, these conditions are no opposites of liberty, no regulations at liberty's cost, but liberty's presuppositions. Legal provisions need not be inroads into liberty. Rather liberty is a product of certain legal provisions.

Smith mentions certain preconditions of the working of the invisible hand: law, free communication, morals, usages, absence of restraints of competition particularly regarding but not limited to governments and banks. In addition to preconditions, Smith speaks of protective measures against poverty in a sense that today would be subsumed under the concept of a "social net." According to Smith, the working of the invisible hand and its preconditions, along with the protective measures against poverty amount to a humane economy. Here follow his preconditions:

---

[42] Mestmäcker, Die sichtbare Hand des Rechts: Über das Verhältnis von Rechtsordnung und Wirtschaftssystem bei Smith, in: Mestmäcker, Recht und ökonomisches Gesetz, 1978, 100 – 131, 107 ff., 112, with references to earlier publications on 737 no. 5; the following footnotes refer to Mestmäcker. See also, for this discussion, Fikentscher, Oikos und Polis und die Moral der Bienen, eine Skizze zu Gemein- und Eigennutz, Festschrift für Arthur Kaufmann, 1993, 71-80.

[43] Smith, The Theory of Moral Sentiments, 1759/2005.

[44] Smith, An Inquiry into the Nature and Causes of the Wealth of Nations, 1778/2007.

[45] Convincingly demonstrated by Mestmäcker (Fn. 42) with references.

(1) The requirement of a functioning legal system consisting of general rules and based on justice, is stated both in "Theory of Moral Sentiments"[46] and in "Wealth of Nations"[47].
(2) Free communication between the participants of the market has to be present.[48]
(3) Principles of general morality have to be obeyed.[49]
(4) General rules and usages of societal contact and self-containment tend to neutralize selfish interests.[50]
(5) Foreign monopolies and monopolies at home have to be absent.[51]

Obviously with Edward Coke's anti-royal Statute of Monopolies of 1624 in mind, Smith identifies as monopolies what today would be called restraints of trade or restraints of competition. Smith addresses the power of British and other governments and "merchants and master manufacturers" who because of their wealth receive the "greatest share of public consideration" and yet use this public concern not for their own better insight in public politics but for the promotion of their own private gains.[52] Merchants of this kind, according to Smith, always try to restrain competition and deceive and suppress the public.[53] Smith thus anticipates the slogan "too big to go bankrupt" (Holzmann, AIG, HypoRealEstate, Fanny May, Freddy Mac, Bayerische Landesbank, the state of Greece as an EU member, etc.). To prevent banks from committing or participating in such abuses, Smith proposes administrative and legal controls. Such restrictions and controls may correctly be regarded as curtailments of "natural" freedom. But the use by some of "natural" freedom to endanger societal liberty and safety in a legal sense will rightfully be prevented by government. Freedom without legal justice will dissolve human society.[54] Here, Adam Smith describes – *nolens volens* as it were and forced by his own logical progression – the freedom paradox. However, Plato's warning against the working of freedom to cause injustice and tyranny does not come to mind here. Plato's skeptical attitude vis-à-vis value-deprived democracy seems to be based on his teacher Socrates' trial and sentencing by a formally democratic Athenian court and Plato's ambivalent position regarding the Thirty Tyrants.[55]

---

46 Smith, The Theory of Moral Sentiments, 1759/2005, 175 (cit. Mestmäcker at 108 Fn. 42).

47 Smith, An Inquiry into the Nature and Causes of the Wealth of Nations, 1778/2007, 687 ("exact administration of justice"). See for this also Mestmäcker (Fn. 42), 114, 127.

48 Smith, The Theory of Moral Sentiments, 1759/2005, 326; a discussion: Mestmäcker (Fn. 42), 110.

49 Smith, The Theory of Moral Sentiments, 1759/2005, 112, 304. Mestmäcker (Fn. 46) 111 draws attention to the point that Smith attempts to combine individual and social ethics.

50 Smith, The Theory of Moral Sentiments, 1759/2005, 175.

51 Smith, An Inquiry into the Nature and Causes of the Wealth of Nations, 1778/2007, 687.

52 Smith, An Inquiry into the Nature and Causes of the Wealth of Nations, 1778/2007, 267.

53 Ibidem and 462, 493, 570; for a comment see Mestmäcker (Fn. 42), 130.

54 Smith, The Theory of Moral Sentiments, 1759/2005, 86; see also Mestmäcker's summary (Fn. 42), 131. For the following see also Mestmäcker's summary (Fn. 42), 127.

55 For the trial see Plato's dialog Kriton and for the Tyrants Plato's Republic (Politeia), and the evaluation by Popper, The Open Society and Its Enemies, Vol. 1: The Spell of Plato, 1995, 91 f.

(6) Last but not least, Smith goes beyond the precinct of economic freedom and enters the field where markets cannot properly work and less privileged members of society need – in modern terms – a social net. In a society of law-supported liberty, says Smith, land owners and workers will find their group interests generally safeguarded. But the land-owners will be uninformed for lack of interest in matters *politiques*, and the workers, though interested, will suffer from lack of information and education while promoting their interests. This points to the need to reinforce those groups' chances to repair societal defects. According to Smith, there is a need to establish publicly financed institutions for public utility ends whenever private profit does not cover the cost of establishing, maintaining and protecting collective goods such as schools and other installations and environments that are "more than worthwhile" having in a society.[56] It is striking how Smith, against the background of his law-founded and law-maintained economic liberty principles even thinks of social cost (including collective goods) economy, public utilities, social want and means of overcoming that want.

Still today, social net economy consisting of social cost economy including an economy of collective goods (*Sozialkostenwirtschaft*), economy of distributing want (*Bewirtschaftung*), developing economy (supported by affirmative action – *Entwicklungswirtschaft*) and public control of economy (*Wirtschaftsaufsicht*), all mentioned by Adam Smith as addenda to a fair and workable free economy, may be regarded as its necessary amendments. Even today, these elements of social net economy draw the line between establishing, maintaining, protecting and (if necessary) reconstituting free and fair markets on the one hand, and (exchange value) socialism on the other.[57]

To avoid misquoting Adam Smith for unlimited "natural" freedom, the above-mentioned requirements should be respected. To refer to Adam Smith as a protagonist of unfettered economic freedom is mistaken and does not do justice to, nor indirectly follow from, the texts he wrote. Being an 18th century writer, the most strident words he used for rejecting unlimited economic liberty are directed against monopolies and social injustice.

Modern industry and business not only often misquote Adam Smith and his plea for legally controlled liberalism, but instead invoke a more or less unlimited freedom of economic behavior. At times, in the economic-political debate the market-tailored democracy is placed above the democracy-tailored market. Worse, economic leaders sometimes do not conceal their lack of interest in a political order that has been installed and is held responsible for establishing and maintaining legally and morally guaranteed and controlled freedom. "Wall Street" and its imita-

---

[56] Smith, An Inquiry into the Nature and Causes of the Wealth of Nations, 1778/2007, 687 and 788 (schools).

[57] See Smith's remark on "pillars", The Theory of Moral Sentiments, 1759/2005, 86. The text above reflects the outline in Fikentscher, Wirtschaftsrecht (Economic Law), Vol. 2, 1983, 28, 50 - 55; translation into Chinese by Zhang Shiming, with the author's preface, in: Selected Works by Fikentscher in the Chinese language, Vol.1, 2009.

tors ought to be blamed for any couldn't-care-less attitude to democracy or other forms of organized society that set out to provide for exactly that freedom which these circles untiringly claim. Political indifference and even mockery on the side of some business leaders is a not infrequently described historical and present-day fact. Criminal charges do happen, but they are rare. In Chapter 4 below (under 4.2) some material is mentioned. A sometimes heard industrialists' statement is that business actually does not care about what the solution might be, but rather only cares about being able to safely plan things of importance.

An especially intricate liaison may exist between such self-centered industrialism and socialism, most of all use-value socialism, the central concept of Marxism, in more detail described below (near note 71). Use-value socialism has a problem with cost because it cannot calculate cost. What is more pleasant for a business leader, or a governmental employee, not to have to pay attention to cost? After the year 2000, the governments of certain Mediterranean north-rim countries had little qualms in disobeying EU rules of limiting national debt in relation to national income. Some international banks are said to have assisted governments in disregarding eventual breaches of pertinent European law. Under the theory of national sovereignty developed by Justice O.W. Holmes, wrong committed abroad in principle does not affect U.S. law.[58] There may be an unholy alliance between business disrespecting democracy and (use-value) socialism disrespecting cost. This kind of economic liberty would not have been included in Adam Smith's liberalism because of its immorality.

Beneath this issue lurks the question of who has the final say in a free democratic, organized society, who owns the prerogative of leadership and of gearing in a political organism: business or government. In his work on the historical, ideological and political background of U.S.-American antitrust, Hans B. Thorelli addresses this constitutional problem.[59] Developed from English common law, between 1880 and 1890 the "trust problem" gained enough public awareness in U.S. to be included in the legislative agenda of Congress.[60]

The "trust problem" was the catchword for monopoly power of big businesses and their combinations and arrangements. There was public resistance against the "new feudalism" of the "trusts"[61] The question was raised whether trust power would endanger democracy, and whether democracy and rule of law would persist.[62] In one of his summaries, Thorelli – in formulations that could have been laid down by Adam Smith and should have been laid down by Thomas Jefferson –

[58] For relevant case law and evaluation see, e.g., Fikentscher, Rechtswissenschaft und Demokratie bei Justice Oliver Wendell Holmes, Jr., Eine rechtsvergleichende Kritik der politischen Jurisprudenz, Juristische Studiengesellschaft Karlsruhe, Schriftenreihe Heft 96, 1970; also idem (Fn. 41), Vol. II, Anglo-amerikanischer Rechtskreis, 189 ff. with materials.

[59] Thorelli, The Federal Antitrust Policy: Origination of an American Tradition, 1955.

[60] Thorelli (Fn. 59). The Sherman Act was passed on 2 July 1890, 26 Stat. 209, 15 U.S.C. 1 – 7.

[61] Thorelli (Fn. 59), 317.

[62] Thorelli (Fn. 59), 327, 565.

remarks: "In business it helps to distinguish liberty from license", and "Antitrust is a mission of morale."[63]

What during the last decades of the 19th century mainly applied to smokestack industries, railways and oil business, today concerns private and public finance. Heiner Geißler points to the fact that until 1990 business in merchandise and services acted on the forefront of national and international economy, with banks assisting by serving production and trade of these goods by payments and credit. Since about 1990 banks and other financing institutions took over the lead and relegated production and trade to a secondary role on the global economic stage.[64]

Now, Geißler says, citing U.S.-American sources, the tail is wagging the dog. Geißler does not mention the parallel to the antitrust policy debates of the 1890ies. They were not limited to the U.S. as is demonstrated, for instance, by the German Supreme Court decision of February 4, 1897, RGZ 38, 155 – Holzstoff –, and the German *Reichstagsdenkschrift* of 1906/08.[65] The story and its meaning are identical: "The trusts" are about to wrest societal leadership from organized society. There may be two differences, though: In the 1890ies "the trusts" still were mainly national and active in production and trade of merchandise and services, whereas in the 1990ies "the trusts" are global and active in finance. But the threats of economic monopolization to democracy and to the rule of law are similar.[66] Antimonopoly law is assigned the task of safeguarding political leadership, outweighing the legal-political task of trade law with its rules to keep up fair commercials dealings. Antitrust is the interface between grand politics and economy.

1.4.2 The environment- and culture-conscious free and fair market economy, its institutional character, and its societal elasticity limits

For the drafting of a free and fair economy, fit to meet the needs of different cultures and environments and supported by a social net, some results from the foregoing deliberations and arguments may be considered. If not, consequences e.g. for economic, legal or political sanctions in case of deviations could not be drawn. Whoever would prefer to reject one of the aforementioned premises should engage in drafting another economy. Alternatives might be drawn from examples such as Emperor Diocletian's centrally administered economy including maximum prices

---

[63] Thorelli (Fn. 59), 608; all quotes with further references, among them Cook, The Corporation Problem: The Public Phases of Corporations, Their Uses, Abuses, etc. 1891, 230; Andrews, Individualism as a Sociological Principle, 2 Yale Review 13 – 27 (May 1993); idem, The Combination of Capital, 4 International J. of Ethics, 321 – 334 (April 1894).

[64] Geißler, Frisst der Kapitalismus seine Kinder?, Weimarer Reden, 28 February 2010, http://www.thueringer-allgemeine.de/ta/ta.staedtenews.volltext.phpb?/kennung=on1tal of 1 March 2010.

[65] For more details Fikentscher, Wettbewerb und gewerblicher Rechtsschutz: Die Stellung des Wettbewerbsrechts in der Rechtsordnung, 1958, 166 – 170.

[66] Rule of law is used here for *Rechtsstaat* in the meaning of everybody's (including foreigners') constitutional right under Art. 19 (4) German Constitution to sue the government for protection against contractual or tortuous violation of the rights of the minority as such, the subordinate administrative unit against the higher administrative unit, and human and other individual rights; cf. Fn. 18.

against the declining monetary value,[67] a theocratic *iustum pretium* ("just price") economy which was attempted for some time in the papal church state in central Italy during the 15th and 16th century and given up after its failure,[68] the German and Allied occupation powers' fixed prices and coupon system between 1936 and 1948,[69] the Russian 100% paradox-exposed free economy of the years 1990 ff.,[70] or the near to 100% paradox-exposed free economy on the global financial and capital markets between 1990 and the beginning of the financial and economic crises of the years 2006 – 2010, the complete history of which has not yet been written. The main question remains: Are there discernible criteria of a "humane" economy characterized by a cost-controlling invisible hand and yet socially safeguarded wherever cost cannot be adequately governed by that invisible hand?

One essential criterion is a decision in favor of the economic standard of exchange value instead of the use value. Despite a considerable literature, the history and importance of this distinction seems not to have been sufficiently clarified, at least not to this generation. To students of the 1968er generation the difference between the two value concepts was clear and did not need to be explained. Some modern Neomarxist postulations refer to it and point to a century-old debate.[71] A popularized story goes like this: In ancient Greece, somebody enters the *agora* (= the market place) and wants to sell his sandals. He asks himself what he may charge for them. He meets Aristotle who happens to be there and asks the famous philosopher what he may ask for the sandals. Aristotle's answer is that everything has two values, an exchange value and a use value. The exchange value can be ascertained by comparing the offers on the market and calculating the average. The

---

67 Gaius Aurelius Valerius Diokletianus, born around 240 A.D., Roman emperor 284 – 306. The maximum price system proved to be ineffectual.

68 The so called pasquinades – graffitti that ridiculed the papal economic administration – contributed to the abandonment of the religiously reasoned fixed-price system. An ancient statue, discovered in Rome in 1501, received in public the nickname Pasquino.

69 Huber, Wirtschaftsverwaltungsrecht, Vol. II 1964, 197; Rauschenbach, Wirtschaftsrecht mit Kartellrecht, 1965, 202 ff.; Fikentscher (Fn. 57), Vol. 2, 441 ff. with additional references.

70 Sachs, Lecture, Report, in: Law Quadrangle, The University of Michigan Law School, 38 (1995) No.1, 3 – 4 (on the failure of his being consulted by the Russian government in 1990 after the end of socialist centrally-planned economy; Sachs had advised to abruptly replace the – still essentially Marxist use-value-oriented – Gosplan-planned economy with a 100%, paradox-exposed free market system; see also Sachs, The End of Poverty: Economic Possibilities for Our Time, 2005, as another „big push" example, this time to overcome poverty; a critical comment in: Easterly, 44 Journal of Economic Literature 96 – 105 (March 2006, No.1)).

71 Mandel, Entstehung und Entwicklung der ökonomischen Lehre von Karl Marx, 1968; idem, Marxistische Wirtschaftstheorie, 1968; idem, Der Spätkapitalismus. Versuch einer marxistischen Erklärung, 1972; Hofmann, Verelendung, in: Mohl et al. (eds.), Folgen einer Theorie, Essays über Das Kapital von Karl Marx, 2nd ed. 1967, 27; Markovic, Entfremdung und Selbstverwaltung, in: Folgen einer Theorie op.cit. 178 – 180; Gerfin/Hickel (eds.), Karl Marx, Das Kapital, 3 vol, 1971. For a discussion see Leptin, Marx und Neomarxisten – Vorstellungen über eine neue Wirtschaft, Markenartikel 1973, 362 ff.; Schimmelbusch, Kritik an Commutopia, 1971; Fikentscher, Zur politischen Kritik an Marxismus und Neomarxismus als ideologischen Grundlagen der Studentenunruhen 1965/69, 1971; idem (Fn. 41), Vol. 3, 1976, 504 – 567; idem (Fn. 57), Vol. 2, 55 – 57; idem (Fn. 7), 447 f., 456, 461.

average is what the offeror of the sandals might expect. So it would be useful to look around and hear what the competitors are asking. The other type of value is use value. It indicates the degree of how much the sandals are useful for the present owner of the sandals who is offering them for sale. When the offeror asked Aristotle: "And how much would this be", Aristotle answered: "This is what you have to find out by asking yourself how much you like your sandals. There is no way to ascertain a use value in terms of a yardstick or currency".

Marx rejects an economy – and life as a whole – at exchange values because this would enable owners of things and offerors of services to reap a surplus value from needy people by exploitation. Instead, an economy – and life as a whole – based on use values was his ideal to be achieved by revolutionary abolishment of (non-personal) ownership. To determine the use values of things Marx did not indicate precise methods but seemed to rely on ascertainable "scientific," politically established procedures, to be carried out by activities of the revolution-minded cadres. Marx did not make proposals on how cadres should proceed in case of eventual discord about the use values of things and services. He could not propose a cadre-intern dialog because this would mean turning (empiricism-safe) use values into (empiricism-exposed) exchange values. On this issue, Rudi Dutschke, a neomarxist political leader, deviated from Marx under the impression of Dubcek's "Prague Spring" of 1968 which Dutschke witnessed. Back in Germany, Dutschke – apparently influenced by Dubcek – proposed cadre-intern dialog on use values while pursuing traditional dialog-free class struggle towards the outside. Outside of the "top-cadres of the metropolies" as Dutschke put it, the economically and politically non-operational character of the use value remained for Dutschke unquestionable and to be determined by the top cadres, that is, by a political dictatorship.

Around 1960, the Soviet Russian economist Evsei Liberman (1898 – 1981) predicted that socialist economy was bankruptcy-bound since its planning was based on use values so that no control of cost existed and consequently production tended to be uncontrolled and too expensive.[72] Liberman also criticized the dependence of use value determination on the decisions of cadres too far removed from economic reality. Instead, he proposed barter exchanges between factories, the so-called "contract system," which was made reality for example in the GDR.

Under Liberman' influence, the central "scientific" planning of economic values by Gosplan (the central economic planning institution for the "Socialist Camp" seated in Moscow) started being based on average world prices and average world cost (that is, on exchange values). Only for the barter system and for distribution to the consumer an alleged use value economy was upheld in the "Socialist Camp". In the GDR, mentioning the name of Liberman in institutions of education (universities, schools) or in public lectures became prohibited. Still, the politically concealed reference to world market prices and the impossibility of controlling cost sufficed for Liberman's prediction in 1989 to become true, the bankruptcy of socialism. A

---

[72] For more details, see Fikentscher, Blöcke und Monopole in der Weltpolitik! Die Herausforderung der Freien Nationen, 1979, 100 – 119; idem (Fn. 57), Vol. 2, 55-57; idem (Fn. 7), 108, 447 f., 456, 461.

fair economy needs control of cost by competition and therefore must be founded on exchange values throughout.

This does not solve the social problem, it causes it: An economic system built upon the invisible hand of competitive rivalry, law, morals, free communication, control of restraints of competition, state instead of business prerogative, ethnological substantivism, empirical fact-mindedness and cost-controlled by exchange values instead of cost-free use value fiat may duly be called a liberal one. What then is a *neo*liberal economy?

When in June 1948 Konrad Adenauer, Ludwig Erhard and the German political majority decided in favor of a free economy for the three Western occupation zones and in 1949 for the fledgling Federal Republic of Germany, a thoroughly liberal economic system was rejected. A totally liberal economic system was then called "Manchester-liberal," "elbow-liberal", or "100%-liberal." By contrast, the free economy found fitting for post-war West-Germany was at that time called, by academics, "Freiburg-liberal" or "ORDO-liberal," and because of the need to have a practical name for political usage, by almost everybody, "social-market economic-liberal" or shortened "neoliberal". "Neo-" meant to avoid the sophisticated concepts of Freiburg School and its ORDO-liberalism, and to indicate that the German post-war economy was not thought to be "Manchester-" or "elbow-liberal," but subject to economic control by antitrust and other laws, including laws providing for a "social net." The use of the term "neoliberal" for unfettered ("Manchester-" or "elbow-") liberalism by trade unions and anti-globalization advocates today is a-historical and confusing.

A large share of the public opinion in English-speaking countries since World War II mistook and will probably always mistake German neoliberalism as a kind of socialism, the distinction between use value socialism and exchange value socialism being widely disregarded or simply ignored. On the other hand, as indicated, Middle and Western European and South American leftist thinkers, politicians, parties and trade unions mistake German neoliberalism as 100%-, Manchester- or elbow-liberalism, opposed to "neoliberalism". A clarification of terms may thus be helpful. It may be gained from briefly tapping into "new economic institutionalism".

Early classical economists were, more or less, "naïve" empiricists. Adam Smith and his contemporaries observed economic facts and drew observations from these observations.[73] During the second half of the 19th century, the marginalist revolution turned classic economics into a science that postulated economic behavior under certain fixed theoretical requirements.[74] A later generation of theoretical economists focused on the "firm" and entrepreneurship.[75]

---

[73] See the list of names and the discussion of meanings of their theories in Fikentscher (Fn. 3), 140, 145.

[74] Rössler (Fn. 23), 34 ff.; Gregory (Fn. 26); Appadurai (Fn. 26); Schneider (Fn. 23).

[75] The discussion was opened by Coase, "The Nature of the Firm," Economica 4 (1937), 386 and Eucken, Grundlagen der Nationalökonomie (Foundations of national economy), 6th ed. 1950; for a comment, see Fikentscher (Fn. 57), Vol. 1, 587. See also Ackerman, The Future of Liberal Revolution, 1993. For the following, see the earlier version in Fikentscher 2004 (Fn. 5), 37–42.

1.4.3 New economic institutionalism

At this point in the development of economic thought the concept of the institution was introduced as another aspect of the inside-outside-of-the-firm debate. Of course, the term institution was well known. French, German and other brands of institutionalism all had their philosophical, legal, and economic histories.[76]

In economics, the term "institution" has been used with a double meaning. First, it was used to encompass all factors that normatively influence a present state of facts (economic and other) and, in particular, its development from one stage to another. Douglass C. North, as author or co-author, published a series of books and articles on influences of these "institutions" on economy, and finally extended the theory of institutional change to incorporate ideology and culture.[77] In this sense, "institutions" amount to what Malinowski describes as the "hemming in of natural propensities."[78] Depending on the context, the terms "norms" and "culture" also describe what is meant by institutions in this sense.

Second, "institutions" have been used, particularly in an economic context, as a source for directing human behavior, as a behavioral beacon, so to speak. In this sense, "institutions" are seen as being equipped with an entelechy (of "inherent" guiding values), similar to the guiding functions of natural law. In this sense, institutionalism is exposed to all criticism that has been brought forward against religious and secular versions of natural law, including "nature-of-things law."[79]

Since cultural anthropology prefers the term "norm" over "institution," and while an empirical social science is critical of every sort of entelechy, the present text will proceed in the Malinowskian manner of asking the normative question only where it has to be asked. The central difference between the (normative, entelechian) institutional approach of Douglass C. North and the approach applied

---

[76] Cf. the material collected and discussed in Fikentscher, Maurice Hauriou und die institutionelle Rechtslehre, FS L. Raiser, 1974, 559 – 576 .

[77] North, Structure and Change in Economic History, 1981; idem, Institutions, Institutional Change and Economic Performance, 1990, 118, where North states that "Institutions provide the basic structure by which human beings throughout history have created order and attempted to reduce uncertainty in exchange"; idem, Institutions and Credible Commitments, 149 Journal of Institutional and Theoretical Economics (JITE), 1993, 11 (11-13); for a more detailed history of the development of institutional thought in economics and North's share of it, Kantor, Politics and Property Rights: The Closing of the Open Range in the Postbellum South, 1998, 5 ff.; for formulating the same idea, that competition needs "imperfections", Borchardt/Fikentscher, Wettbewerb, Wettbewerbsbeschränkung, Marktbeherrschung, Stuttgart 1957, Fn. 89, use the term "mini-monopolies" homologous to "institutions" and "transaction cost." On North's way from "institutions"to "mental models" see Fikentscher 1995/2004 (Fn. 7), Fn. 24 and 25; and North himself, in his article Some Fundamental Puzzles in Economic History/Development, Arthur/Durlauf/Lane (eds.), The Economy as an Evolving Complex System II, 1997, Santa Fe Institute Studies in the Sciences of Complexity Proceedings, vol. XXVII, 223 – 238, e.g. 230 (shaping belief systems).

[78] See Fikentscher 1995/2004 (Fn. 7), Fn. 6 ff., and the discussion there.

[79] See a longer version of the text in Fikentscher (Fn. 5), Fn. 19, and in Fikentscher (Fn. 41), 504 – 542. The criticism is upheld.

here is as follows: Mental models are models. In anthropology, ideational generalities (as opposed to material cultures) are called mind-sets or modes of thought. These modes of thought are no models, but results drawn from empirical observation of real world phenomena, tested, in interviews and otherwise, according to anthropological methodology. Modes of thought are thus middle types, not ideal types.[80]

The institutional approach has attracted considerable interest. "New Institutional Economics" or "New Economic Institutionalism" has become a name for a scientific search for neglected factors of economic influence. The view has been sharpened for details, if not for mini-details, under the theoretical influence of post-Marxism or other forms of "postmodernism," sometimes in ground-breaking historical studies of non-ideological interest. To the latter kind belongs Avner Greif's study on "cultural beliefs" and societal organization by use of a comparison of eleventh- and twelfth-century Genovese and Maghribi sea-trading habits. Greif calls the Genovese approach to trade "individualistic" and the North African Maghribi approach "collectivistic," and in his book drafts a law and economics model from those two cultural beliefs. Greif attributes the final success of the Genovese and the falling into oblivion of the Maghribi way of trading across the Mediterranean Sea, accompanied by the growing wealth of Genovese commoners, to the more efficient and trade-promoting character of the formers' organizational development, based on their cultural belief in the role of the individual.[81]

In anthropology, the terms collectivism and individualism have distinct meanings and should not be used without a firm grounding in the respective mode of thought. For example, Lin Yutang, the famous critic of the "Chinese mind," identifies Chinese "collectivism" with what he calls "the absence of the social mind." To him, collective thinking by way of the social mind is what characterizes "the West," whereas Eastern "individualism" prevents modernization.[82] This amounts to the opposite use of the two terms. Anthropologically, it is safer to use the distinction between *attached* and *detached* "cultural beliefs" (to use Greif's terminology). The first "belief" may grant subjective rights of a person against another person under a trust-ensuring law common to both, the second will not.[83] Greif's punctilious investigation is a good example of the exploitation of "culture" for the purposes of economic theory.

---

80 Fikentscher (Fn. 7), 15.

81 Greif, Cultural Beliefs and the Organization of Society: A Historical and Theoretical Reflection on Collectivist and Individualist Societies, 102 Journal of Political Economy 1994, 912 – 950.

82 See the discussion of Lin Yutang's culture comparison (Yutang, My Country and My People, 1st ed. 1939, (3rd printing 1975)) and, on the different meanings of individualism and collectivism, Fikentscher (Fn.11), 339 ff.

83 In a similar vein – markets and property rights instead of the rule of the state – , Cooter, The Theory of Market Modernization of Law, International Review of Law and Economics 16 (1996): 141–172; idem, The Rule of State Law and the Rule-of-Law State: Economic Analysis of the Legal Foundations of Development, in: Bruno/Pleskovic, World Bank, Washington, D.C. (eds), Annual World Bank Conference on Development Economics, 1997, 191-218, reprinted in: Buscaglia, Ratcliff/Cooter (eds.)., The Law and Economics of Development, 1997, 101-148.

As a consequence of the development of scientific theory, a second question would concern the systematic context of this cultural "addition" to economics (North, Kantor, Greif), all still in line with the assumption that culture is an *institution* with certain impact on economics. Since anthropology is the science of cultures in their meaning for human behavior, Rudolf Richter and Jean Ensminger have convincingly suggested that anthropology should take better notice of the rising role of culture in economics, a role demonstrating the influence of economics upon anthropology. However, neither author has so far offered a definition of culture.[84]

The result of this brief presentation of "new economic institutionalism" resembles the concept of ORDO-liberalism in Walter Eucken's terminology, however with one or two differences.

A first difference can be found in the circumstance that new economic institutionalism carries with it a touch of the older neoclassic model thinking. The type of fair economy presented here instead prefers the naïve empirical approach of the economic classicists and of the ORDO-liberals. But market,[85] market share, firm, entrepreneur, competition, restraint of competition, social net and all major concepts of social market economy can also be expressed as institutions. The same holds true if ORDO-liberalism is expanded to include the spheres of environment and culture.[86] FairEconomy is a field of activities carried on by the use of institutions.

Another difference may be seen in the degree of closeness to economic policy. ORDO-liberalism includes goals of economic policy. For new economic institutionalism this is not always so. But it is hard to deny that new economic institution-

---

[84] Richter (ed.), Views and Comments on the 'New Institutionalism' in Sociology, Political Science, and Anthropology, Editorial Preface, JITE 154,1998, 694; idem, Institutionen ökonomisch analysiert: Zur jüngeren Entwicklung auf einem Gebiet der Wissenschaftstheorie, 1994, e.g., 64 f., where Richter expresses his consent with North. North said that efficiency and development of an economic system depend on historical and nationally characteristical institutions and their change (e.g., The Netherlands, England, Spain), on insecurities and transaction cost, and on imperfection or absence of competition, in contrast to the neoclassic theory for which the world is frictionless, has no institutions and functions perfectly. Cf. Ensminger, Anthropology and the New Institutionalism, JITE 154,1998, 774-789. A still much-quoted *definition of culture* has been given by Tylor, Anthropology: An Introduction to the Study of Man and Civilization, 1881, 1; see 1.1.2 above; slightly rephrased for the study of the modes of thought as backgrounds of the cultures at footnote 12, above, and in Fikentscher (Fn. 7), 23, 95.

[85] North, The Evolution Of Efficient Markets In History, Economic History 9411005, EconWPA 1994; idem, Institutions, Institutional Change and Economic Performance, 1990.

[86] *Environment*: Fikentscher, Die umweltsoziale Marktwirtschaft – als Rechtsproblem, 1991; idem, Free Trade and Protection of Environment as an Integrated Economic Value System: Outline of an Environment-conscious Social Market Economy: A Lawyer's View, 1991, Juristische Fakultät der Universität Stockholm, 1992. – *Culture*: Fikentscher, Die Rolle des Marktes in der Wirtschaftsanthropologie: Marktorganisation und das globale Wirtschaftsrecht, in: Engel/Möschel (eds.), Recht und spontane Ordnung, Festschrift für E.-J. Mestmäcker zum 80. Geburtstag, 2006, 199 – 230; idem (Fn. 3).

alism – in a perhaps more distant manner than ORDO-liberalism – envisages policy goals as well. At the very least, new economic institutionalism is equipped and could be used to analyze the requirements of many kinds of economic liberalism, including the Freiburgian species. Institutions cannot retreat to pure descriptiveness and deny any normativity.

The same test could be repeated with the teachings of Hernando de Soto, the *other* famed institutionalist next to Douglass C. North. The main institution de Soto is concerned with is property, and in terms of methodology his concern clearly is an empirical one. What could be a more striking economic institution than property, as it can be observed and grasped in land registers, boundary posts and stones?[87]

1.4.4 Markets

The categorization of "environment- and culture-conscious social market economy" as a subspecies of an empirically understood new economic institutionalism leads to a distinction between the objective and the individual market as two different institutions. The distinction is explained elsewhere,[88] as are its considerable consequences.[89] It suffices here to repeat the essentials:[90]

There is a difference between the statements "This is my market", and "The steel market is in good (or bad) shape." In the first phrase, the speaker wants to circumscribe a situation of rivalry, either on the market side of the speaker's buyers, or on the side of the speaker's suppliers. In the second phrase, the speaker wants to describe a conglomeration of substitutable merchandise or services that can be identified by good, area and time; he who mentions the market of pharmaceuticals, car tires, energy, second hand attire or transportation does not think of competitive rivalry, but of an entity usable, for example, for statistical purposes, from which conclusions of strong or weak rivalry cannot be drawn.

The market in the *individual sense* (= individual market or subjective market) is defined by one criterion only: whether its participants compete. There has to be a rivalry between the members of an individual market for it to exist. The individual market does not answer the objectively asked question what "the" market may be, rather it answers the question posed to a businessman, "What is *your* market?" This question is put to an *individual*, a *subject* active or preparing for activity in business. The addressee of this question may perhaps answer: „*My* (!) market is

---

87 See the discussion of de Soto's institutionalist positions in: Fikentscher (Fn. 5), 25-33.

88 Fikentscher, Mehrzielige Marktwirtschaft auf subjektiven Märkten: Wider das Europa- und das Weltmarktargument, in: Immenga u.a. (eds.), Festschrift für E.-J. Mestmäcker zum 70. Geburtstag, 1996, 567-578; idem (Fn. 5), 119-178; prepared – but not precisely enough – is the idea of the individual market in: Fikentscher/Borchardt, Wettbewerb, Wettbewerbsbeschränkung, Marktbeherrschung, 1957, 25, 51 f., reprinted in Fikentscher, Recht und wirtschaftliche Freiheit vol.1: Die Freiheit des Wettbewerbs, 1992, 115, 135 ff.

89 Fikentscher, Markt oder Wettbewerb oder beides? Gewerblicher Rechtsschutz und Urheberrecht Internationaler Teil 2004 Heft 9 (FS R. Krasser), 722-731.

90 For this, see the remainder of this subchapter.

not easy. Although I serve about a dozen more or less regular clients, competition is on the alert. It consists of five firms, and next year there may be six or seven of them."

Markets in the *objective sense* are defined by three determinants: a good (merchandise or service), a geographic area, and a period of time. To illustrate, in *United States v. Columbia Steel Co.*, 334 U.S. 495 (1948), the court defined as relevant market the product of certain steel products, the area of eleven states of the U.S., and the period between 1937 and 1946. When ice cream vendors and beverage vendors agree to raise prices during a football game, *the* market consists of "refreshments," the area in and around the stadium, and the time between 1 p.m. and 5 p.m. There are markets for cardboard packaging materials, mid-price used cars, and daily journals. Markets in the objective sense such as the healthcare market or the insurance market may indicate a prima-facie case for existing or potential competition, but most of them are, in both respects, competition-free, since between many market participants there is no rivalry to be seen or to be expected. Still, for statistical purposes, or for political plans to integrate formerly separate (individual) markets such as those that led to the creation of the EU, of or ASEAN, or other industrial policy aims, objective markets may be of no small interest.[91] The test question for the ascertainment of an objective market reads: "What do these business people have in common with regard to technically defined goods they offer or buy, and with regard to a given area and a given time frame?" But a rival tension, a zero-sum game by which the one party wins and a second loses that which the one wins, is not involved. As soon the rival tension becomes apparent, the market turns into an individual one, and of course substitutability is often the factor that opens competitive rivalry and thus individual (= subjective) markets.

Economic and legal literature rarely distinguishes between objective and subjective (= individual) markets. Often both kinds of markets and their institutional nature are interchangeably used on one single page, and its author is not aware that she or he is speaking of two different things. Case law, discussions of cases, market theories and economic issues often confuse the two concepts as well.[92] However, it is obvious that economic issues concerning competition and restraints of competition involve rivalry and thus the individual market concept. Therefore, for the following discussion of free and fair competition, the individual market and the com-

---

91 In 1994, in an interview in Hualien, Taiwan, I learned that Taiwanese marble did not compete with Australian marble because of shipment cost. When I asked the same question in 2002 in Darwin, NT, one of Australia's northernmost ports, the answer was that Taiwanese marble was being shipped to Australia in considerable quantity and at competitive prices. Thus, a market that had been objective, the Western Pacific marble market, eight years later had turned both bigger and individual; in between, there must have been a period when there was a reasonable chance for both marble producers soon to become competitors, a period of "potential competition." Today, the world marble market still is an objective one, although there may be, depending on distance, transportation cost, and consumer taste, a competitive potentiality for individual marble markets here and there.

92 With consequences shown in the article cited above (Fn. 89).

petition in it are addressed. Whenever there is talk of objective markets, this term will expressly be used.

A consequence of the individual market as an economic institution is an inevitable readjustment of the alleged dichotomy between perfect competition and monopoly. Rivalrous economic competition raises the question what the rivals compete for. There must be something to compete about.

Neoclassic economic model thinking postulates that there are two extremes: perfect competition and perfect monopoly. Perfect competition requires an unlimited number of indefinitely small market participants, a 100% identical good, complete information of all participants, and zero time of competitive reaction. A perfect monopoly is defined by a single firm and the absence of challenge by others of the economic conditions the monopolist is able to dictate. The market power of a participant of the perfectly competitive market is zero, the market power of the monopolist is 100%. However, if a participant of perfect competition is exposed to the conditions which define perfect competition, the participant has no chance to improve its position and will stay inactive. Perfect competition is total discouragement of any move on the market and thus utter stagnation – and hence absence of competition. Therefore, *both* perfect competition and monopoly are forms of absence of competition, and perfect competition must be a misnomer. But what is competition, what does rivalry mean?

Scarcity of offered (resp. demanded) goods causes two or more buyers (resp. suppliers) to try to obtain one and the same good (resp. merchandise or service). Therefore the buyers (resp. suppliers) outbid each other by offering the potential supplier (potential buyer) better terms. The best offer will lead to a deal. The transaction leads to making the winner richer than before. The winning buyer receives at bit more property in goods than she had before; the winning supplier receives more property in money than she had before. This is the usual manner of participating in an individual market. In each case this participation requires to have something to offer, goods or money. Therefore the participants are not indefinitely small and they are not utterly powerless. They are not "perfect competitors." This is not the place to rehash the theories of incomplete, workable, effective, intensive competition, incomplete markets, market deficiencies, market failures, contested markets, markets for lemons etc.[93] All these nescient descriptions of the fact that perfect competition is no competition and that competition involves participation of buyers and suppliers who have something to offer they own have one premise in common: competition requires property and is about property.

How much property does a market participant have to consider herself fit to engage in marketing? If there is too much property, the participant is too big to be a good player in the market place, and may be a monopolist or a member of a competition-restrained oligopoly. If the participant is too small, the market suffers from "atomization" and does not work effectively.[94] Thus, a curve may be drawn from

[93] Cf. Borchardt/Fikentscher (Fn. 88), in the reprinted version 89-159.

[94] Bakhoum (in a forthcoming publication), a statement made for certain situations in developing markets, but a cogent one for other markets as well.

too little market power for effective competition, rising to an optimum of competition-favoring market power, then falling to less and less intensive competition due to more and more market power, with monopoly and no-competition at the end of the curve. This is not a preordained structure to be encountered in and confronted with reality but a simple empirical comparison. In political practice, from this curve derives the task of human society organized in a superadditive unit, such as a state, to watch the distribution of property and market power flowing from it, so as to remain as much as possible in the neighborhood of that optimum. If successful, this society enables its members to meet their needs, resulting in a competition-defined Pareto-Optimum.

It follows that the preparation of competition for having workable markets is too weak and inadequate when there are not enough people with enough resources to share in the socially required markets. Therefore, economic policy aims at quantitatively and qualitatively augmenting markets. Markets do not grow from nothing. In Germany, after 1948, Adenauer and Erhard were politically active creating individual markets and filling them with life in order to feed and dress the people. On the other side of the optimum, economic policy is obliged to reduce market-damaging power, through cutting back that power using the instruments of antitrust and rules of fair competition.

Both economical-political endeavors, the build-up and the maintenance of markets, develop over time. Timeless neoclassic models are meaningless for the pursuit of such policies. Similarly, the proximity of Coase's theory of the firm to perfect competition prevents it not only from relating to time, but also from being applicable to competition.

1.4.5 A principled basis for free and fair economics

What are the reasons for judging a business practice, competitive or factually close to competition, to be "unfair"? Congruent to legal history, the answer will look for qualitatively unfair trade practices first, and next for quantitative restrictions upon business behavior, ending by answering the question whether there is a common ground for reasons. Each part of this double question has to be subdivided in two sections again, the first with regard to those (more numerous) legal systems which use the concept of unfairness as main focus of said deliberation, and the second with respect to the common law countries which in the wake of the British case Mogul Steamship Co. v. McGregor, Gow and Co., 23 Q.B.D. 598 (1889) affirmed (1892), A.C. 25, reject a fairness test and use a tortious act approach instead ("Mogul Steamship legal systems").

In Germany, the search for justification of an anti-unfair competition legal policy dates back to the discussion preceding the enactment of the first Law for the Control of Unfair Competition of 1896. Yet, its official "Motives" mention only the offense against good faith in business, breach of general law and order, and the "obvious" parallels to deceit, criminal egoism, and financial abuse (*Untreue*).[95]

95 Fikentscher, Wettbewerb und gewerblicher Rechtsschutz, 1958, 114 (Fn. 26).

Adolf Lobe seems to have been the first to try to derive the distinction between fair and unfair competition from the essence of competition itself.[96] Lobe started from the truism that competition results from business activity. Thus, for him to distinguish between fair and unfair competition, a comparison of relevant business activities of the competitors has to deliver the test. About two decennia later, the idea that a comparison of business activities ought to produce the criterion brought Eugen Ulmer to propose that a business activity making use of a legally unacceptable advance ought to serve as the basis for the judgment of the unfairness of that business activity.[97] In this way, the business act the fairness of which is at stake needed a justification of having the character of a meritorious contribution to general welfare and normalcy, and the business act to be prohibited had to be seen as a non-meritorious one. The burden of proof was on him who alleged the unacceptability of the advance. Later developments of the discussion turned around the necessary degree of non-meritoriousness for being judged as making use of an unacceptable and therefore unfair advance; only grave violations of normal decency of market behavior were regarded as fitting that negative standard.[98] Based on Art. 1382 Code Civil as a general clause of torts law, French law essentially follows the same principles.[99]

Legislation against quantitative restraints of competition including monopoly control was in preparation in many industrial countries before the First World War since it was gradually understood that restrictive practices such as loose agreements in restraint of trade (national and international cartels, exclusive arrangements, discriminations, etc.) and business combines of identical restrictive effect may work just as detrimental to a functioning market as qualitative unfairness of business behavior, the latter even more radically so because of their quantitative, competition-reducing nature. In Germany, preparations were made in the Reichstag of 1904, but during the First World War 1914 - 1918 the initiative stalled. After a rather ineffective "Cartel Ordinance" of 1923 that (by a requirement to register) encouraged cartelization rather than controlling it, and after Hitler's utilization of Germany's highly cartelized and concentrated industry and business for preparing and waging the Second World War between 1933 and 1939, the Allied decartelization and deconcentration laws of 1945-47 laid a foundation for a German antitrust law, first by being continued as German law *verbatim*,[100] and since 1958 as a stim-

[96] Lobe, Die Bekämpfung des unlauteren Wettbewerbs, Vol. 1: Der unlautere Wettbewerb als Rechtsverletzung, 1907.

[97] Ulmer, Sinnzusammenhänge im modernen Wettbewerbsrecht, 1932.

[98] Fikentscher (Fn. 95), 114 ff.

[99] For a theoretical and comparative introduction as well as for the details of French antitrust law, see Krasser, Das Recht des unlauteren Wettbewerbs in den Mitgliedstaaten der Europäischen Wirtschaftsgemeinschaft: Frankreich (in the series ed. by Ulmer, Gutachten erstattet im Auftrag der Kommission der Europäischen Wirtschaftsgemeinschaft vom Max-Planck-Institut für ausländisches und internationles Patent-, Urheber- und Wettbewerbsrecht in München, Band 4: Frankreich, 1967).

[100] Fikentscher/Gleiss, Weitergeltung des Dekartellierungsrechts, Wirtschaft und Wettbewerb, 1955, 525-533; reprinted in: Der Markenartikel 1955, 450-459.

ulus, not as a model, for a German Law Against Restraints of Competition. Also since the year 1958, German antitrust law became gradually superimposed, but not repealed, by EU law.[101] To many lawyers of the German tradition, the central idea of illegalizing restraints of competition appeared to be close to banning unfair competition. Taken together, the quantitative protection against the forestallment of free competition and the qualitative protection against the distortion of fair deals, looked like a promising pathway for a German post-war economy. It meant a "see-it-fresh" public policy favoring ordinary, recognized and decent business behavior, in short, what can be called legitimate trade.[102]

As regards the "Mogul Steamship legal systems", at face value no general fairness test exists in the business law of these systems. Achieving very similar outcomes to those of their colleagues on the European Continent, British judges in 1889/1892 resorted to a theory of tortious business acts. Just as in the Continental European unfair competition laws, a business act of decidedly non-meritorious nature, granting an unacceptable advance over competitors or competition-related business partners, was the object to be judged. However, the line of reasoning is in part different. In concise terms (skipping a wealth of theoretical and case-related debates) the Anglo-American law of unfair trade relations including the law of unfair competition is as follows:

Unfair trade practices are regarded wrongful acts and sanctioned under law and equity (cease and desist or other injunctive relief, damages, treble damages, fines, administrative orders, etc.). Whether or not a commercial act is wrongful depends on whether the act meets the requirements of a nominate tort or falls under the scope of prima-facie-tort liability (from which innominate torts may arise).[103] Nom-

---

[101] Cf. Fikentscher, A Transnational Antitrust Convention and the Recent European Antitrust Proposals: Exercises in Economic Anthropology, in: Jones/Matsushita (eds.), Competition Policy in the Global Trading System, 2002, 341-386 (Chap. 18); idem, Das Unrecht einer Wettbewerbsbeschränkung: Kritik am Weißbuch und VO-Entwurf zu Art. 81, 82 EG-Vertrag (*The Wrong of a Trade Restraint: Critique of the White Book and of the Draft Regulation for Art. 81, 82 EC Treaty),* Wirtschaft und Wettbewerb 2001, 446-458.

[102] Fikentscher (Fn. 22, 95), 117-119 (the monograph turned the law of cartels, as it was called at that time, from a sidefield of corporation law into a field of torts law); also idem, Systemfragen im europäischen Recht der Wettbewerbsbeschränkungen, in: Wirtschaftsordnung und Rechtsordnung, Festschrift für Franz Böhm, 1965, 257-278 (on the suitability of the new German understanding, system and implementation of the law of restraints of competition for the beginning European law of restraints of competition, in contrast to the French industry policy "planification" and the British abuse approach); idem 2001 (Fn. 101).

[103] Oppenheim, Unfair Trade Practices: Cases, Comments and Materials, Trade Regulation, 1950, 43, 46-58, 68 ff.; Graf von Westerholt/Gysenberg, Das Recht des unlauteren Wettbewerbs in den Mitgliedstaaten der Europäischen Wirtschaftsgemeinschaft (ed. by Ulmer, Gutachten erstattet im Auftrag der Kommission der Europäischen Wirtschaftsgemeinschaft vom Max-Planck-Institut für ausländisches und internationales Patent-, Urheber- und Wettbewerbsrecht in München), Band 6: Vereinigtes Königreich von Großbritannien und Nordirland, 1981, 10-16; Ohly, Richterrecht und Generalklausel im Recht des unlauteren Wettbewerbs – ein Methodenvergleich des englischen und des deutschen Rechts, 1997; O. W. Holmes, Jr., in Aikins v. State of Wisconsin, 195 U. S. 194, 25 S. Ct. 3, 49 L. Ed 154 (1904); Prosser on Torts (1941) 5 f.

inate torts in trade and commerce are passing-off, misrepresentation, and misappropriation.[104] Judge-made law has developed the two latter from the first category (passing-off). Generally speaking, case law also gradually widens the scope of all three.[105] If an act does not amount to a nominate tort, courts examine prima-facie-tort liability, a broad field of tortious behavior from which hitherto unnamed ("innominate") torts may be derived. European Continental lawyers would speak of a "general clause", in contrast to the "enumeration principle" underlying the limited number of nominate torts. Still, it is the dominant opinion in Anglo-American law and equity that there is no general concept of "unfair competition" since there is neither room for such concept between the nominate torts and the freedom of trade and commerce, nor the necessity to fill such a gap; Bowen, L.J., in Mogul Steamship., Ltd. v. McGregor, Gow & Co., 23 Q.B.D. 598 (1889), affirmed (1892) A.C. 25, Lord Esher dissenting.[106] Instead, recourse is sought in the even wider and also more imprecise general clause of prima-facie-tort liability; Allan v. Flood, (1898) A.C. 1; Quinn v. Leatham, (1901), AC. 495; Lumley v. Gye, 2 Ell. & Bl. 216 (1853). Mogul, Allan and Quinn were often referred to as the "House of Lord's Trilogy", Mogul speaking in favor of enumerated nominate torts, and Allan and Quinn as footsteps to the development of new tortious actions in business law.[107]

Bowen's case law positivism makes it easy to overlook seemingly shaky values such as "unfair" and "just". It preempts H.L.A. Hart's stance in the positivism debate between H.L.A. Hart and Patrick Devlin in the 1950ies.[108] To delineate right and wrong in British business law, Bowen, L.J., contents himself by relying on the enumerated nominate tort actions of English law. Of course, this reluctance is only understandable because English judges are free to create new tort actions "out of nothing".

Prima facie tort theory of liability covers all facets of human behavior[109] and therefore also trade and commerce.[110] Because of the limited number of nominate business torts, this broad idea of innominate (unnamed) torts is of particular importance in trade and commerce, both involving competition and non-competition. Prosser summarizes that

> "(i)t is now generally felt that tort law is broader than any named categories and that some more or less vague general principles run through it, however difficult they may be to formulate. There is no necessity whatever that a tort must have a name."[111]

---

[104] Westerholt (Fn. 103), 91-123; Oppenheim (Fn. 103), 425- 619; Fikentscher/Ramsauer, Traditionswissen – Tummelplatz immaterialgüterrechtlicher Prinzipien, Urheberrecht, Gestern – Heute – Morgen, für A. Dietz zum 65. Geburtstag, Ganea, etc. (eds.) Munich 2001, 25-41.

[105] Westerholt (Fn. 103), 13, 15, 91 ff.; Oppenheim (Fn. 103), 43, 425 ff.

[106] A theoretical formulation of this dissent in: Callmann, What is Unfair Competition, 28 Geo. L.J. 585 (1940); for this debate see Oppenheim (Fn. 103), 62 – 64.

[107] On the „Trilogy", see Oppenheim (Fn. 103), 46, 52 ff.

[108] On this debate, e.g., Fikentscher, Methoden des Rechts (Fn. 41), Vol. 2, 1976, 54 f., 321, 430.

[109] Holmes (Fn. 103).

[110] Oppenheim (Fn. 103), 46.

[111] Prosser (Fn. 103), 5-6.

Examples of trade and commerce related tort action developed on the basis of prima facie tort liability are an interference of contractual relations,[112] certain infringements of intellectual property,[113] and certain misappropriations in connection with the right of privacy.[114] Prima facie tort theory of liability, particularly in the range of trade and commerce, largely functions as a default mechanism wherever nominate torts in that range are absent. Therefore, the often heard statement that Anglo-American business law or legal policy does not know a concept such as "unfair" is misleading, and a reference to Mogul would be in vain, since the prima facie tort theory of liability is the broader principle.[115]

Prima-facie-tort liability is grounded on the assumption that "(i)t has been considered that, prima facie, the intentional infliction of temporal damages is a cause of action which, as a matter of substantive law, whatever may be the form pleading, requires a justification, if the defendant is to escape".[116] This legal and equitable assumption, again in a form of a principle that would be called a "general clause" in Continental law, comes close to Art. 1382 French Code Civil (of 1804), according to which an act that inflicts damage upon another obliges him by whose "faute" (= culpable unlawfulness) it occurs to repair that damage. Holmes' rendition of the prima facie tort theory of liability also resembles § 826 German Civil Code, a provision that serves as a device offering remedy whenever a wrongful act calls for appropriate legal compensation and because of the "enumerative" nature of German torts law that "nominate" tort law is silent.[117]

As a result – with a view to the widespread of both Anglo-American common law and of European Continental laws and their respective transplants – there is in most

---

[112] Oppenheim (Fn. 103), 34-40.

[113] Oppenheim (Fn. 103), Chapt. 3, 117 ff.

[114] Fikentscher/Ramsauer (Fn. 104).

[115] A recent example: The Economist, Against Fairness, 3 July 2010, 14; it is noteworthy that the anonymous writer of this article uses the same argument against fairness as Bowen, L.J., who wrote for the majority in Mogul that instead of resorting to an imprecise colloquial term such as fair it is preferable to go for the more formal notion of justice (p. 14 left column), that is, to torts law. Both Bowen and the Anonymous fail to notice general torts law, in European Continental language the "general clause", of prima facie tort. Then why not accept fairness of commerce? It would not hurt free enterprise. Another modern follower of the Mogul doctrine, however unaware of the "trilogy", is David Gerber, Anthropology, History and the "More Economic Approach" in European Competition Law – A Review Essay, IIC 2010, 441-449.

[116] O. W. Holmes, Jr., in Aikens v. State of Wisconsin, 195 U.S. 194, 25 S.Ct. 3, 49, 49 L.Ed. 154 (1904).

[117] As to differences, in French law, negligence suffices while Holmes mentions intentionality. German law requires intentionality (as Holmes does) of the act (but not of the offense against the "good mores"), but in contrast to French and Angloamerican common law adds the test of (objectively) offending "the good mores". A remarkable difference relates to the burden of proof of unlawfulness and culpability on the side of the defendant: French and German law see the burden on the plaintiff's side, Angloamerican law on the defendant's. The defendant is the one who has to "justify" the "infliction" of "damages" by showing the reasonableness and merits of his business conduct. Hence, unexpectedly, Angloamerican law gives – at least procedurally – an even more efficient protection against what in substance is unfair competitition, in spite of some lip service to the "liberty of competition" contained in many a case.

countries of the world a legal rejection and ensuing control of unfair acts committed in trade and commerce (including in competition) in a "general-clause styled manner." This justifies further investigation of what "unfairness" of business conduct means. Before going on to that investigation, however, the question has to be answered whether, compared to the above, anything is different when the offense does not consist in qualitative "unfairness" but in a quantitative "restriction of competition."

Why should restraining competition and impeding another merchant's business in competitive or non-competitive relationships be condemned at all? Are there parallels to unfair competition in the meaning characterized in the foregoing text?[118] It is the same principle of rewarding a merchant's respectable contribution to ordinary trade and commerce that induces a transfer of economic evaluation into business law. What is reproached against a restraint of trade (including competitive trade) are the unjustified advances following from unmerited market power, such as from a mutual understanding to raise prices or lower quality, exploiting a monopoly by vertical agreements, or otherwise distorting trade. Possessing and utilizing comparatively greater market influence or acquiring greater market power by agreements in restraint of trade means to be permitted to work less in order to stay in business. Restraining competition or using existing restraints of competition grants undeserved power in the market and unearned advances in relation to other participants of a market. It leads to market inequalities. Therefore these advantages should not be rewarded. Consequently, the same principle of meritoriousness of participating in ordinary trade and commerce and the consequential refusal to honor undeserved advantages unites qualitative and quantitative distortions of generally agreed-upon business behavior.[119] This principle can

[118] For the following, see, e.g., Fikentscher (Fn. 22); a more modern version, also with respect to European law, idem, Das Unrecht einer Wettbewerbsbeschränkung: Kritik am Weißbuch und VO-Entwurf zu Art. 81, 82 EG-Vertrag. Wirtschaft und Wettbewerb 2001, 446- 458; it should be noted that in the 1957 book according to the terminology of that period, the term „Marktbeherrschung" (market domination) is not used in the sense it is used today: as a synonym for monopoly, near-monopoly, or substantial impediment of effective competition (e.g., in the "SIEC test") but in the sense of restraint of competition (not even "substantial" but at least "appreciable").

[119] In the words of 4 Restatement § 766, there is a general duty not to interfere purposely with another's reasonable expectations of trade with a third person, whether or not the expectancies are secured by contract unless the interferences is privileged under the circumstances, Oppenheim (Fn. 103), 67, 1307. In the United Kingdom, the Mogul decision opened a wide field of entrepreneurial liberty in the choice of business practices, but a step-by-step expansion of the passing-off tort claim provided for redress of unusual and unacceptable competitive behavior, Westerholt, op.cit. 13 with cases and references. In France, *concurrence déloyale* was not developed and interpreted as a guiding principle, but outlawed as unacceptable in a case-by-case method of an interpretation of Art. 1382 Code Civil as a general clause. In Germany, the search for a basic principle underlying unfairness first found followers of a general principle of meritoriousness of partipation in ordinary trade and commerce (e.g., Nipperdey, Wettbewerb und Existenzvernichtung, 1930), then of the idea that unfairness in business means making use of undeserved advantages (Ulmer, Warenzeichen und unlauterer Wettbewerb in ihrer Fortbildung durch die Rechtsprechung, 1929), and at present rather rejects a positive concept of *Leistungswettbewerb,* without however giving up the guiding principle of prohibiting the use of improper and disapproved advantages (Baumbach/Hefermehl, Wettbewerbsrecht, 23rd ed. 2004, § 1 UWG (H. Köhler).

be said to be at the bottom of business law of most nations and cultures. Of course, the legal consequences of disobeying this principle may be different from nation to nation, from culture to culture, depending on local traditions, experiences, pre-existing economic structures inside and outside of the relevant territory,[120] its size, climate, ethnographic data and overt and covert modes of thought.

1.4.6 The social aspects of the invisible hand

As discussed above,[121] the social aspects of competition and market belong to the moral premises of the invisible hand. Otherwise, John Holland's breakfast example would not work. Wherever the social aspects of competition and market are not heeded, three instruments of economic policy shortage economy, development economy, and surveillance of economy have to be put to work.

In a similar context, the social sides of competition and market were mentioned before, when the establishment of markets was addressed as a public task. The task consists in equipping people with enough money in their pockets to go to the markets to be established for feeding, clothing and answering the needs and preferences of those who opt for them.[122]

A third idea leads to the same end: the limits of elasticity. The origin of this idea again is competition. Competition as guided by the invisible hand necessarily involves a certain elasticity, itself a social aspect of the invisible hand.

Elasticity is generally discussed in at least two contexts, as simple elasticity and as cross-price elasticity.[123] Simple elasticity shows up in situations such as these: If due to a housing shortage the rent for four-room apartments increases, people looking for an apartment may think about opting for three-room apartments. If chinaware traditionally produced in the Bavarian Forest can no longer compete with chinaware imported from China, buyers will buy the latter. In both cases there may be enough elasticity to switch to the cheaper offer. But there are social limits: If the family that looks for an apartment to rent is so large that three rooms are simply not enough, and if chinaware rises in price so that the consumer is no longer willing to pay for it regardless of its origin, consumers may change to using paper plates or start spooning from the opened tin can. There are social limits, sheer hunger and cold among the most serious ones. Beyond these social limits, the elasticity of the invisible hand and with it the invisible hand itself as the most social distributor of needed goods no longer work.

---

[120] For instance, whether "bigness as such" is an offense depends on whether a given economic structure needs improvement. The IG Farben and the "Ufa" (movie industry) deconcentrations under Allied occupation antitrust in post-war Germany are historical examples.

[121] In connection with reading and misquoting Smith (chapter 1.4.1).

[122] Ibidem.

[123] Triffin, Monopolistic Competition and General Equilibrium Theory, 1949; Küng, Zur Lehre von den Marktformen und Marktbeziehungen, in: Konkurrenz und Planwirtschaft, 1946; Machlup, The Political Economy of Monopoly, 1952, 9; Borchardt/Fikentscher 1957 (Fn. 88), note 20, in the reprint of 1992, 140.

Cross-price elasticity is composed of simple elasticity and substitutability. The cross-price elasticity indicates the relationship in the sales of one good to another. The price of good A drops when the producer of a comparable good B reduces B's price. The relationship represents the degree by which one good is replaceable by another.[124] Both simple and cross-price elasticity describe the same phenomenon of a competitive reaction that helps define a market. Moreover, it defines where a market and its "self-healing forces" end. Where in spite of moving market data elasticity can no longer be ascertained, the invisible hand can no longer be relied upon. Stepping over this line means entering the realm of the social net Adam Smith considers a framing condition of the market mechanism he describes.[125]

The limits of elasticity are absurdly but strikingly illustrated in a sketch by famous Karl Valentin (a German humorist, † 1948). He meets his partner, Lisl Karlstadt:

> "Listen, Lisl, I am so happy, I finally found a job"
> Lisl: "Wow. Where? What are you doing?"
> Karl: "I'm now the gardener of Count Rembremerding."
> Lisl: "And what do you have to do for Count Rembremerding?"
> Karl:" He has a fountain in his garden, and in the spring I have to turn it on, and in the fall I have to turn it off."
> Lisl: "And what do you get for that?"
> Karl:" When I turn it on, I get one mark. And when I turn it off, I get another mark."
> Lisl: "And can you make a living from this?"
> Karl: "A living – yes. But how (*Leben schon – aber wie*)."

In an economic science, the elasticity theorem is being applied to meet all kinds of purposes. In the situation told in the sketch, it is attached to the property-competition-optimum curve described above. Its use here is the differentiation between competitive and social cost economies. The use of the elasticity theorem for the distinction between competitive and social cost economies facilitates the fixation of definable contents of exchange value socialism, and thus enables politics to reject use value socialism, *iustum pretium* economies and other economic and political dictatorships.

When at the outbreak of the French Revolution, so the story goes, messengers reported to Queen Marie Antoinette of France that people rioted in the streets of Paris crying for bread, and she allegedly asked: "Why don't they eat cake?", she disregarded the laws of elasticity. The revolutionaries could not change to cake because cake was more expensive than bread. There was no market that could have provided for a substitute for bread. In 1948, the "father of the German economic miracle", Ludwig Erhard, was asked: What is the "social" element in your Social Market Economy? He is said to have answered: "The Social Market Economy is social because it is a market economy, the word social need not be added." Did Ludwig Erhard, like Marie Antoinette, disregard elasticity? The economic history of post-war Germany tells how Erhard, after having stated the free competitive

[124] Borchardt/Fikentscher (Fn. 88), 139 (in the reprint).

[125] See 1.4.1. above.

market system as the principle, admitted and introduced free (individual) markets only after careful examination of whether on both sides of the market, buyers and sellers, there was enough market power of individual firms to engage in competition. In terms of the optimum curve proposed above, Erhard examined whether the firms on either side of the individual market operated close enough to the optimum point on the curve of competition-relevant exclusively owned resources.[126]

Before this stage was reached, Erhard had followed the rules of centrally-planned economy. It was in the memory of many Germans from WW I- and post-WW I times, reestablished under Hitler in 1936 and confirmed and rigorously administered by the Allied occupation powers, including the U.S.-American, between 1945 and June 1948.[127] Of course, another question is whether during the period between 1936 and 1948 a centrally-planned economy was necessary. For Hitler this type of economy, called *Bewirtschaftung* (coupon economy) was part of his preparation for war. After WW II, continued *Bewirtschaftung* seemed necessary as an answer to extreme shortages in all areas of the economy. Both Erhard and the occupation administrations at least subconsciously knew about the humanity-contingent limits to the market drawn by elasticity.

A contemporary group of German legal and economic scholars unintendedly seem to revive some kind of *Bewirtschaftung* as the leading and most important type of economies, placing the free and fair market type of economy in the tradition of Adam Smith, English and U.S.-American mainstream, Walter Eucken, Franz Böhm and Ludwig Erhard on the second row and subordinating free and fair economy as a function of government-administered general welfare (*Gemeinwohl*). However, in the writings of this group, references to legal or economic *Bewirtschaftung* literature of the years 1914 through 2000 are scarce. It might be that trying to find a theoretical access to the public law of economic regulation, these authors were simply not aware of entering the treacherous terrain of economic order systems. What they say is not so new and original as it appears at first sight.[128]

---

[126] See Fn.69 above. Some branches were permitted to enter market freedom as late as after the Korean War.

[127] See esp. Huber and Rauschenbach (Fn. 69).

[128] Lepsius, § 19 Ziele der Regulierung, in: Fehling/Ruffert (eds.), Regulierungsrecht, 2010, 1055-1987, with a comparative outlook on the U.S.-American development of "regulated industry" economics and law and differences in systematic respect, at No. 31; idem, § 1 Regulierungsrecht in den U.S.A: Vorläufer und Modell, in: Fehling/Ruffert op. cit. 3-75; idem, § 4 Verfassungsrechtlicher Rahmen der Regulierung, in: Fehling/Ruffert op. cit. 143-213; Eifert, Regulierungsstrategien, in: Hoffmann-Riem/Schmidt-Assmann/Vosskuhle (eds.), Grundlagen des Verwaltungsrechts, 1996-2011, § 19 No. 126 f.; Holoubek, Vom Wirtschaftsaufsichtsrecht zum Regulierungsverwaltungsrecht?, Gutachten, Österreichischer Juristentag Wien 2009, Band I/1, 19 f. - U.S. American sources: Breyer et al., Administrative Law and Regulatory Policy, 6th ed. 2006; Sunstein, After the Rights Revolution, 1990; Rabin, Federal Regulation in Historical Perspective, 38 Stanford Law Review 1189 ff. (1986); a comparison in: Masing, Die U.S.-amerikanische Tradition der "regulated industries" und die Herausbildung eines europäischen Regulierungsverwaltungsrechts: "constructed markets on networks" vor verschiedenen Rechtskulturen, 128 AöR 558 ff. (2003).

In some of their formulations they come close to a return to principles discussed in the wane of World War I – almost ninety years ago.

The stimulus for a revival of *Bewirtschaftung* may have another source, that is, an attempt to find a theoretical answer to the economic issues of public utilities. The quest for a tenable public utilities theory is supported by comparative views of U.S. American regulated industries laws and economics. Common to the German and the U.S. American theoretical discussion is the assumption that in the field of public utilities (in German sometimes called *Daseinsvorsorge* = provision for existence) a free and fair economy of individual markets does not provide for a necessary justice of production and distribution.

German law makers introduced "regulation laws", putting up "regulation administrations", similar to U.S. federal and state public utilities and regulated industries laws and policies. State-run planning and care was to "regulate" the demand, and to plan production and distribution. The intent to establish common legal principles for at least most of the "regulation" may be understandable. But is this degree of *Gemeinwohl* paternalism adequate to explain economic reality, and is it defendable to interpret economic theory in general by deducing from public utilities research? Isn't again the tail wagging the dog?[129]

Speaking in theoretical terms: Isn't the fixation of the limits of elasticity enough and sufficiently indicative to separate a free and fair market system as a principle to strive for from non-elastic situations of social want such as those of the rioters of the French Revolution and Valentin's happy garden hand turning the fountain-on-and-off?[130]

Out of the multitude of pressing issues raised by public utilities and regulated industries economics, policies and law, with respect to the theme discussed here – rules of free and fair global, but culture-oriented trading – only one issue shall be addressed: the relationship of principle and exception in view of market competition and the social needs of public utilities. For some of the regulation theorists, a free and fair market is not the principle and regulation not the exception. Instead, common welfare (*Gemeinwohl*) is the header for governmental decisionism how to serve economic needs best. Convincing reasons speak in favor of instituting a competitive market as the rule (especially for testing its social adaptivity due to its flexibility). Instituting a marketless social distribution system can only serve as an emergency brake. That system should look at comparable markets for as-if competitive data. The argument is made that both market and its imitation comes down to regulation.[131] The following reasons argue against such indiscriminate "regulatory" understanding:

---

[129] Cf. text near note 68, above.

[130] Ockham's razor says „no." (Ockham's razor, called after the English scholastic William of Ockham, requires approaching the result of a logical deduction on the shortest possible way and avoiding unnecessary detours). Did Normannic verticality leave traces in "regulated" law (cf. Fn. 20)?

[131] E.g., Lepsius, (Fn. 128), § 19 Fn. 1, 28, 43, 58 f.

(1) Competition is not a law of nature. A competitive market is never "emergent." It only works under some specific conditions of culture, the most important condition being superaddition, that is, the understanding of a unit of the competitors in addition to the sum of the competitors, and therefore an inside-outside distinction, common law and morals, free communication, control of restraints of competition, state instead of business prerogative, and a social net – as Adam Smith has duly remarked or implied.[132] Adam Smith's and his followers' numerous value-laden preconditions for the working of the invisible hand cannot be discredited as being "rationalist." If there is a law of nature contained in a competitive market it is that it is bound to abolish itself.[133]

(2) To let government decide how to best spread the amenities of welfare across the nation borders on decisionism without compass. Common welfare (*Gemeinwohl)* amounts to a social goal too loosely knit to be practical. It is also exposed to the danger of being abused. There are much debated historical examples of abuse, from classical Greek sophism over the unsuccessful *iustum pretium* policy of the Church State to the various "realist" movements, socialist use value fiat and *Bewirtschaftung* (see above). F.A. von Hayek's concept of "competition as an open-goal process of discovery" marks the opposite of politically prefabricated *Gemeinwohl* allegations (because it has no system-immanent answer when competition "discovers" restraints of competition). But it is just as ambivalent as *Gemeinwohl*. Both extremes show the necessity of value-consistent guideposts of rule and exceptions, of contents of "freedom to" instead of the emptiness of mere "freedom from".

(3) Under the cultural conditions discussed before, a free and fair competitive system should be the principle, the methodological rule. Then, from the conditions it may be derived when never the rule should not apply, but – for example – a distributive system of social support is in place. From the methodological rule follows that an antitrust proceeding against abusive behavior of a monopoly or of members of a factually competition-restricted oligopoly,[134] for example in a public utility branch, is preferable. Laws for doing so exist and need only be applied, to the numerous cases that exist, too.

Referring to the situations of social want that cannot be cured by free and fair competition because elasticity is keeping them out of reach of its "self-healing" forces, historically the classical (and most primitive) instrument of first resort is to distribute the want among the needy ones. After 1933, the efforts of the Nazi German government were directed towards complete independence from imports (so-called "autarky"). It appeared that some lacunas of self-sufficiency could be closed, for example by the invention of plastic (catchword: *Ersatz* = replacement) but that for some import articles this did not work out. For example, the *Butterlücke* (lacuna of

---

[132] More on superaddition in Fikentscher (Fn. 1), Chap. 9 III, p. 327 ff.; idem (Fn. 5), 57 ff., 158.

[133] This is called the freedom paradox; details in Fikentscher, Die Freiheit und ihr Paradox, 1997.

[134] Expressed in the technical language of the classical theory of market forms and behavior: *durch wettbewerbsbeschränkten Zustand nach innen* und *durch Wettbewerbsbeschränkung nach außen hinreichend unabhängiges homogenes Oligopol der wenigen*; see Sullivan/Hertz (Fn.4).

butter) could never be closed between 1933 and June 1948. The remedy was a coupon system by which every citizen was guaranteed a certain share of the butter available nationwide. A paper document contained the name and address of every citizen including children on preprinted squares, similar to today's newspaper ads, for instance: 125 g butter/week for an adult or 100 g butter/week for a child. The retailer cut off the little square from the document (the *Lebensmittelkarte* = food chart, coupon sheet) and spent the evening by gluing all the little scraps onto big pieces of paper which were turned into the competent food administration agency. Not only was money needed to go shopping but also the food chart had to be taken along and presented to the shop owner. In the beginning the food charts contained only a few items such as butter, but month after month more and more articles were included, month per month, and stayed there until June 1948 when Ludwig Erhard, against the will of the occupation powers, had the coupon system abolished overnight (June 20/21, 1948). It appeared that there was enough demand and supply, including of butter, so that the economy returned to exchanges of goods against hard currency. German total *Bewirtschaftung* ended in June 1948, only in some sectors the instrument is still in use. Today, many European countries suffer from demographic changes, so that support for families may be granted by money transfers or issuance of coupons, for example for school books or tuition.

Thus, the simplest manner to deal with social want is *Bewirtschaftung*, distributing the want by dividing the available supply by the number of buyers, or otherwise trying to restore balance between the powers on either side of the market. A translation into the English language could be "shortage economy." During WW II, Great Britain used a coupon system similar to the German type. For a short while, the European Economic Community returned to *Bewirtschaftung* during the oil crisis of 1974 by using a kind of coupon system because of a shortage of gasoline. But every coupon system asks for a remedy of augmenting resources on the goods or on the money side of the markets, depending on where the imbalance has grown. These attempts to redress and overcome imbalances and to replace *Bewirtschaftung* by normal functioning of the market may be called economic development policy, development aid, foreign aid, industrial policy,[135] economic reinforcement, market restitution, etc.; for German usage, in contrast to *Bewirtschaftung* the term "*Entwicklungswirtschaft*" (= development economy) has been proposed (and accepted).[136]

Together, shortage economy and development economy form the basic stock of government-planned regulated economy including "regulated industries." Both cannot deny their origin and background in the economy of a freely and fairly competitive market economy (in contrast to parts of modern German regulation theory).[137] For the mainstream of national and international economic policy the-

---

[135] On the ambivalent concept of „industry policy" and its relationship to antitrust policy and law see, e.g., Fikentscher, Recht und wirtschaftliche Freiheit, Vol. II, 1993, VII – XIX. There is a traditional conflict of policy between France and Germany.

[136] Fikentscher (Fn. 57), Vol 1, 43 f.; Vol. 2, 31 ff., 33.

[137] See e.g., above, text following Fn. 132.

ory, however, both derive from classic market theory, as two exceptions which are rooted in lacking the elasticity of an (individual) market. Among the duties of the government is to step forward from merely distributing social want among the population to attempting to overcome that shortage by development policies.

There is a third type of planned economy that as a preparatory step should be added to both shortage and development economies, namely public surveillance of eventual deviations from general market performance. The purpose of such governmental surveillance is to warn against imminent deviations in order to take preventive, timely measures. Usually, no special agencies are established for this purpose. Rather, the task is entrusted to the competent ministries and the like. But the function is different from distributing the want and taking steps to overcome it. The German term is *Wirtschaftsaufsicht* (= economic surveillance). Against this background, three fields of economic regulation may be distinguished: shortage economy, development economy, and economic surveillance.[138]

The common feature of these three regulatory duties of any government responsible for a country whose written or unwritten constitution provides for a market economy is that all such regulation becomes necessary by the elasticity innate in the market concept. Therefore, the philosophy behind these regulatory functions is the necessity to protect people who would like to participate in the market but cannot do so because market elasticity is preventing them from such participation. The elasticity-caused dissociation from the market mechanism is what prevents these citizens from being market participants. They would like to, but they cannot. It is not market avoidance or market-dodging that makes them a case for the social net, but a market essentiality. The door to return to market conditions, back to the principle of the working of the invisible hand, possibly in form of as-if-competition, remains open.[139] Until that door in the direction of market conditions has been passed a social net economy – indispensable as it may be – does not provide for the framework of a free and fair competitive market economy.

A different philosophy stands behind another escape from the laws of the market. It is not induced by the limits that elasticity establishes for the functioning of every market (and thus "regretted" by the victims of exclusion from market flexibility), but sought for by those who would like to avoid cost to be paid for every market participation (and thus "welcomed" by cost-dodgers striving to be excluded from market rules and morals as well as shunning the exigencies of FairEconomy). This sometimes pleasant, sometimes unavoidable retreat from markets is at the

---

[138] Fikentscher (Fn. 57), chap. 9, 17 and 24.

[139] Here lies a crucial difference to the theorists of common welfare regulation who deny a linkage to a competition principle. It is interesting to note that the antitrust concept of as-if-competition, important in many public-utility cases and in U.S. American law, not only in antitrust (Sullivan/Hertz Fn. 4), but also in subsidy control cases of the U.S. Fair Trade Commission as "constructed value" or LTFV (Less-Than-Fair-Value), finds little attention in German regulation discussions; see for an example the golf cart case, cit. in Fikentscher 1983 (Fn.61), Vol. 2, 345. In US law, antitrust is to outweigh and balance regulation law. Therefore, to call US law a "precurser" and "model" of regulation law (see Fn. 132 above) does hardly reflect reality.

center of the issue of "social cost."[140] How far do the rules inherent in FairEconomy extend, and what happens beyond those limits?

Social cost may arise when a firm succeeds in externalizing cost in a way that burdens other people, other entities, or simply nature, instead of the originator of the cost. When a laundry shop directs its exhaust of steam etc. into the open air so that neighbors may suffer, these eventual damages are externalized cost. The same holds true when a chemical plant pollutes a creek or river or the ground water by letting liquid waste run into them. Costs are reduced for the firm, but burdened upon outsiders. This is not the place to discuss pro and cons of social cost, however.[141] The issues here at stake are the non-marketability (in principle) of social cost and the place of social cost economy vis-à-vis a free and fair market economy.

Social cost economy can be divided into four kinds of phenomena all of which discharge the originator of the cost from having to carry them and thus characterize him as cost-avoider and consequently as non-market participant.[142] All four kinds involve firms which avail themselves of collective goods: (1) There are users of cost-qualified "club" public goods such as congested highways, public parks or public swimming pools: although a fee for the use may be charged to "run" the "club", the cost caused by the use is higher than the fee so that social costs arise. (2) This is all the more the case for "pure public goods" including "meritorious goods" such as fire brigades, lighthouses and mandatory vaccinations: every captain uses the advantages of the presence of a functioning lighthouse and hereby saves cost but does not pay for it. (3) For cost-free collective goods the situation of cost is not different: in the "tragedy of the commons" cases individual profits are not paid for but the use may ruin the common source of the profits, as in an emptied common fish pond or a cut down rain forest. (4) "Free goods" may not be exposed to such tragedy, but to being burdened with externalities such as filling outer space with rocket debris, spoiling a landscape with sprawling settlements or factory outlets, contributing to climate change or abusing copyright fair use.

In every single of these situations costs are being externalized that should be carried by the user of the collective good who saves cost while profiting from the use. The "trick" is to dissociate from the market. As a rule, profit drawn from a market involves corresponding cost, and relating one to the other is the essence of (individual) market participation that keeps the invisible hand at work, thus minimizing cost. Ducking out of bearing cost spoils the game and the invisible hand's

[140] On this discussion, involving the authorities Milton Friedman, Ronald Coase, Knut Borchardt, Robert D. Cooter and many others. Cf. the discussion at Fikentscher (2004) 179 – 200, 191 f., and the terminology developed there, with references.

[141] Pro, e.g.: Friedman; assumably contra: Elliott, Strengthening Science's Voice at EPA, 66 Law & Contemp. Probs. 45 (2003); idem, Toward Ecological Law and Policy, in: Chertow/Esty (eds.), Thinking Ecologically: The Next Generation of Environmental Policy, 1997, 170.

[142] For the following, see the chart in Fikentscher (Fn. 9), 192. Authors writing in this field differ widely as to terminology. Even basic concepts such as property and good are defined and used differently. The present text uses the terminology developed in Fikentscher (Fn. 9) 179-205 (with references). It has been proven useful in many discussions.

merits.[143] Therefore, in the field of social cost market essentialities are missing so that a social cost economy does not provide for the framework of a free and fair competitive market economy.

The foregoing deliberations demonstrate the need to focus on a general principle of attainment, of bringing about something, of acting the normal generally accepted decent way, of contributing some activity to the "wealth of nations" which is so firmly founded on the wealth and best possible well-being of the individuals. Anthropologically speaking, it is a matter of reciprocity for somebody who engages in economic activities in the widest sense to be permitted to ask for something as long as she or he is willing to contribute.[144] Being addressed for granting something without receiving something, and be it a peppercorn, or a friendly face, or a promise of reliability, such as asking somebody to rely on a credit that induces the creditor to irretrievably eat the bread of tomorrow, is regarded with a deeply rooted mistrust.

A consequence in the present context is the organized society's duty to cut back the discharge of externalities upon outsiders and free goods, whether tragedy-exposed or not.

In later chapters additional consequences will be put forth, as related to concepts such as consideration, reciprocity, gift-giving, non-seriousness, gaming, buying mere chances, inviting to accept risks without due liability, ominous negotiations, and theocratic determinism such as a *iustum pretium* economy. The basis of all this is the acknowledgment of the human ability to form a positive or negative statement, a judgment, a proposition in the sense of empirical Parmenideian-Platonic subject-object evaluation of morality. Again, as in the discussion of Adam Smith's conditions of economic freedom, anthropological and philosophical deliberations emerge and claim attention.[145]

---

[143] At this point, another disadvantage of the unprincipled regulation theory comes to the fore: It has to be neutral as regards social cost. This neutrality forsakes cost control by the invisible hand. Therefore chances are that unprincipled regulation produces at too high a cost. Any similarity of method or effect of regulatory common welfare decisionism and Marxist use value fiat should be avoided, cf. Fn. 68.

[144] On this *allgemeine Leistungsprinzip* (=general principle of ordinary recognized decent businesss behavior, of attainment, of prestation, of merits, of meritoriousness) see the discussion, mainly during the years 1920 ff. (cf., Fn. 73, 123 above).

[145] Parmenides, a pre-Socratic philosopher (540 – 470 B.C.), is said to be the founder of the School of Elea type of epistemology, that is, a theory of getting to know things if only tentatively and incompletely. He distinguished three preconditions of getting to know something: the observing subject, the object to be observed, and "thinking". By thinking Parmenides meant the observer's critical approach to the object to be observed, with the intent to get an understanding judgment about the object. He thought that a human being is able to form merely three kinds of critical judgments, the judgment of whether something is true (or not), whether something is good (fitting, adequate, just, moral, appropriate; or not) and whether something is pleasing (beautiful, appealing, attractive, or not). In the first part of his dialog "Parmenides", Plato (427-347 B.C.) reports Parmenides' epistemology. Plato uses Parmenides' epistemology throughout his own writings ("dialogs", "letters") and tries to improve this method by introducing Socrates' (470-399 B.C) art and practice of dialog. Classical Greek and modern "Western" thinking therefore anchor in Parmenideian epistemology. It facilitates logical proposition, comparison based

1.5 Links between freedom and fairness of a market economy, and the risk and liability mechanism (a preview of Chapters 2 to 4)

There are links between the principles of freedom and fairness of a competitive (= individual market) economy on one hand and the mechanism of risk and liability on the other. Freedom itself is discussed in this Chapter. Rules on freedom and fairness are addressed in Chapter 2. Risk and liability are discussed in Chapter 3. Chapter 4 on sanctions mentions some possible consequences without which liability might appear ineffectual.

Competition is the essence and the focus of a free and fair market system. But competition does not encompass the range of human activities that is called economy. There is, so to speak, an upper limit of competition beyond which competition cannot meet its purpose to eliminate by bankruptcy from participation in economic activities those wasteful firms that cause more cost to general or individual welfare than good ("good" in the sense of ordinary and acceptable contributions). Beyond this limit of workable competition are firms that are "too big to fail", systemic, so that they must be kept alive artificially at taxpayers' expense by the public authorities that should have performed those firms' business in the first place or should have deconcentrated them. There is also a lower limit to the working of competition (as presumably the most effective and just distributor of scarce goods to the places where they are most needed) where this distribution cannot satisfy the needs which to meet an economy exists. The upper and the lower limit are of an elastic nature and pose issues of political and legal choice and evaluation.

As far as competition is permitted to work between these two limits, the usual risks of competition prevail. Whenever such a risk becomes reality, liabilities follow. From the attachment of risk and appertaining liability to competition the contents of liability follow, for example, the amount of damages to be born or repaired (whosoever has to carry the liability under the applicable principles and rules of the law). Part 3 of this book addresses risk in a framework even considerably broader than competition.

Beyond the aforementioned elastic limits of competition the mechanism of risk and appertaining liability does not work. These are fields of political responsibility and political steering (a "political liability", as it were, sometimes giving rise to the call for "more state").

Whenever an economic activity triggers either legal liability to private persons, or "political liability" (in the sense used above) to the general public and the risk

on a *tertium comparationis*, systems going beyond dichotomies, perspective, harmony using horizontals and verticals, superaddition ("the whole is more than the sum of the parts"), and thinking along a directionality of time (*Zeitpfeil*) and thus historical perspective. In this, Parmenides' epistemology differs from Aristotelian entelechy (the theory of immanent meaning of things). Historically, Arab, African and other non-Western philosophies comparatively studied Aristotelianism, not (or much less, or refuting) Parmenideian-Platonic-Neoplatonic epistemology; Fikentscher 1975-77 (Fn. 41 above), vol. I (1975) 235-325; idem 1995/2004 (Fn. 7 above) 157 ff., 181 ff., 419 ff; see also Fn. 41 above; Chapter 4, below, Fn. 34.

affects the legally or politically wrong side, that activity is wrong. In business, activities that are wrong are called unfair.[146]

In other words, whenever somebody acts in business without being exposed to the limiting and controlling effect of competition, the damage done by such action is unfairly inflicted – either by causing unjustified social cost or unjustified individual damage or both. The reason is avoidance of exposure to the risks inherent in competition. This avoidance gives rise to the typical unfair margin resulting from harvesting where one has not sown.

In this way, competition, its elastic limits, risk/liability, and fairness are linked.

1.6 Conclusion

The results of the foregoing checklist of the essence and requirements of a free and fair competitive market system may be summarized as follows:

(1) Economics are contingent upon anthropology. Competition does not consist of natural data, and a market is never simply emergent. Both are concepts produced by human cultures and therefore tied to cultural requirements including culture change. Against the background of Adam Smith's theory of the working of an invisible hand for turning individual egoisms into common welfare, it is noted that Smith himself mentions as preconditions of the working of the invisible hand: persons engaged in egoistic business activities, law, morals, free communication, usages, absence of restraints of competition particularly regarding but not limited to governments and banks, and additional protective measures against poverty in a sense that today may be counted under the concept of a "social net." These preconditions are based upon the following sources:

(2) The requirement of a functioning legal system consisting of general rules and based on justice is stated both in "Theory of Moral Sentiments"[147] and in "Wealth of Nations"[148].

(3) Free communication between the participants of the market has to be safeguarded.[149]

(4) Principles of general morality have to be observed.[150]

---

[146] A register of examples of unfair activities in the context of the crises 2006-2009 in: Fikentscher, Finanzkrise, Wettbewerb und Regulierung, GRUR Int. 2009, 635-646. One of the examples concerns the handing out of credits that carry the risk of becoming „toxic". There is a limit posed to responsible credit-giving, seen both individually and in global dimensions: How much credit does the planet take? The upper limit of competition comes in sight. This issue cannot be explored here in more details; it is to be discussed elsewhere. Basel III can only be a modest beginning (see part 4, below).

[147] The following footnotes are repetitions. They are repeated here for sake of convenience.

[148] Smith, An Inquiry into the Nature and Causes of the Wealth of Nations, 1778, 687 ("exact administration of justice") (cit. Mestmäcker, Fn. 42, 127, 114).

[149] Smith, The Theory of Moral Sentiments, 1759, at 326; a discussion at Mestmäcker (Fn. 42), 110.

[150] Smith, The Theory of Moral Sentiments, 1759, 112 and 304. Mestmäcker (Fn. 42), 111 draws attention to Smith's attempts to combine individual and social ethics.

(5) General rules and usages of societal contact and self-containment tend to neutralize selfish interests.[151]
(6) The absence of foreign monopolies and monopolies at home is inevitable.[152]
(7) Smith goes beyond the precinct of economic freedom and enters the field where markets cannot properly work and less privileged members of society need – in modern terms – a social net. It remains the government's task to reinforce that societal part's chances to overcome the social defects.[153]
(8) According to Smith, there is a need to establish publicly financed institutions for public utility ends (*Daseinsvorsorge*), whenever private profit does not cover the cost of establishing, maintaining and protecting collective goods such as schools and other installations and environments that are "more than worthwhile" to have in a society.[154]

    All these essentials of a free and fair competitive market economy are valid now as much as they were at Adam Smith's time.
(9) In continuation of the social requirement under (8) of availability of public utilities a more modern distinction may be added: Where the competition-immanent elasticity of market reactions does not work, this limit of elasticity evokes the need for legal instruments to distribute the social want, to address the want itself by adequate means of economic development, and to prepare these measures by effective observation and control of economic on-goings. Further implications of the foregoing characteristics of competitive markets include:
(10) Market in the sense of this book is the individual market, not the objective market.
(11) Free and fair competition can only be secured on the basis of exchange values, not of use values. For political ends, use values have to be prescribed (the "Gosplan ideology") and thus require dictatorship. Use values discussed in a political context are exchange values.
(12) ORDO- and neo-liberalism may be expressed in terms of New Economic Institutionalism. This has advantages in stressing the role of environment and of culture and cultures in formulating the requirements for a global free and fair competitive market economy, and in a more precise examination of the roles of property and property rights for the same requirements.
(13) On this basis, the concepts of perfect competition and monopoly can be readjusted.
(14) In turn, this leads to a better understanding of the essence of competition, aided by a new theory of a competitive optimum.
(15) The result is an improved description of the working of a freely and fairly competitive market and its limits of elasticity. Competition, its elastic limits,

---

[151] Smith, The Theory of Moral Sentiments, 1759, 175.

[152] Smith, An Inquiry into the Nature and Causes of the Wealth of Nations, 1778, 687.

[153] See Mestmäcker's summary (Fn. 42), 127.

[154] Smith, An Inquiry into the Nature and Causes of the Wealth of Nations, 1778, 687 and 788 (schools), cit. Mestmäcker, 127 (Fn. 42).

risk/liability and fairness interlink by avoidance of exposure to the risks inherent in competition. This avoidance gives rise to the well-known unfair margin resulting from harvesting where one has not sown.

(16) The criterion of elasticity of the market is an appropriate tool for defining the "social net."

(17) A social net economy has two parts: the shortage, development, and adherent observation activities of the government triggered by the elasticity criterion, and the economy of social cost. The first concerns victims of dissociations from markets, the second cost-avoiders and externality-originators. The first are market-seekers, the second market-dodgers. Yet both react to social cost economic laws. Sound governmental economic policy should help the market-seekers to get into a market, and force the market-avoiders to internalize their externalities, hereby preserving collective goods (incl. environment and cultures) and decreasing cost.

(18) It seems important to let an underlying principle, and a legally fixed relationship of rule and exception, guide the prerogatives of competitive market behavior. The underlying principle is the principle of attainment, i.e., of being willing to contribute to human achievements in ordinary trade and commerce. The rule-and-exception methodology is to place the working of free and fair competition first, and the exceptions of governmental regulation second.

(19) The concept of free and fair competition used in this paper is derived from an empiricist approach to observed economic behavior in the sense of economical-anthropological substantivism, not from a neoclassic model approach which characterizes economical-anthropological formalism.

(20) European and German philosophy of competition law with free and fair competition differs from U.S. American economic philosophy. Expressed in catchwords, the European and German tradition builds upon the trilateral system of society, state and government, while the U.S.-American tradition starts from a bilateral system of society and government. The historical background of this difference is the one between the horizontal-vertical construction of Frankish pledge-of-faith organized society on the one hand and the retained ducal, more centralized tradition as part of the Normannic version of the borrowed Frankish pledge-of-faith on the other. In competition law, this leads to a European understanding of antitrust as a means of stabilization and reinforcement of the horizontal-vertical structure of organized society and of fair trade law as a means of a general control of unjustified getting ahead in business, whereas in the U.S.A. antitrust is an instrument used by the government in the perennial combat between government and business for the prerogative of power, while a general fair trade law comparable to the European one is practically non-existent.

(21) In politics, economics and law, many searches are under way to trace the causes of the present financial and economic crisis, and proposals are made to prevent future crises of comparable or even larger dimensions. These proposals look similar to levers of an apparatus, or dials of a machine, the user of the machine being invited to adjust the dials. Few authors speak of the machine

itself to which the dials are attached. The present text is about the machine. Chapter 1 is devoted to some anthropological and economic foundations of a crisis-resistant fair and free economy, it describes and explains the mechanism the working of which should be reset. For this it does not suffice to point to the concepts of market and competition as if they were fixed and unqualified entities, grown from nature, "emergent" as the jargon goes. On the contrary, the mechanism the dials of which are to be adjusted is a highly qualified object of the social sciences.

A rivalry-defined and therefore individual and competition-identified market; framed by law, moral, societal usage, communication, trust, and both environmental and cultural consciousness; based on a general principle of ordinary decency and recognition for humanity; protected against restraints of competition such as monopolies and competition-restrained oligopolies; equipped instead with property rights and other positions apt to be competed about, so that there is a competitive optimum in the relationship between *property* and *change of property* ("the optimum curve"); expressed in exchange values (instead of use values) and therefore aware of cost; a market concept that despite its cognoscibility in terms of New Economic Institutionalism follows from substantivist empiricism and not from neoclassic model-building ("the theory of the individual market"); and supported by a social net and risk-controlled economy where competition does not work, either because social cost derive from actual poverty or because "too-big-to-fail situations" prevail (both combined to a "theory of competitive elasticity"). – Is this too much to ask?

The freedom and fairness of this market concept forms the focus of the mechanism defined above and below. Whoever prefers to turn the dials differently had better first redefine and redesign the machinery.

2 Rules on Competition after the Crisis

This chapter aims at framing ideas on how to improve the rules on restrictive and unfair business practices in the aftermath of the financial crisis. If something was rotten in the international legal framework for the financial industry, then it is necessary to turn to the fields of economic law. Many scholars and legislative initiatives have focused on specific laws for capital markets and the supervisory authorities. This chapter looks into another direction and goes to the very roots of economic law: the basics of business behavior are regulated by the most general laws of contract, property, liability, and competition. These fields form the legal ground on which an economy flourishes. In this chapter the focus lies on rules regarding competition law in its two main aspects, the rules that deal with collusion and market power (known in the U.S. as antitrust law) and the rules that deal with unfair business practices. All these rules are based on a concept of a market economy that leaves the decision-making to the market participants. We have learned, as the first chapter in this book has shown, that market participants know best and that the principles of supply and demand for exchange values are fundamentals of human culture. Yet, the challenge is to find well-suited rules to ensure that the market economy works. The ideas presented here center around the concept of Fair-Economy: In business players need freedom, but business as such also needs a minimum standard of fairness.

We proceed in five steps: firstly, we argue that a free market needs some regulation. Free markets depend upon regulation that ensures its necessary (systemic) conditions. Secondly, we turn to the rules on restrictive business practices, called antitrust law in the U.S., competition law in Europe. These rules are seen as basic rules guaranteeing free markets. Yet, it is necessary to rethink the rules – they are outdated since they were shaped for an industrial age, but may not fit the finance-driven business-world of today. Thirdly, we suggest focusing on a second set of rules that is necessary to make markets work and not derail: rules on fairness. The fairness principle needs to be clarified, and we try to give ideas on how "fair" may translate into a legal concept. Fourthly, we examine one area in financial markets where the fairness principle has been disregarded, namely in business-to-consumer transactions between banks and private persons. Finally, we shortly touch upon enforcement issues. Here, the focus will be on the international dimension of the rules and on the possibilities of private enforcement. This, however, will be explored in more detail in chapter 4 of this book.

2.1 Freedom needs regulation

If you think of the global economy as a game with different players who interact to advance in the game you may also consider the question what makes a good game. The answer is: The quality of the game depends upon its rules. Good rules are based on agreed principles. Such principles, democratically agreed upon, whether explicitly by law or implicitly by a societal contract, form the foundation of the whole market economy system. If the economy does not comply with them it will collapse. Freedom is the very basic principle that politics and rule-making has to stick to when trying to design rules for the market economy. The market depends upon, or better: *is* free decision-making by the economic players. Markets work through the voluntary co-operation of men who decide autonomously about the price they are willing to pay to satisfy their wants and needs. To watch markets at work means to watch individuals taking decisions, i.e. exercising their free will. There is no doubt about freedom being the cornerstone of the market economy. Yet, despite all the praise sung to freedom by the apostles of the market economy, the concept of freedom remains blurry.

2.1.1 The two dimensions of freedom

In order to devise rules necessary to sustain freedom the concept must be clarified in the first place. Freedom actually entails two notions, the objective and the individual dimension. The first dimension of freedom concerns its power as an objective principle: the market economy is characterized by the virtues of this "objective" freedom.[1] Freedom claims primacy as the key organizing principle for social interactions in economic affairs. Freedom in this respect commands a general absence or limitation of government intervention. The economy shall be shaped through the autonomous decisions of the individuals participating in that economy. Therefore, whenever someone starts to define new rules or "press buttons on the machine" of economic policy, the alert goes off and suggests to abstain. The objective value of freedom may also be endangered by a market structure that is dominated by private entities. Restrictions to economic freedom may stem from public sources as well as private ones. Turning to private restrictions of economic freedom in its objective sense necessarily implies to define at what point the concentration of power in private hands becomes a structural problem for freedom. To determine when private entities restrict freedom is a most delicate endeavor: It is necessary to avoid unnecessary harm to the individual freedom of these entities.

Individual freedom constitutes the second dimension of freedom: economic freedom entails the right of the individual market participant to decide autonomously.[2] This gives the market participant a right to be free from governmental intervention and coercion by public or private bodies. Examples may be a governmental order not to sell certain goods or pressure by a potent business partner to grant exclusivity. This individual right entails a freedom *from* as well as a freedom *to* as the expression of the fundamental personal right to self-fulfillment in economic affairs. Business has often been in the shadows of other expressions of this right, such as free speech, and certainly the other freedoms have attracted more consideration by constitutionalists. Yet, as a field for self-fulfillment man's engagement in business is probably the first and most important field for everyone in daily

1 Cf. Fikentscher, Wirtschaftsrecht, 1983, Vol. 2, 57 ff.
2 Cf. Fikentscher, Wirtschaftsrecht, 1983, Vol. 2, 131 ff.

life. After all, satisfying hunger is most elementary for every human being, and satisfying hunger is, as shown in the first chapter, one of the very starting points of economic transactions. The two dimensions of freedom prompt followers to safeguard the decision making process against structural restrictions and the individual against coercion.

2.1.2 Systemic regulation

Rules seem to be a necessary contradiction to freedom. Legislation or governmental action in business matters primarily means a restriction of the dynamics of free exchanges. "Real" liberals therefore have a bias against government intervention in general. Rightly so! And yet, even for a free-market-advocate as determined as Milton Friedman it was natural to accept at least some form of regulation: "The existence of a free market does not of course eliminate the need for government. On the contrary, government is essential both as a forum for determining the "rules of the game" and as an umpire to interpret and enforce the rules decided on."[3] This statement may serve as a wake-up-call to those business leaders who overshoot their legitimate bias against government intervention and dismiss all forms of governmental action. The question is not whether rules for the market economy are necessary. They are. But: what rules are necessary?

The philosophical concept behind the regulation of the economy is the "freedom paradox": Unlimited freedom or an exercise of individual freedom without any restriction may eat up freedom. Karl Popper in his critique of Plato was the most sharp-sighted philosopher to remind us of the freedom paradox in the 20th century. He illustrated the dangers of freedom with the example of a democracy in which the majority freely votes in favor of replacing the democratic system with a dictatorship.[4] Popper called for institutional safeguards to protect the democratic system against the dangers of majority voting. He expressly addressed politics to protect the principles of equal rights and individualism against the dangers of unfettered power: "Politics, I demand, must uphold equalitarian and individualistic principles".[5] If an individualist like Karl Popper and a free-marketeer like Milton Friedman ("rules of the game") accept it that some rules are necessary to control power one seems to be on intellectually safe and still liberal ground to turn to the rules necessary for a market economy.[6]

---

3 Friedman, Capitalism and Freedom, 1982, 15.

4 Cf. Popper, Die offene Gesellschaft und ihre Feinde, 7th ed. 1992,Vol. 1, 147 f.

5 Ibid., 197.

6 For the sake of justice it may well be noted that Popper and Friedman of course both warned about too restrictive rules and too much government intervention. Popper spoke of a "paradox of state planning": giving the state too much power to plan the economy may restrict the basis of the plan, namely the freedom to enforce these plans (Popper, Die offene Gesellschaft und ihre Feinde, 7th ed. 1992, Vol. 2, 152). He expressly writes: "State intervention shall be restricted to what is really necessary for the protection of freedom." (Ibid., 152). Let us keep that in mind.

Friedman gives us an idea when talking about the "rules of the game" and the function of government as an umpire. "Games" need a common understanding of the players of the most basic questions. When people first decided to play soccer they probably did not have an offside rule. However, they must have had an understanding that the ball must be kicked by foot into a goal and that the number of goals decides who the winner is. With a lack of such a basic framework the game would not have been soccer (or football). It simply would not have worked, or at least would not have worked as a forum to find a champion by unleashing the forces of rivalrous sportsmanship.

Translating this into the world of business means to provide for rules that ensure the basic possibility of taking decisions autonomously. There needs to be a common understanding that free negotiations on supply and demand constitute the economy. It would not be a market economy if this common understanding was not present. The very characteristic of soccer is to use your foot to kick a ball into a goal. The very characteristic of the market economy is that private persons decide autonomously on what they are willing to give and take in the exchange with others. If people do not have the choice to decide freely or are hampered in taking their decisions, the market fails. Rules have to be designed so as to ensure that decisions may be taken freely and autonomously. So, while freedom is seen as the paramount principle governing the market economy, a free market still does not sustain itself without further ado. It is necessary to have rules that ensure a continued process of free interactions. Rules saving the freedom of the market from the predatory forces of freedom may be called "systemic regulation": These are rules guaranteeing that the system works and the markets do not fail.

It is a particularly difficult task to identify the principles that are inherent to a system and those that are more far-reaching, i.e. not necessary as *systemic* regulation. For the sake of illustration: In road traffic, you may do without a speed limit (and yet it may be beneficial to have one for some reasons), but it would be hard to imagine traffic on roads without principles on who gives way at the crossroads. At intersections with heavy traffic, the system would collapse. The distinction between systemic principles and additional rules is important to avoid a common misunderstanding on regulation: All rules are perceived as restrictions of freedom. But they are not! Systemic rules are enabling freedom. Intervening rules that are not systemic normally do restrict freedom. They may have some legitimacy or not, may prove to be beneficial or not, yet they are not necessary, and thus they are beyond the scope of this project that tries to look at the very basic legal framework of the market economy.

2.1.3 Challenges to the freedom principle

The design of the basic framework of the market economy suggested here is a design based on freedom as the key principle (the objective dimension) and aiming to ensure freedom for the market participants (the individual dimension). Systemic rules keep this system working. Yet, the goal to design a regulatory framework for promoting freedom has come under attack from two sides: The non-regulators and the hyper-regulators.

Some businessmen and libertarian thinkers denounce all forms of regulation as undue intervention.[7] They are ignoring the "freedom paradox". The financial crisis may serve as a signpost to them that markets without systemic rules such as the financial markets are bound to fail. Law-makers were tempted to follow the concept to refrain from all sorts of regulation, and they were not only tempted by powerful lobbying and concerns for retaining successful business centers.[8] Another reason was the complexity of financial markets: Transactions become more international; they are driven by highly specific financial mechanisms; there is no longer a clear structure of attributing responsibilities; and thanks to modern economics, the complexity is known as well as the danger of over-enforcement. In short: the economy became complex to a degree that seemed to make it difficult to submit it to certain rules. Complexity was a key motivation for law-makers to keep their hands off the financial markets. Only after the breakdown of important banks like Lehman Brothers the powers of law-making were re-discovered. Up to that point legislatures took (and are still continuing to take) the libertarian stance in order to avoid mistakes in regulating an extremely complex field. (Ironically, the knowledge of the difficulties to *tame* financial markets did not save taxpayers from governments trying to *steer* or even *outwit* financial markets: It was politicians setting incentives to invest in subprime housing and it was public sector entities that fared particularly badly in their investments during the crisis).

Yet, rule-making is about reducing complexity. It was one of the big mistakes of the past to think that "globalization" and "finance" are too complex to be governed by politics. If things seem to be too complex, this is either a calculated distraction of those who fear that politics starts regulating. Or it is a sign for institutions that are not up for the job. Certainly, all rules that are proposed for regulating the economy will be imperfect rules. This is inherent to rule-making: rules contain general formula for a number of individual cases that have specifically distinct advantages and disadvantages. Rules cannot take account of all the individual circumstances. Yet, they express principles that are thought of as the right principles to govern a certain class of cases. Taking account of the specifics of a case is the task of those institutions applying the more general rules to the individual cases, e.g. attorneys drafting contracts, authorities applying rules or judges deciding conflicts. The solution to the problem of regulating complex matters is not to abstain from systemic regulation but to place more confidence in the law-enforcers.

The other challenge to systemic regulation based on the principle of freedom stems from economic scholars who promote welfare-standards as the criterion of

7 Ackermann of Deutsche Bank for instance advocates an internationally agreed regulation and – acknowledging the lack of such international agreement – speaks in favor of peer-review mechanisms, i.e. a form of self-regulation of business; cf. Ackermann, Wettbewerbliche Aspekte der Bankenstützung und Regulierungsreform in: FIW, Wettbewerb in der Finanzkrise – Lehren für die Zukunft, 2010, 70 ff. While an international solution is desirable it seems to serve as a tool drawing attention away from a more realistic national or European regulation.

8 Some argue that the British government resists all sort of European regulation on banking to keep London as a financial centre, cf. the study by nef, Subverting Safer Finance, 2011, http://www.neweconomics.org/sites/neweconomics.org/files/Subverting_Safer_Finance.pdf.

regulation. Advice on economic policy during the 20th century was often based on bold assumptions and value judgments. The influential papers and books of renowned economists from former times often contain more references to literary and political writing than mathematic formula. This qualitative approach kept the tradition of Adam Smith who started as a philosopher. The trend though was reversed in the 1980s: Economics turned to quantitative and model-based research. Instead of starting from the principle of freedom, economists analyze the effects of governmental measures or business practices. This kind of research contributes enormously to the understanding of how markets work. It is an extraordinary tool to refine rule- and profit-making.

The seemingly exact science of models, formulae and prognoses misled some scholars into the belief that they can provide exact advice on how to regulate the economy in order to produce certain market outcomes. Accordingly, an effects-based approach replaces the process-oriented approach. Efficiency or welfare-standards are promoted as the aims of economic policy instead of clinging to the freedom principle. It is misleading to consider this "more economic approach" as an approach that is an objective one, free from normative assumptions.[9] Relying on (purported) welfare effects sets efficiency as the new standard instead of a more principled regulation that openly discusses normative values and individual rights.[10] Law-makers are advised to institute detailed legislation with specific measures. Whether it is possible to design an economic policy that achieves certain pre-defined aims remains doubtful. Thinkers who favor a dynamic, innovation-friendly business environment, such as Friedrich von Hayek, would certainly have opposed such a regulatory approach: it deprives the free market economy of its essential asset – the power to come up with new and surprising developments.[11]

The result of an approach based on effects-analysis and welfare-criteria is two-fold: Firstly, interventions aim at very specific issues, thereby restricting individual freedoms and replacing the freedom principle of market economies with a more detailed concept of a welfare-economy. This paradigm shift is often concealed under the seductive force of exact models, while it is forgotten that models are but a reduced version of complex realities. Secondly, abstention from legislation may also be a consequence of the new science of law-making: The experts are often able to point to type-I-errors and say what may go wrong. Accordingly, law-makers for fear of running into false positives (banning activities that are productive) refrain from acting at all, which leads to false negatives (activities that should be banned

---

[9] Cf. Zäch/Künzler, Efficiency or freedom to compete? Towards an axiomatic theory of competition law, ZWeR 2009, 269 ff. with a fundamental critique of the "more economic approach" in antitrust law.

[10] See Drexl, Ronald Dworkin, ökonomische Effizienz und das Kartellrecht in: Wettbewerbspolitik und Kartellrecht in der Marktwirtschaft, FS für 50 Jahre FIW, 2010, 175, 188.

[11] Hayek, Wettbewerb als Entdeckungsverfahren, 1968; the English version "Competition as a Discovery Procedure" can be found at https://itunesu.mises.org/journals/qjae/pdf/qjae5_3_3.pdf, taken from The Quarterly Journal of Austrian Eeconomics vol. 5, no. 3 (fall 2002): 9–23.

are not banned). In recent years the balancing of false positives and false negatives seems to have tipped.

Taking account of all the positive contributions of modern economic research it remains vital to see that economic policy needs a value judgment at its bottom. The fashionable scientific approach is not value-free:[12] it often confuses an empiric analysis of effects with a normative argument of principles; and it replaces the Hayekian freedom principle by a model-based welfare-standard.

2.1.4 Market requirements and market failures

Two kinds of systemic rules may be distinguished: Firstly, rule-makers need to provide the basic framework that enables citizens to satisfy their needs accordingly in a free exchange. Secondly, rule-makers need to fight market failures. The decisive questions for translating the freedom principle into law are: What are the systemic requirements for establishing and guaranteeing a market? What constitutes a market failure? How can law-making institutions support markets and fight market failures? Instead of viewing state and market as antagonistic forces (as in the Normannic model, see 1.2 above), the state has a vital role in creating and ensuring the working of market forces.[13] This is all the more true when market forces have been unleashed and are free to reassemble: Deregulation needs the companionship of freedom-guaranteeing regulation.[14]

These questions need to be under constant debate, not just by economic and legal scholars, but by the general public and politics. It seems that after the financial crisis too few decision-makers asked these fundamental questions to find out what went wrong and instead focused on the cure of symptoms.

As seen in Chapter 1, Adam Smith came up with ideas regarding the basic framework for a market economy that the state has to guarantee:[15] a functioning legal system, free communication, principles of general morality, general rules and usages on societal contacts and self-containment, the absence of monopolies, a social net for underprivileged classes. Milton Friedman saw it as vital to maintain

---

[12] On the underlying assumptions of this approach see Drexl in: Drexl/Kerber/Podszun (eds.), Competition Policy and the Economic Approach, 2011, 312 ff.

[13] Fikentscher, Finanzkrise, Wettbewerb und Regulierung, GRUR Int. 2009, 635, 646; Fikentscher, Culture, Law and Economics, 2004, Chap. 2. Similarly, the opinions prepared by Hellwig, Zimmer and Höfling for the 68. Deutscher Juristentag also refer to the governmental responsibility for markets, yet focus on strengthening supervisory bodies instead of going to the very roots of how markets work in: Hellwig/Zimmer/Höfling, NJW-Beil. 2010, 94 ff. Also note the reviews by Mülbert, Finanzmarktregulierung – Welche Regelungen empfehlen sich für den deutschen und europäischen Finanzsektor?, JZ 2010, 834 ff. and Liebscher/Ott, Die Regulierung der Finanzmärkte – Reformbedarf und Regelungsansätze des deutschen Gesetzgebers im Überblick, NZG 2010, 841 ff. Schmitz, President of the Federal Association of German Banks, acknowledges that there is no financial market without adequate regulation and control, cf. Schmitz, Finanzmarktkrise und Reorganisation von Banken, ZIP 2010, 1199 (1202).

[14] Sullivann/Hertz, The AT & T antitrust consent decree – should Congress change the Rules?, High Technology Law Journal 238-244 (1990).

[15] See supra Subchapter 1.4.1.

law, prevent physical coercion so that individuals are free to decide, to enforce contracts to give their decisions meaning, to deal with monopolies that reduce choice and to avoid "neighborhood effects", i.e. the externalization of losses.[16] Most macro-economic mainstream thinkers today accept a couple of conditions for functioning markets that are close to the common denominator of Smith and Friedman: People need property rights that grant them the power to exchange goods; external effects are to be avoided; transaction costs should be as low as possible, i.e. a state should provide for a marketplace; information should flow freely so that decisions are well-informed; market power needs to be absent so that there is no coercion of individual decisions. These requirements are commonly agreed as the requirements of the first theorem of welfare, leading to ideal competition. It is accepted that market failures prompt a state response. Such failures are – according to common economic wisdom – due to external effects, indivisibilities (as is the case with natural monopolies), information deficits, and missing or delayed adaption in the markets.[17]

There may be disagreement on one point or the other in economic theory. It is essential however, that there is a form of regulation that actually enables freedom since it provides the basic requirements for the market process and corrects market failures. This sort of systemic regulation needs to be constantly updated so as to serve the current needs of the markets. Identifying key failures in the financial crisis leads to a revision of the legal design of such rules. It may be noteworthy at this point to see that not all of Adam Smith's ideas were taken up later. Friedman, as a representative of mainstream economic thinking of the 1980s and 1990s, did not turn to notions of self-containment or general morality that can be found in Smith's work.

Legislatures often fail in performing tasks such as fighting market failures. Wrongly set incentives or "market failures" harm the business of politics in similar ways as markets ("government failure")[18]. There is a reservation towards any regulation that has to be dealt with. Constitutionalists always need to work on improving the mechanisms of government, and they profit from the insights of Public Choice Theory and Institutional Economics. These strands of economic thinking inform institutional reform, yet they are still often ignored when governmental authorities or public interventions are designed.

One institutional solution to minimize government failures is presented in more detail in Chapter 4 of this book: More trust should be placed on private initiative and private law enforcement with the help of civil law courts. Since public overseers have largely failed to prevent the crises, it is time to turn to a more decentralized and better-informed mechanism of "regulation". The task of guaranteeing market requirements and of remedying market failures, i.e. systemic regulation, should largely be left to the market participants themselves, only supported by government agencies. The collective wisdom of those present in the market may serve this aim

---

16 Friedman, Capitalism and Freedom, 1982, 14.

17 Cf. Fritsch/Wein/Ewers, Marktversagen und Wirtschaftspolitik, 7th ed. 2007, 82.

18 Cf. Fritsch/Wein/Ewers, Marktversagen und Wirtschaftspolitik, 7th ed. 2007, 420 ff.

better than the simple knowledge of a central government. Private enforcement of rules is Hayekian "catallaxy" – the spontaneous order that flows from the coordination of information in the market.[19]

2.1.5 Summary

Markets are based on the freedom principle: the autonomous decision-making of the market participants needs to be free from interventions and coercions. Regulation may step in as systemic regulation to enable the autonomous decision-making process, i.e. regulation may be freedom-enhancing. The role of the state to guarantee freedom and to correct market failures is overlooked by those who advocate a non-regulation approach. Moreover, the freedom principle is challenged by market engineers who believe in replacing the discovery procedure of markets with a fine-tuned effects-based policy. The decisive question with a view to necessary reforms is: what is necessary for preserving the autonomous decision-making process? Adam Smith and the economic scholarship ever since have presented core ideas. It is the task of the legal scholar to translate their findings into modern rules that fit the business world of today.

2.2 Rethinking competition rules

The most important set of legal rules guaranteeing the freedom of the market place are the rules on competition or antitrust. These rules protect freedom of acting in the market place against restrictions by private players. Rules on antitrust, as embodied in the Sherman Antitrust Act in the U.S., in Art. 101 and 102 TFEU, in the Chinese Anti-Monopoly Law, or in the Japanese Antimonopoly Act, are accepted as the fundamental economic legislation. In general, antitrust laws prohibit that competitors co-ordinate their competitive parameters by forming cartels and they declare illegal other restrictive business practices such as the abuse of a dominant position or vertical agreements between undertakings that lead to market entry barriers. Most competition law regimes also include merger control. With a view to the aspects of how markets function competition law tackles the issue of market power: Most competition provisions these days serve the idea of remedying market power or take market power as the threshold to apply intervening rules. Market power grants undertakings the possibility to act irrespective of customers, i.e. customers no longer have a choice (and respectively in the case of buyer power). Their decision-making becomes irrelevant and so does the invisible hand of the market since one side is dominating the outcome anyway. The possibility to defy control of the market forces may stem from collusion with competitors or external growth based on financial means or the abuse of an already existing dominant position.

If competition law is the legal cornerstone of the market economy, and if the market economy has come close to crash, it may be the right time to reconsider the

---

19 Cf. Hayek, Law, Legislation and Liberty, Vol. 2, 1976, 107 ff.

capacity of this cornerstone. It is timely to reconfigure competition law and to sketch some ideas that may shape a competition law that is apt for the finance-driven business world of today.

2.2.1 Competition and market power

Both, the objective guarantee of freedom and the subjective right of the individual to engage in economic activities are served by the mechanism that is the blood circuit of the economy: competition. Competition is the tool that makes markets in the individual sense work. Competition law keeps the competition going and prevents private parties from restraining economic freedom. When markets are opened up and freed from state intervention, competition law has the power to prevent private parties from replacing state barriers to trade with their own barriers. But what then, is the essence of the mechanism that shall ensure freedom? According to Friedrich von Hayek's famous definition, competition is seen "systematically as a procedure for discovering facts which, if the procedure did not exist, would remain unknown or at least would not be used".[20] This definition highlights the surprising power, the dynamics of the free interaction of individuals. Yet, it does not really give us a sense of what happens in a competitive market. Borchardt/Fikentscher have identified key elements of competition and have described competition as "the autonomous pursuit of rivals that mutually affect each other in their economic success for contracts with third parties by employing favorable conditions".[21] The freedom in business is a freedom to compete on the merits: the best one shall win. The essence of competition is the rivalrous fight for consumers (or suppliers) through the use of competitive parameters.

The fruits of competition are manifold: Companies are forced to enhance their efficiency, they need to innovate. Consumers profit from choice, quality and low prices. Profits in society are distributed according to an objective criterion, which is success in business. The contestable position of every undertaking keeps the economy and also the society dynamic and free from tyranny. Ever more countries recognized this in the past and opened up their economies for a free trading system, securing it against private restraints with a regime of competition law enforcement.

Competition law is based on the principle that rivalry among competitors is in danger of being distorted in cases when market power occurs: if one of the market players becomes too strong it no longer needs to rely on the merits of conducting business, on efficiency and innovation, but may succeed due to its strength. The bargaining for favorable conditions is replaced by a one-sided imposition of conditions, be it in a cartelized market or in a market with a monopolistic or oligopolistic situation where customers or suppliers are reduced to mere price takers without any influence while the other side may fix conditions and prices. Market power is

---

[20] Hayek, Competition as a Discovery Procedure, 1968.

[21] Borchardt/Fikentscher, Wettbewerb – Wettbewerbsbeschränkung – Marktbeherrschung, 1957, 80.

defined as the possibility to act irrespective of the reactions of customers, competitors or other market participants.[22]

The focus on market power helps to analyze the financial crisis as well. Traditional antitrust law thinks of market power situations as in the famous Microsoft case: One company has the leading role in a market, e.g. by being the sole relevant producer of operating systems for personal computers in the world. The sheer market power is perceived as problematic, but it does not yet necessarily prompt a state reaction, since this could be a disincentive for companies to strive for success. In this case there are network effects that cause a monopoly that comes close to what is called a natural monopoly. However both artificial and natural monopolies are restraints on competition "by fact", in a structural way, and subject not only to adequate abuse control but also to adequate inhibition. Antitrust laws were applied once Microsoft abused its position and relied too strongly on its power instead of its innovative and efficient thinking. What is the case in financial markets? Actually, few companies (if any) hold a dominant position on one of the many markets in the financial sector (with the notable exception of the three leading rating agencies). Yet, the concept of market power applies to the whole sector: it is no longer a single entity that has grown into a position of a strength that may invite to abuse. It is a whole sector that has taken the rest of the economy hostage. Financial institutions do not wield market power in the traditional sense, in these tiny little units defined as markets by competition authorities. Financial institutions have the power to influence *all* markets and extend their reach into very many transactions (and in particular the important ones). This horizontal power is similar to the power of the energy sector on which many industrial producers depend. Learning the lessons of antitrust means to cast a critical view on entities that became too powerful in business. Antitrust laws were applied to break the monopolies in energy and to distribute power in the energy sector on more shoulders. The financial sector rests on many shoulders, yet it still is a power block.

Competition was defined as the autonomous pursuit of rivals for favorable conditions. Today, the economically important fights have a strong link to financing issues. The pursuit is no longer an autonomous one, but the man from finance sits at the table as well and has an important say in the transaction. Competition laws need to have a critical eye on this "market" power, and needs to find out whether it makes a difference that it is not one undertaking (as in the operating systems business) but different undertakings that play such a role.

2.2.2 Competition law enforcement in financial markets

Imagine a policeman who is positioned at a crossroads to keep traffic running smoothly without accidents. Now, a gargantuan traffic jam builds up and several people are severely hurt. What would you expect the policeman to say? Naturally, he will claim that this jam was not his fault but caused by the drivers. Even if his claim holds true the outcome undermines his legitimacy as a traffic regulator. The

---

[22] Cf. ECJ, Case 85/76, [1979] ECR 461, para 38 – *Hoffmann-LaRoche*.

obvious cause for the traffic jam may have been the untamed behavior of the drivers. This, however, may lie in the nature of driving cars. To avoid traffic jams there are speed limits and rules on right of way etc. and there is traffic police. The underlying cause of the jam may have two aspects: The rules may be poorly designed or poorly applied (which may be a question of the enforcer). And still, the policeman will most probably tell you that such things happen, that he remains without fault, and that he will keep on enforcing the rules that did not hinder this jam to happen.

The financial crisis of 2008 was the gargantuan jam of the market economy with several casualties, most notably Lehman Brothers and the passenger on the Lehman Brothers bus. As seen above, the competition laws are perceived to be the fundamental rules of the market economy. The enforcers of these rules and also most academics in the field reacted exactly like the policeman in the example given above: According to officials of the European Commission and the U.S. competition agencies the existing rules are well crafted and were perfectly enforced. They did not see any fault on their side nor any deficits in enforcement or in the set of fundamental rules governing the market economy.[23] The reaction was endorsed by most scholars: Few, if any, saw the necessity of reforming competition rules to avoid future crises. This may take observers by surprise: The market economy is close to collapse, but the basic rules of the market economy remain beyond doubt. The reform program enacted after the crisis did not alter competition laws at all but remained in the domain of banking law, for example for restructuring ends. Answering the financial crisis with regulatory measures in the supervisory law for financial institutions misses the point that this crisis affected the whole economy: It was not just the banking sector that was drawn into trouble. The relevant community seems to be of the opinion that the fundamental rules on markets do not have anything to say on drastic market failures in one of the most important sectors of the economy. The silence in this matter is rather breath-taking. For example, conscious parallelism of action of hedge-funds, banks, insurances and/or pension funds betting against the Euro or other currencies is an abuse of homogeneous competition-restricted oligopolies and their eventual concerted action is a cartel (restraint of competition "by fact" or "by measures").

Before the financial crisis, apart from subsidies cases (underlying their own rules) competition law enforcers rarely decided cases from the financial sector despite constantly highlighting the importance of this sector. Taking the European Commission's enforcement record for the years 2003 to 2008 as an example:

---

[23] Cf. e.g. the European Commission's Annual Report on Competition Policy 2010, 10 June 2011, SEC (2010), 690 final, and the European Parliament's Draft Resolution on the report, 31 August 2011, 2011/2094 (INI), both with no mention of necessary reforms in competition law in the light of the crisis. A notable exception is the OECD's 2009 paper "Competition and the Financial Crisis" that addresses issues for adapting competition laws to the changing landscape of financial institutions. The suggestions serve as a starting point and thus remain vague. However, the authors of this paper acknowledge the deficits of competition law enforcement in the past, cf. http://www.oecd.org/dataoecd/52/24/42538399.pdf, 19 – 21.

- In 2004, the Commission took a decision against Clearstream, a company providing clearing services in securities trading, for discriminating against another company.[24] The Commission did not impose a fine since there had not been experience with antitrust in this sector before.[25]
- In 2005, the Commission cleared the acquisition of Telerate, a data provider, by Reuters, one of the leading providers of financial data.[26] Despite a duopoly in the market for financial information the Commission cleared the merger. The only remedy imposed was a license for an infrastructural platform.
- In 2006, the Commission presented a report on securities trading identifying certain concerns.[27] The report remained without consequences.
- In 2006-2007, the Commission undertook a sector inquiry in retail banking.[28] Despite some concerns identified in the report there were no tangible results of the far-reaching inquiry.
- In 2007, the Commission dealt with different cases involving payment cards (Visa, Master Card, Groupement des Cartes Bancaires) with a particular focus on reducing interchange fees.[29]
- In 2007, the Commission cleared the merger of Fortis/ABN Amro.[30] The Dutch banking sector is highly concentrated but the Commission refrained from blocking the merger and only asked for divesting certain commercial banking activities. Restructuring banks under State aid law may even lead to higher concentration.

The activities undertaken did not cast light into those sectors that became relevant for the problems in 2008. The Commission focused on the interests of end consum-

---

[24] COM, 2.6.2004, Case COMP/38.096, C (2004) 1958 final – *Clearstream;* available at http://ec.europa.eu/competition/antitrust/cases/dec_docs/38096/38096_75_1.pdf.

[25] One may note that this argument against fines amounts to a carte blanche for companies in sectors that have not been subject to competition law investigations before. Actually, sectors in which the Commission has substantial experience run the risk of staying in focus – air traffic with the only two merger prohibitions in years (Ryanair/Aer Lingus 2008, Olympic Air/Aegean Airlines 2011) may serve as an example.

[26] COM, 23 May 2005, COMP/M.3692 – *Reuters/Telerate*, available at http://ec.europa.eu/competition/mergers/cases/decisions/m3692_20050523_20212_en.pdf.

[27] COM, Working Document "Competition in EU securities trading and posttrading", 24 May 2006, available at http://ec.europa.eu/competition/sectors/financial_services/securities_trading.pdf.

[28] COM, Sector Inquiry under Art. 17 of Regulation (EC) No 1/2003 on retail banking (Final Report), 31.12007, COM (2007) 33 final, available at http://eur-lex.europa.eu/LexUriServ/LexUriServ.do?uri=COM:2007:0033:FIN:EN:PDF.

[29] COM, 3 October 2007, COMP/D 1/37860 – *Morgan Stanley/Visa*; available at http://ec.europa.eu/competition/elojade/isef/case_details.cfm?proc_code=1_37860; COM, 17 October 2007, COMP/D 1/38606 – *Groupement des Cartes Bancaires*, available at http://ec.europa.eu/competition/elojade/isef/case_details.cfm?proc_code=1_38606; COM, 19 December 2007, COMP/D 1/34579 – *Europay/Master Card*, available at http://ec.europa.eu/competition/antitrust/cases/dec_docs/34579/34579_1889_2.pdf.

[30] COM, 3 October 2007, COMP/M.4844 – *Fortis/ABN Amro Assets*, available at http://ec.europa.eu/competition/mergers/cases/decisions/m4844_20071003_20212_en.pdf.

ers (inquiry on retail banking, payment card cases) or dealt with discrimination cases (Clearstream, Groupement des Cartes Bancaires) with essentially one victim or dealt with cases that came up without its own initiative (the merger decisions). In the merger cases, the Commission did not take a particularly tough stance. The only effort to look into the structural deficits of the financial industry, the report on securities trading, was not undertaken by the Commission itself and remained without consequences. In the preceding years, meaningful enforcement actions in the financial sector were also rare. With this record, it seems fair to state that DG COMP did not keep an eye on the markets that are systemic and extremely powerful for the whole economy. This *laissez-faire* approach may have fostered booms in the financial industry, yet in the long run it did not seem healthy. The thriving financial sector of the years 1991 to 2008 led the Commission to ignore the freedom paradox that explains that markets without a market order may easily collapse.

Similarly, the cases brought by the Commission early after the financial crisis do not seem to get to the core of the matter:[31] Again, the Commission dealt with the merger cases that it had to deal with without meeting a significant decision.[32] The investigation into payment services and interchange fees was continued.[33] The Single European Payment Area, easing bank transfers within the EU, was co-designed by DG COMP.[34] In 2011, the Commission finally opened investigations in matters that seem to have some relevance to the financial crisis: In the Standard & Poor's case the Commission investigates the rating agencies behavior in assigning identification numbers to new securities. Standard & Poor's may have charged excessive prices for the use of these numbers.[35] A similar case involves Thomson Reuters and their restrictions on the use of Reuters' identification codes.[36] Both cases seem worth a look but will hardly change the architecture of financial markets. The Market case and the Intercontinental Exchange case seem a bit more promising: in these cases the DG Competition investigates the agreements of investment banks with infrastructural companies providing financial information. The investigations may help to discover practices in the derivatives market that harm competition.[37] At the time of finishing this chapter, however, this is wishful

[31] The account given here ignores the state aid cases. They consumed a lot of time within DG Competition for the sheer amount of aid handed out to financial institutions during the crises. While the Commission handled these cases with care and a lot of effort, it seems that in the essence the Member States' generous help was confirmed.

[32] Cf. COM, 14 May 2009, COMP/M.5508 – *SOFFIN/Hypo Real Estate*, available at http://ec.europa.eu/competition/mergers/cases/decisions/m5508_20090514_20310_de.pdf.

[33] Cf. COM, 8 December 2010, COMP/39.398, C(2010) 8760 final – *VISA*, available at http://ec.europa.eu/competition/elojade/isef/case_details.cfm?proc_code=1_39398.

[34] Cf. http://ec.europa.eu/internal_market/payments/sepa/index_en.htm.

[35] Cf. COM, Case COMP/39.592 – *Standard & Poor's*, Commitments proposed by the Commission available at http://ec.europa.eu/competition/antitrust/cases/dec_docs/39592/39592_1727_3.pdf.

[36] COM, Case COMP/39.654 – *Thomson/Reuters*.

[37] Cf. speech by Almunia at CASS Business School, 16 May 2011, 4 available at http://europa.eu/rapid/pressReleasesAction.do?reference=SPEECH/11/337&format=HTML&aged=1&language=EN&guiLanguage=en.

thinking. The Commission's work in the area of financial services after the collapse of Lehman Brothers remains "unremarkable"[38]. As late as 2012, the Commission blocked a merger in the financial sector (Deutsche Börse/New York Stock Exchange).[39] When it turned out in 2012 that the London Interbank Offered Rate (the BBA-LIBOR) was manipulated – possibly only the tip of the ice-berg in a sector that had not been subject to competition law scrutiny – the Commission's reaction was primarily regulatory: the Commissioner for Internal Market suggested new legislation while vigorous antitrust enforcement may have sufficed.[40]

Neither before the turmoil in the financial markets nor after it had the competition law authorities brought meaningful cases that helped in "making markets work better"[41]. The European Commission did not come up with initiatives to reform competition law so as to give it more meaning for the financial sectors. The economic crisis did not prompt an answer from the enforcers "policing" the markets. For them, it was business as usual while for business it was the most unusual period in decades.

2.2.3 Competition rules for a finance-driven economy

The rules that govern the market economy today were established under specific historic circumstances, most of them modeled at the turn of the century – from the 19th to the 20th and in the years after World War II. The first modern antitrust law was the U.S. Sherman Antitrust Act of 1890. Politicians felt that the power of the trusts was so far-reaching that the economy was about to derail. The rules were destined to control the strong industrial conglomerates holding power over oil or steel or other resources at the time. The motivation to introduce European rules on competition was triggered by similar considerations. Actually, the first European competition laws were integrated in the European Coal and Steel Treaty of 1952, and they were motivated by fears of too strong industrial conglomerates.

The interpretation of rules is formed in the specific historic context that first motivated the introduction of the rules. Freeing the interpretation from the historic situation and modernizing it is a challenge for enforcing authorities and judges. There are limits to stretching rules to new contexts, and sometimes rules have to be amended in order to fit their original task in a changing environment.

The business of the 1950s is no longer the setting for the enforcement of competition rules. In those days, financial institutions played a role in the economy, of course, but did not wield the same influence as today. Many forms of financial institutions and transactions did not even exist. Banks acted as servants to the real economy, and doing business was about the exchange of goods. Power lay with the

---

38 Jestaedt/Polland, The Application of European Competition Law in the Financial Services Sector, 348, 356 JECLP 2010.

39 COM, Case COMP/M.6166 – *Deutsche Börse/NYSE Euronext* (not yet published).

40 Cf. http://ec.europa.eu/commission_2010-2014/barnier/headlines/news/2012/07/20120725_en.htm.

41 This is the claim of DG Competition on its website http://ec.europa.eu/competition/index_en.html.

industrial undertakings. Business was concentrated within national borders. In this setting, cartels were seen as the biggest danger for free competition. Dominance was defined as the market power of a single undertaking. Merger control did not yet exist since the business of acquiring companies was not of overwhelming importance. The dangers for the free exchange of goods and services, based on the autonomous decision-making by individuals, were completely different from today.

In a parallel field of law, international trade law, the changing circumstances of doing business were partly reflected: In the 1940s policy-makers saw problems of exchanging goods as most pressing, and the 1947 General Agreement on Tariffs and Trade (GATT) was the result. In 1995 only, provisions on services (GATS) and intellectual property (TRIPS) were added to the trade agenda, realizing at that time that there is more than just tangible goods driving the economy. Service providers such as telecommunication-companies or companies holding vital IP rights such as big pharma had grown to considerable importance for the national economies. Now, fifteen years on, all these companies are partly in the grip of investment banks, private equity funds, banks and other financial institutions.

Since the game changed, it may be wise to rethink the rules of the game. Any reform may bear in mind that the economy centers on catering to human needs. Such needs can be satisfied with goods and services. In a competitive market economy, financial institutions therefore would be servants, not central players. Important issues in reconsidering competition law rules may relate to five aspects that characterize today's new economic environment: financial power as a key to distort competition; the systemic relevance of certain institutions; the way how decisions are taken; the actors; the international dimension. The suggestions sketched here are not meant to be a blueprint but food for thought. They do not represent an overly elaborate concept yet.

2.2.3.1 Financial power

At present, competition law makes market power the most important criterion for interfering with certain business practices. It may serve the task of competition rules to add a criterion relating to economic or financial power.

The basic idea of competition rules was to stop the accumulation of power by single entities and to reduce economic (and also political) pressure that may distort the free market activities. In the law-making process market dominance became the threshold for power. The practical result of today's focus on market power is that market definition is the number one battlefield of competition law suits, particularly in abuse and merger cases. Yet, with markets defined very narrowly nowadays in many cases, the focus is shifted away from the possibility to pressure business partners. The focus rests with the influence of the undertaking on a very specific stage of the production or distribution process of one specific product or service. This may go hand in hand with the efficiency orientation of antitrust rules and may serve to optimize the production process, yet it does not see the bigger picture. To illustrate this with an example from the retail business: When a supermarket chain aims at buying another supermarket chain the antitrust authorities end up defining hundreds of local markets due to a narrow geographical market definition in the retailing industry – end consumers are thought to take a 20-minute-ride for shopping.[42] Even if the authorities check the overall effects of the merger[43] it is hard to imagine that such a merger is blocked *completely*. In several cases, the authorities asked the merging parties to divest certain stores to competitors. The overall concentration of the supermarket business got out of focus. The general economic power of the big retailing chains cannot be represented with the proxy of traditional market definition. One idea to come to terms with such situations would be a tougher stance on competition-restricted oligopolies, particularly on homogeneous oligopolies and "oligopolies of the few". The restraint of competition by oligopolies may be caused by their mere existence, their structural impact, not depending on their specific actions.[44] It may prove fruitful to reconsider the thoughts on market power laid down in earlier decisions such as *Alcoa* in the U.S.[45] and *Continental Can* in Europe[46].

In the financial industry, the problem may be even more pressing. Financial strength is key to market developments, and even big industrial firms make huge parts of their profits through financial activities.[47] Economic success, even for industrial companies, depends on financing issues. Efficiency and innovation no longer suffice to achieve market dominance or even to survive. The cases of profitable companies taken over by smaller rivals that are equipped with credits by investors and that shift the credit debt to the newly bought company after the acquisition are telling examples for a finance-driven market economy. Competition laws that focus on market shares have little to say on this.

Real market dominance in the traditional sense is a rare phenomenon only. In the financial markets, there are normally enough important players (apart from bottleneck service providers that came under scrutiny recently). In real-economy-markets where financial institutions hold assets, e.g. as investors, they normally will not have a whole industry under their control. Does this mean that they are not powerful? Maybe, market shares are no longer as important as credit volume, liquidity or other financial indicators.

Competition legislatures have already shown a bias against financial strength in that they submit mergers to a notification procedure as soon as the companies reach certain thresholds (mostly turnover thresholds). The right of an agency to prohibit a merger actually is the right to prohibit external growth on the basis of financial strength. Internal growth (normally through good performance) is desired and not subject to intervention while external growth of companies (through the use of financial means) is seen as problematic enough to submit it to state control. This

---

[42] Cf. COM, 3 February 1999, Case COMP/M.1221, C(1999) 228 final – *Rewe/Meinl*, para 18.

[43] The European Commission does that, yet this impact of the merger is usually not made the ground of the decision.

[44] For an early idea of this cf. Borchardt/Fikentscher, Wettbewerb, Wettbewerbsbeschränkung, Marktbeherrschung, 1957, 10 ff.; see also the text following Fn. 22 above on the difference between restraints of competition "ley strategy" and "ley fact".

[45] United States v. Aluminium Co. of America, 148 F. 2d 416 (2d Cir. 1945) – *Alcoa*.

[46] ECJ, 21.3.1973, Case 6/72, [1973] ECR 215 – *Continental Can*, 242 – 245.

[47] It is reported for instance that the financial arms of car-makers contribute about a quarter to the profits.

distinction between internal and external growth is not self-explanatory since the result may be the same – the substantial lessening of competition or market dominance. However, law-makers who introduced merger control laws may have had a feeling that the input of financial means does not comply with competition on the merits. In picking up this thought it makes sense to find a better proxy for economic strength than market shares.

2.2.3.2 Systemic relevance

During the crisis it turned out that some financial institutions had become too big to fail or were of systemic relevance. Their failure would destabilize the real economy to a high degree or even take whole countries into trouble. If competition law is about controlling market power the mere existence of companies that are "too big to fail" is definite proof that the rules may not suffice or were not enforced vigorously enough. Assessing financial power more critically than before, as suggested above, may provide a helpful tool in this regard.

Discussions in Europe have centered on the question whether competition authorities should deconcentrate financial institutions. The European Commission has accepted structural remedies, i.e. the divestures of undertakings, in abuse cases already.[48] The British Competition Commission ordered a divestiture of ownership in airports in 2009.[49] The U.S. gained some experience throughout the past but the last case dates back to 1984 (AT&T).[50] Deconcentration measures pose many legal and economic problems and may take a long time with expensive court battles.[51] Nowadays deconcentration measures would require an international effort of regulators. It may still be an issue worth considering, yet its practical impact will probably remain low for the financial sector. In some of the cases governments may influence the future size of undertakings through intelligent privatization policies.[52]

Maybe the ultimate remedy of deconcentration is not the golden tool for competition agencies. Private enforcement would not profit from this. The initiative and action would rest with the state and all the intricacies of public intervention. It is important to take a closer look to the structural situation in a sector, the intersectoral implications of behavior and the interdependence of companies. The rationale of competitive assessments is to sanction or avoid pressuring in the autonomous decision-making process. If organizations are of systemic relevance their mere

---

[48] Cf. COM, 26 November 2008, Case COMP/39.388 and 39.389 – *German Electricity Wholesale Market (E.on)*.

[49] Competition Commission, 19 March 2009, BAA airport markets investigation report, available at http://www.competition-commission.org.uk/rep_pub/reports/2009/fulltext/545.pdf; note subsequent rulings by the Competition Appeal Tribunal and the High Court of Justice – Court of Appeal.

[50] United States v. AT&T, 552 F. Supp. 131 (D.D.C. 1982).

[51] Cf. Thomas, De-merger Regimes in Europe. Are National deconcentration powers an appropiate tool for enhancing competition in the EU, JECLAP 2011, 201 ff.

[52] Thomas makes this point for the U.K. airport case, but it may also be applicable to financial institutions, particularly now after several banks depend on state aid.

existence destroys future options since the freedom to decide against this organization is no longer given. Competition law needs to keep markets working by avoiding such constraints. In practice this may mean to take "worst case scenarios" into account when assessing mergers. It may also be worth to consider situations as a "structural abuse" if the market player in question endangers the functioning of the market.

Competition authorities may also reconsider their stance on oligopolies that are of systemic relevance for the economy. The criteria set out by the European Court of First Instance in a 2002 decision may prove too tough for tackling situations of collective dominance in merger control.[53] The Court established three criteria for assuming collective dominance: The members of the oligopoly need to have knowledge about the other members decisions and strategies (transparency); there needs to be tacit coordination with a sanction mechanism against deviations from the common policy (sanction) and the reactions of competitors or customers may not counter the oligopoly policy (countervailing market power). These criteria, set forth in a case dealing with holiday tour operators, completely miss the point of financial markets: Firstly, transparency is not a matter of access to competitors' information, but granted by the market data themselves. Strategies of financial institutions may differ, but they all follow the same data and pass the flow of information on to their debtors. Secondly, tacit coordination will normally not be necessary since decisions in finance do not follow the same strategic patterns as in classic industrial business environments. Decisions here are taken within seconds, often by computer programs. The perception of the Court is a different one and may prove right for decisions on holiday package pricing. Thirdly, customers of financial institutions normally adapt completely to the requirements of financing. It would be hard to perceive alternative reactions.

All these considerations aim at taking the specific characteristic of some financial institutions into account, namely their systemic relevance. This is justified due to the aim of "making markets work better" which means to take systemic risks into account.

2.2.3.3 Form of decisions

The founding fathers of modern competition laws placed a lot of emphasis on restrictive agreements, imagining the heads of powerful companies assembling in a hotel room, discussing conditions and fixing prices for the upcoming months. This idea may still be valid for some sectors and the cartels discovered in the past years provide proof that the classic cases still have to be fought vigorously. Yet this kind of decision-making process is unimaginable for the financial sector. Decisions in banking and investment are often taken within seconds and partly by computers or at least following strict conditions. The scope for decisions is reduced for the individual trader or banker. So, the process of decision-making is much faster than in traditional businesses but also more static. Does that mean that there is no need for

---

[53] CFI, 6 June 2002, Case T-342/99, [2002] ECR II-2585 – *Airtours/First Choice*.

competition law to step in? Arguably, the opposite is the case: if a business no longer works on the basis of autonomous decision-making but on narrowly defined possibilities to press buttons, competition law needs to bring back some of the spirit of free exchanges.

Two aspects seem worth considering: transparency and the form of decision-making.

High transparency in the financial sector leads to the domino effects that hurt the real economy so hard. Regulatory bodies believe in transparency as a key to avoiding problems. This belief may stem from the idea of perfect competition with perfect information. Yet, perfect competition is an illusion – and for lack of rivalry even a case of non-competition. Information asymmetries will always remain. In other competitive surroundings competition lawyers learned that transparency does not necessarily serve efficiency and innovation but leads to a reduction of the competitive pressure. Therefore, anti-competitive information exchange between competitors may be seen as a hard-core violation of competition rules in many jurisdictions. Governments may be ill-advised when asking for transparency, the disclosure of competitive strategies and the collection of millions of market data. While government agencies and consumers will have difficulties to digest this information they may serve as paradigmatic for the behavior of market players. Transparency does not necessarily lead to markets performing better but it definitely leads to less room for surprising competitive advances.

The problematic behavior in a transparent financial market, however, will not amount to classic agreements or concerted practices in the competition law sense with physical contacts and a co-ordination (with notable exceptions as in the LIBOR case). It is more likely to find parallel behavior which according to current competition law standards cannot be prohibited. Yet, one may contemplate to lower the standard of proof for tacit collusion in cases where decision-making does not follow classic ways but is much faster with little need to explicit coordination. The border to parallel behavior may be blurry and courts should take the specifics of the sector into account when assessing cases. Parallel behavior may be an indicator that requirements on transparency and information are exaggerated and that an unhealthy oligopolistic market structure or even a structural restraint of competition in the form of a homogeneous oligopoly exists. Competition authorities should watch such situations with special care. More far-reaching would be a revision of the term "agreement" in Art. 101 TFEU and the standard of proof associated with it. One regulatory lesson to be kept in mind is that the call for transparency by regulators undermines the rivalry of competitors. Decisions are less autonomous if those who decide are enmeshed in close net of transparent information and strict regulation.

2.2.3.4 Actors

When rules for the market economy were devised under European law the addressee was clear-cut as the "undertaking", the firm, usually organized through a strict hierarchy and with responsible persons pulling the strings at one end – as in a privately owned family business. Competition relies on the concept of "control" for determining who the responsible actor is.[54] Yet, while the concept is rather broad in the relevant legal texts, practice centers on shareholding and decisive influence – concepts hard to apply to some forms of financial institutions. Today, we find more and more businesses that have very loose structures. Corporations have hundreds of subsidiaries and consequently all room for maneuvering employees, taxes, strategies and profits. In some companies it is hard to see who actually owns it with diverse shareholders and executives that are controlled by board members who are executives in other companies. In financial institutions, e.g. investment funds, it is particularly hard to follow lines of responsibility and to determine who ultimately calls the shots.

Nowadays, it is no longer the managers of steel companies who call the shots, but employees of banks, hedge funds, investment companies, private equity funds, rating agencies. They make the deals. Yet their activities are not necessarily attributable to single entities but they act in very diverse forms of organization. Even large industrial corporations sometimes depend more upon institutional investors or creditors than on their shareholders.

If competition laws shall fit the modern business world, it is necessary to integrate modern forms of business. Maybe it is worth to return to the Sherman Act's definition of the addressee which is partly anonymous (i.e. rests without a legal definition) or refers to "person". This opens the window to address individuals in a stricter way than in European law where individuals at present do not face any sanctions. The individual taking the decision should be in the focus of enforcers.

Even in merger control where it is vital to find lines of responsibility the individuals taking strategic decisions may be the most promising starting point for identifying entities. The economic, legal, personal or other ties between employees, board members, owners etc. may establish a legal picture of economic entities that is much closer to economic reality than the picture that emerges from reliance on formal legal ties.

Competition law needs to take the relevant actors into focus, and it seems that modern business organization has become so complex that only returning to the individual and its decision-making capabilities serves as a solution.

2.2.3.5 International dimension

The economy is globalized to a degree that makes national rules on business affairs look anachronistic. This is, in part, due to the elimination of tariffs and trade restrictions and other forms of deregulation and liberalization that loosened the grip of the state. Today, companies move from one jurisdiction to another, they invest here and there. At least for large companies[55], the big players in the game, an attribution to a nation is misleading. From a certain size upward and depending

[54] Cf. Whish, Competition Law, 6th edition 2009, pp. 91 f., 823 f.

[55] In the EU, large companies are defined as having more than 250 employees and a turnover or total assets of more than 50 million Euros per year, cf. EU Commission Recommendation, 6.5.2003, OJ, 20.5.2003, L 124/36.

on existing or potential markets (comparable to the "potential competition" test) as connecting factors there are no Turkish, Swiss or French companies, any more. Geographical markets in many sectors are covering several states if not the world. This is all the more true for finance. Although this globalization of the economy is a matter of fact, rule-makers still seem to stick to pre-globalization times or at least appeal to voter's economic patriotism. This is an issue of governance. Traditional national institutions are no longer able to regulate business behavior. Competition law for a globalized world economy needs to strengthen international efforts.

The body of law in this field provides excellent starting points for protecting competition. Competition law is well developed on national (and regional) scale with very effective enforcement mechanisms in many jurisdictions. Today, competition law regimes are in force in most economies, with the U.S. and the EU as leading enforcers, but also including Japan, South Korea, Australia, Brazil, China, India and South Africa. The goals and rules in these countries are in the essence very similar, even if practical enforcement differs. In many of these jurisdictions, enforcement does not just rest with specific agencies but also with private parties in private lawsuits.

The international application of competition law rules is based on the effects doctrine. As soon as there is a genuine effect in the national territory, domestic competition law applies. Through this link national enforcers and private parties may initiate proceedings against international cartels or other unlawful practices. Yet, the outreach of enforcing agencies is still limited by the principle of sovereignty. Real cross-border enforcement only exists if there is a regional competition agency as in the EU. On the international scale initiatives prosper. The International Competition Network, an organization of competition agencies, meets regularly and fosters co-operation and convergence.[56] The United Nations and other organizations have drafted model laws that represent a consensus on what practices should be banned.[57] In the WTO, attempts to integrate an agreement on restraints of competition have mostly failed so far. While politicians managed to reduce state-induced restrictions of international business in the framework of the WTO, they failed to tackle private restraints of international business on an international scale. Yet, in soft law there are a lot of initiatives that recognize the importance of antitrust law.

New solutions to the enforcement issue seem vital. While an agreement on certain binding substantive standards (e.g. against hardcore cartels) seems imaginable, enforcement still needs more consideration. A more coherent international approach, especially to oligopolistic competition and restraints of competition, should also be in the interest of the undertakings concerned, since they run into bureaucratic trouble when confronted with several agencies at a time. The problems of multiple merger filings or multiple sanctioning by national enforcers are telling.

---

[56] www.internationalcompetitionnetwork.org

[57] UN-RBP, OECD, DIAC.

The most elaborate model of international competition rules is the Draft International Antitrust Code.[58] It was drafted by scholars from all over the world in the 1990s and inspired the debate on international competition rules heavily.[59] The Code is meant as a plurilateral agreement in the framework of the WTO. As a development of the past years, an international framework nowadays would also need to take private enforcement actions into account on an international level.

2.2.4 Summary

Competition rules were designed for an economy of another age. Today, they lack the sting to tackle the big issues of a finance-driven economy. Today, market players no longer look like classic undertakings, they act differently, they act more internationally, and the dynamics of the knowledge economy have become more important. The rationale of competition law, to control market power and to keep the decision-making processes in transactions free from coercion, remains intact. Yet, the instruments need to be reconsidered. The crisis has shown that the present competition law regimes have very little to say on the turmoil of the markets even though competition law is still seen as the fundamental law on how markets work. In this chapter, some starting points for a revision of competition rules were presented: Firstly, the focus may be shifted from shares in narrowly defined markets to the financial and economic strength of entities. Secondly, the systemic relevance of actors needs to be taken into account, e.g. when assessing oligopoly situations. Thirdly, the form of making decisions in the financial sector makes it necessary to reconsider the belief in transparency as good for markets and agreement as the central form of competition law violation. Fourthly, competition law may get rid of the rather formalistic idea of undertakings and concentrate on individual persons. Finally, an international enforcement regime, including private enforcement, is necessary, as in many other fields of business law.

---

[58] DIAC; International Antitrust Working Group, Draft International Antitrust Code as a GATT-WTO-Plurilateral Agreement, Munich/Germany 10. Juli 1993 (Fikentscher, Drexl, Fox, Fuchs, Heinemann, Immenga, Kunz-Hallstein, Petersmann, Schluep, Soltyšinski and Sullivan); eight reprints and translations: (Monograph): Special Supplement, The Bureau of National Affairs, Antitrust & Trade Regulation Report, Vol. 64, Nr. 1628, 19 August 1993, Washington, D.C., 2007; World Trade Materials, Vol. 5 No. 5 (September 1993) 126 – 196; Jurist (Japanese law journal) No. 1036 of 15 December 1993; translation by Akira Shoda und Junko Shibata; WuW 1994, 128 – 139 (without comments); Außenwirtschaft – Schweizerische Zeitschrift für internationale Wirtschaftsbeziehungen 49 (1994) Heft II/III, 310 – 325 (without comments); Fikentscher/Immenga, International Antitrust Code. Kommentierter Entwurf eines internationalen Wettbewerbsrechts mit ergänzenden Beiträgen, 1995, 53 – 110; Fikentscher/Kuhn, Internationales Kartellrecht und Lauterkeitsrecht: Dokumente, Entwürfe und Abkommen, International Antitrust und Unfair Trade Law: Documents, Drafts and Agreements, 1990-1996, Max-Planck-Institut für ausländisches und internationales Patent- und Urheber- und Wettbewerbsrecht, 1996, 212 – 299; Fikentscher, Multilaterale Regeln für den internationalen Wettbewerb?, in: Katzenbach/Mayer (eds.), Von der internationalen Handels- zur Wettbewerbsordnung, 1996, 159-17, with an appendix: Entwurf eines internationalen Wettbewerbsabkommens als plurilaterales GATT/MTO-Handelsabkommen, loc. cit. 171 – 219. For procedural issues that may be added see Podszun, Internationales Kartellverfahrensrecht, 2003.

[59] Cf. Taylor, International Competition Law, 2005, 300 ff.

2.3 Markets need fairness

Fairness is the key to a functioning market. The fairness principle is the sister principle to the freedom principle, equally important, equally entrenched in the general concept of the market economy, often referred to by politicians talking about the economy.[60] Yet, from a legal perspective and also in economic scholarly writing fairness is often neglected: at best, it is seen as an elusive idea, at worst as fetters to a thriving economy. If fairness really is a cornerstone of a market economy, the challenge is to translate it into legal rules. The widespread perception of behavior of banks and other financial institutions as "unfair" undermines the acceptance of the market economy. The financial crisis calls for a commitment to the fairness principle, and such a commitment needs to be expressed in modern rules that help to make business-to-consumer relations in financial matters fair.

2.3.1 Three characteristics of fairness

Shakespeare opens Macbeth with the famous words "Fair is foul and foul is fair / hover through the fog and filthy air" and the bard seems to get to the heart of a common discomfort with fairness: it is an elusive notion, barely possible to define and it may even turn out to be the exact opposite of what it claims to be. Yet, Shakespeare has the Weird Sisters equate fairness to foulness. His quote may just serve as a reminder to sharpen the wits before immersing oneself into the fog of modern business.

Admittedly, fairness is a strange thing: most people will share a sense of what is fair and unfair, yet a meaningful definition will be hard to come up with. That is not too troublesome after all, but a very common legal problem. The definitions of "abuse" or "good faith" or "in due time" are elusive as well. Lawyers are well-equipped to work with difficult concepts and this chapter will provide some suggestions how to apply a principle of fairness in economic relations.

Most definitions[61] of fairness entail three characteristics: fairness relates to procedural questions, it concerns the proportionality of ends and means and it goes to the roots of social interaction in a community.

The first core element of fairness is that it relates to the behavior of individuals in social interaction, and therefore relates to the process rather than the result or the outcome of interaction. The rules that are determined by the imperative of fairness

---

[60] Cf. e.g., President Obama in a 2011 speech: "But [Theodore] Roosevelt also knew that the free market has never been a free license to take whatever you want from whoever you can. It only works when there are rules of the road to ensure that competition is fair, open, and honest.", available at http://www.washingtonpost.com/politics/president-obamas-economic-speech-in-osawatomie-kans/2011/12/06/gIQAVhe6ZO_story_1.html; see the UK Coalition Programme for Government (http://www.direct.gov.uk/prod_consum_dg/groups/dg_digitalassets/@dg/@en/documents/digitalasset/dg_187876.pdf); or President Barroso's 2012 speech (http://europa.eu/rapid/press-release_SPEECH-12-596_en.htm). Critically on politician's use of the word The Economist, Against fairness, 3 July 2010, 14.

[61] For a current review of different approaches to the term in European and international law cf. Henning-Bodewig, UWG und Geschäftsethik, WRP 2010, 1094 ff.

are procedural rules to some extent. Typical elements of fairness rules are equal treatment, non-discrimination, equal opportunity or the observation of procedural standards. In an economic setting, the procedural element of fairness guides the attention to the autonomy of the parties of a transaction, their behavior and the framework for entering into and executing transactions. Ideally, the decision-making process of the parties respects procedural standards.

The second core element of fairness is that it describes the relation between ends and means and excludes certain particularly disproportionate constellations. Here, fairness develops its regulating power in situations of rivalry and scarcity, which are defining features of the market economy.[62] "Ends" and "means" in competition may also stand for "risk" and "liability" or "input" and "benefit". If there is a preposterous discrepancy between the risks and the liabilities, or the costs and the benefits of the parties involved in a transaction, there may be unfairness involved. Exposing the other party to a transaction to a very high risk may prove to be unfair, in particular if there is no adequate compensation. In this proportionality aspect, the concept of fairness is close to common sense: neither particularly dangerous means need to be employed nor particularly exorbitant ends need to be achieved. By disclosing the costs of transactions, fairness grounds some over-ambitious ideas. It demands equity (not equivalence): rewards and costs shall depend upon contribution and input – or to put it into the context of an economic order: fairness is about competition on the merits. The reward (which in a market economy is the highest income) shall be given to the most deserving performer, the one who invested and worked hardest for providing a valuable product.

The third core element, next to proceduralism and proportionality, is the role of fairness for the community spirit. A community lives in social peace if its members respect the basic rules and treat each other by and large in a respectful way. If they do not, they behave unfairly, seeking their own advantage at the cost of those they interact with or at the cost of the whole community. At first, they are only the spoilsport, with growing dimensions of their unfairness they become a danger for the whole system. Trust, an essential ingredient for prospering commerce, is lost. Fairness, therefore, has to do with the basic rules that hold a community together and thus is influenced by the community's social values. It is a particularly interesting endeavor to translate this to the international business community. For preventing another crisis, it may prove vital to discover the ethical code of the international business community. Fairness may just be the smallest common denominator, but enforcing fairness may still prove to be a great move forward.

Looking to other fields of business law illustrates the three characteristics of fairness.[63] In mergers and acquisitions the parties to the contract often rely upon so-

[62] Cf. ibid., 11 ff.; Zampetti, Fairness in the World Economy, 2006, 26 ff. Also see Eucken, Grundsätze der Wirtschaftspolitik, 1967, 172 ff.

[63] The CJEU refrains from defining fairness in a meaningful way in the judgment on fair compensation by rightholders according to Art. 5(2)(b) of the Copyright Directive, CJEU, Case C-467/08, 21 October 2010 – *Padawan/SGAE* at para 38 ff. Finding that "fair compensation" needs to take the harm caused into account is meaningless – this is what "compensation" is about.

called “fairness opinions” by independent experts. These experts indicate whether they see the price that is agreed upon as a fair one.[64] There are no clear rules on fairness opinions, but in the guidelines provided for by interested parties, two features stand out: First, most of the recommendations center around questions of procedure, transparency, conflict of interest and acceptance by the parties. These are purely procedural questions that point to the first of the core elements of the principle of fairness. Secondly, the explanation on the standard of what is called a fair price is very vague. One scholar refers to a statement by Judge *Easterbrook*, stating that “fairness is a range, not a point”.[65] So, how do experts giving fairness opinions help themselves? They weigh the interests of the parties, strive for a proportionality of the different factors and turn to a comparison with other transactions that were deemed fair.[66] Here, proportionality plays a role (second core element), but also the communal spirit (third core element): the community of M&A-investors shares a certain sense of what is a fair price even though it is “a range, not a point”. The communal standard is seen as a valuable yardstick for determining other transactions. Underlying is the assumption that the market economy by and large produces fair deals; otherwise one could not refer to comparable transactions. So, even in the field of M&A, this pool of allegedly ruthless sharks, there seems to be a communal sense of fairness, which may be relied upon in opinions. The trust placed upon experts judging on the price is telling as well and may squash some of the concerns regarding the enforcement of rules on fairness by judges. If individual experts are called upon to assess the price of a transaction, why not rely more often on judges to define what fairness means in a specific case?

The three characteristics in sum lead to an abstract definition of fairness for the business community. *Fairness means the respect for the communal standards that ensure competition on the merits*. This definition points to the community aspect of fairness and its value for keeping the business community together. It also relates to the proportionality aspect since it aims for competition on the merits, i.e. a market behavior that is performance-oriented. Finally, with addressing standards it takes up the procedural aspect of fairness, the thought of providing a basic framework. This definition will stand challenges from cultural perspectives since its normative basis is the acceptance of the principles of the market economy. Societies that base their economy on free markets and on competition also believe in certain procedures (for competition needs rules), in a meritorious distribution of rewards (for this is what competition is all about) and – for reasons of self-preservation – in respect for a certain social form of interaction.

---

[64] As quoted by Fleischer, Die Fairness Opinion bei M&A-Transaktionen zwischen Markt und Recht, in Grundmann a.o., FS für K. J. Hopt, 2010, 2753.

[65] Cf. Fleischer, Die Fairness Opinion bei M&A-Transaktionen zwischen Markt und Recht, in: Grundmann a.o., FS für K. J. Hopt, 2010, 2753, 2772.

[66] Cf. DFVA, Fairness Opinions: Principles for Management and Supervisory Boards of Target and Bidder Companies, 2008, http://www.dvfa.de/files/die_dvfa/kommissionen/application/pdf/fairness_opinions_e.pdf; IDW Standards, Grundsätze für die Erstellung von Fairness Opinions, 2011, http://www.idw.de/idw/portal/d302226.

2.3.2 Fairness, freedom and market failures

To make fairness a cornerstone of the economic setting is necessary for reasons of legitimacy and trust. Yet, it is also consistent with the freedom principle since both principles share their roots and mechanisms.

2.3.2.1 Why fairness is necessary

Fairness has moved philosophers for centuries, so it is not a new concept to be introduced into the world of social interaction. The current discussion was sparked by John Rawls and his model of society built on the *fair* modalities of social co-operation ("justice as fairness").[67] Rawls' idea of fairness is too well-known to present it in detail here. It suffices to remind readers that Rawls imagined the members of society to negotiate the principles of justice and the modalities of co-operation behind a "veil of ignorance" – rational individuals, mutually disinterested, not knowing about their actual position in society. According to Rawls, such an (imagined) "original position is the appropriate initial status quo which insures that the fundamental agreements reached in it are fair"[68]. This fascinating definition of fair – fair is what we would agree to if stripped of our actual interests – may serve as a yardstick for more targeted definitions in economic relations.[69] While Rawls revived the ideas of a social contract, justice and fairness in academia, fairness did not get the place it deserves in economic law.[70]

In our context, it is not necessary to review this debate for a detailed analysis. The findings of philosophers, diverging as they may be regarding the borderlines of this term, share a common ground: that fairness is a vital principle of social (and accordingly economic) interaction for lending legitimacy to these interactions: People accept a certain setting for their interaction due to their belief that this setting is a fair one. The setting investigated here is the market economy, a constituent aspect of the social order in modern democracies. In a democracy, legitimacy relies on the general acceptance of the people that the chosen institutions and settings work well enough and can be trusted.[71] This form of consensual acceptance of basic institutions becomes all the more relevant since the electorate normally is not called upon to meet the basic decision about the economic system. Here, acceptance of the general setting actually replaces democratic decisions about systems. Stiglitz and

---

67 Rawls, A Theory of Justice, 1972; Justice as Fairness, 2001.

68 Rawls, A Theory of Justice, 1972, § 4 (p. 17).

69 Fairness is also a topic of FRAND-terms that determine the licensing conditions in standard-setting organizations. The yardstick is "fair, reasonable and non-discriminatory". The determination of licensing fees relies on an "ex-ante-situation" that may well be compared with Rawls' original position; cf. e.g. Mariniello, Fair Reasonable and non-Discriminatory (FRAND) Terms: A Challenge for Competition Authorities, 7 JCLE 523 ff. (2010).

70 Rawls himself largely refrained from statements on economic institutions (cf. A Theory of Justice, 1972, § 42) but at least seems to accept the market economy as a system that – as a general concept – is in accordance with a fair society.

71 We shall see later that some scholars derive legitimacy from efficiency rather than fairness, infra.

Charlton write about agreements in international trade: "In a democracy, any trade agreement must be freely entered into and the citizens of the country must be persuaded that the agreement is essentially fair."[72] There is no reason to reduce this to agreements of international trade. One of the more troubling and more profound consequences of the financial crisis was a demise in trust in the market economy: Less people believe in the market economy as a good idea. They lose their confidence that the market economy provides a good mechanism in handling the problem of scarce resources. They feel that the rules governing this system are not "fair". In 2011, protest marches became a regular feature of Wall Street. With this lack of acceptance of the economic system the figures for acceptance of the democratic system as such are also dropping.[73]

Fairness is the basis of consent.[74] Introducing fairness as a principle offers the chance to raise acceptance and legitimacy (and thus to preserve the market economy). This offer makes it necessary to design the rules for economic transactions behind a "veil of ignorance", i.e. to introduce fairness in the rules. Otherwise the international market economy will lose its appeal as the organizing principle for handling resources.

Acceptance does not only relate to the system as such. A market economy is also built on mutual trust of the market players, a general confidence that in most transaction the partner will turn out to be a fair trader. Precautionary measures would otherwise drive transaction costs (for instance for drafting waterproof contracts) to inefficient levels. Such confidence in the overall fairness of the system and its disciplinary function for the market participants is all the more important if transactions become complex: in face-to-face transactions in tribal societies with personal knowledge of the goods and the traders, it may have been possible to oversee the details of the transaction and to screen the contractual partner. The respect for communal standards was a matter of survival, and consequences are no longer felt imminently. Today, the complexity of transactions requires the delegation of responsibility to others. And this delegation prompts a trust in those who take that responsibility and in the incentives of the economic system to act fairly. The confidence to let others deal with personal economic matters ultimately clings on the fairness principle as the governing principle for the working of the market.

2.3.2.2 Why fairness is consistent

If fairness is defined as *the respect for the communal standards that ensure competition on the merits*, it describes the basic normative quality of rivalry for scarce resources. In a modern economy, such rivalry is framed as "competition". One

[72] Stiglitz/Charlton, Fair Trade For All, 2005, 81.

[73] According to a representative study, only 48% of Germans in 2010 thought that the economic system had stood the test. Only 52% were content with democracy. Cf. Bundesverband Deutscher Banken, Führung, Verantwortung, Vertrauen, November 2010, https://www.bankenverband.de/publikationen/ods/fuhrung-verantwortung-vertrauen/fuhrung-verantwortung-vertrauen/download.

[74] Cf. Franck, Fairness in International Law and Institutions, 1998, 25 ff.

often reads that competition needs to be fair, yet, it would be more precise to say that the economy is fair if the markets work according to the principles of competition on the merits, i.e. award the price based on performance. Competition with the best one winning, granting new opportunities to market entrants is a tool of fairness. Using Rawls' "original position" one may easily come to the conclusion that competition on the merits is a fair concept that respects Rawls' principles of justice.

Competition teaches us another aspect that is important for rules that relate to fairness, merits, or performance: fairness is not a substantial objective standard to be applied, but it sets a procedural standard for the given situation. Transactions, thus, are not called unfair for their objective unfairness (e.g. in the sense of a concrete distribution of wealth), but for disrespect of the legitimate expectation that the parties follow certain communal rules.

It is often asked how to distinguish or how to integrate "free" and "fair" competition. Competition rules ("free") ensure the general possibility of competition by setting the framework. The focus is on market power as an obstacle to the autonomous decision-making process. Rules on unfairness deal with the micro-aspects of competition: how do rivals compete? Who is rewarded for one's own performance? Do market players respect the courtesy of business? As Fikentscher pointed out as early as 1958, the common idea of free and fair competition is the defining principle of performance.[75] Competition establishes a meritocracy of the business-world: whoever convinces the customer with his cost-performance-ratio is awarded the contract. To be able to perform requires the freedom to find original ways of performing. Competition laws prevent the replacement of performance through power. To measure one performance against others without frustrating everyone for future performances requires fairness of everyone participating. Laws against unfair behavior in business need to take care of the ratio between performance and success.[76] Freedom and fairness, therefore, are intrinsically linked with the idea of a market economy.[77]

More fundamentally, the idea of free and fair in business both stem from a common root: the principle of economic service. Economic service, as spelt out in the first chapter of this book, is the elementary reason for economic interactions. Fairness does not only provide legitimacy to the organizing mechanism of economic service, but – together with the principle of freedom – also keeps engagements sustainable and fends off restrictions to cater the needs. Put differently: trading a credit default swap in London's city ultimately needs to be seen as an economic service that caters the most basic needs of man. The framework we provide for such transactions does not only need to ensure the freedom of the trader but also his fairness.

---

75 Cf. Fikentscher, Wettbewerb und gewerblicher Rechtsschutz, 1958, 113 ff.

76 Cf. Fikentscher, Wettbewerb und gewerblicher Rechtsschutz, 1958, 117.

77 For a modern understanding of the relationship cf. Ullrich, Anti-Unfair Competition Law and Anti-Trust Law: A Continental Conundrum?, EUI Working Paper LAW No. 2005/01.

2.3.2.3 What fairness has to do with market failures

We learned that state intervention in business is necessary to remedy market failures. As seen above, the situations usually accepted as market failures do not mention "unfairness". So what is the relation of fairness regulation to the concept of market failure?

Admittedly, if the rules do not serve as a disincentive to acting foul the market will not immediately collapse. Fairness is a long-term investment into the functioning of the market, its deficit leads to an erosion of the legitimacy of the market economy and to a frustration of market participants, but the game may continue for a while. Restricting freedom takes much faster effect. Thus, fighting unfairness as a systemic task is often overlooked due to a tendency towards short-sighted governance.

Another reason for this blind spot in economic policy may be found in a preoccupation of economic theory with numbers: economists are much better in measuring quantities than in assessing quality. Unfairness, the disrespect for the standards ensuring competition on the merits, constitutes a "qualitative market failure", the game continues, but it is not a good game. This is hard to put into figures and models, since normative value judgments become necessary. While restraints of freedom nowadays are often measured in terms of efficiency, i.e. with welfare models, it is hard to draw up a similarly convincing model for violations of the fairness principle. Yet, in a broad sense, the disrespect for the standards that ensure competition on the merits may still constitute a "qualitative market failure". The responsibility of lawyers is to define the situations of unfairness that constitute such long-term "market failures" that need to be remedied by systemic regulation. Here, normative statements are in place, and law-making needs to be reclaimed from economists.

2.3.3 Challenges to the fairness principle

The fairness principle meets criticism from three sides: Some argue that fairness as a term is too elusive to form the basis of the economy. Another critique claims that fairness restricts freedom. And finally some scholars would prefer efficiency as the basis for legitimacy of an economic system. All three claims do not stand.

2.3.3.1 Too elusive?

The claim that "fairness" is too elusive to be made a principle of economic policies[78] disregards the ambiguity of most abstract terms. Sure, fairness is not easy to define, but this is true for most other "principles" as well, be it freedom, welfare, efficiency or justice. To give meaning to these terms is the challenge for lawyers, particularly judges and academic writers. The definition of such terms evolves over time. Cases and precedents are needed to define the boundaries; litigation will provide showcases for unfair behavior. The deficit of a meaningful enforcement of fairness in the past cannot lead to an abstention in introducing such rules. Furthermore, in some fields of law fairness has been used successfully as a yardstick, as shown above.

[78] E.g. The Economist, Against fairness, 3 July 2010, 14.

2.3.3.2 Restricting freedom?

It is a misunderstanding to criticize that fairness restricts freedom. True, rules set limits for individual behavior. So does the criminal law provision not to steal. As pointed out earlier, the decisive factor for establishing an economic order is to restrict the rules on systemic regulation. The fairness principle and the freedom principle are such pillars of systemic regulation of the economy. Both principles are needed to keep markets working, and they both are complementary: While the freedom principle guarantees the autonomous decision-making space for individuals, the fairness principle guarantees a certain quality of decisions and therefore the legitimacy of the whole market system. The excesses of free-marketism that eat up the acceptance of the market economy are prevented by a sound and low-key fairness regulation.

2.3.3.3 Making people worse off?

The third challenge to the fairness principles comes from economic scholarship. Louis Kaplow and Steven Shavell reject the fairness approach in their notable pamphlet.[79] They suggest to deduct the legitimacy of an economic system from a welfare approach. Human well-being, so they say, makes people believe into a system, and thus enhancing total welfare is the only yardstick for law-making in the business world. Fairness should not play a role in selecting the right rules, according to the authors, since it is detrimental to the cause of welfare. The economic system is to be designed according to welfare standards (such as efficiency), producing the desired results for the people participating in that system.[80]

This approach is oriented towards the achievement of distinct results. The approach is not oriented towards the process of decision-making, it is not about the structure of the market, it is about the performance in the very end and starts from this perspective. It may be noted that this differs considerably from Hayek and other liberals who see the market process as a discovery procedure that finds its own solutions.[81] With their approach, Kaplow/Shavell could justify strong interventionist rules, if one assumes that there were clear paths to welfare (an assumption rightly doubted). Of course, total welfare is an aim worth striving for, and an economic system does lose legitimacy if it does not cater to people's basic needs. Yet, this is what the idea of economic service is all about – no need to argue: If a system fails to do so, it fails to perform its very basic function. Yet, it is one matter to define the basic function of economic service, and another to define the guiding principles of the legal regime governing the economy.

Of course, an excessive fairness-legislation would cause problems. So Kaplow/Shavell send a welcome warning message to law-makers who wish to introduce

---

[79] Kaplow/Shavell, Principles of Fairness versus Human Welfare, Harvard Law School, Discussion Paper No. 277, 3/2000; Kaplow/Shavell, Fairness Versus Welfare, 2002.

[80] Cf. from an Asian perspective agreeing with Kaplow/Shavell *Liu*, In Fairness We Trust? – Why Fostering Competition Law and Policy Ain't Easy in Asia (19 October 2004). Available at SSRN: http://ssrn.com/abstract=610822 or doi:10.2139/ssrn.610822.

[81] Cf. Hayek (Fn. 11); Zäch/Künzler (Fn. 9).

rules on fairness, reminding them that the positive sound of that notion needs to be translated carefully into law.

Yet, the welfare advocates err on three points:[82] First, they overestimate the power of welfare in making people happy. According to behavioral research fair treatment features prominently in the individual perception of happiness.[83] It does not serve the purpose of human well-being to exclude fairness as a principle. Second, Kaplow/Shavell need strong opposition if they try to establish an interventionist system for selecting rules that foster human welfare for the economy: Human welfare as an absolute goal will not be achieved at large scale since resources are limited. Economic decision-making is about scarcity and distribution with limited information. This calls for a procedural solution rather than a substantial one.[84] Third, the lack of complete information prevents a perfect steering of the millions of economic processes taking place every day.

2.3.4 Fairness as an international concept

The definition of fairness provided here calls for respect for the communal standards that ensure competition on the merits. With reference to "communal standards" the definition introduces a cultural element into business legislation. This may trigger fears of either cultural imperialism, or differing national standards in a globalized environment, or of an "airy-fairy" element in business law. These fears, however, are unfounded.

Firstly, all rules contain cultural elements since law itself is a matter of evolution under specific cultural conditions. Setting a purely efficiency-related standard for business legislation does not solve this problem but simply decides in favor of one concept. An efficiency-standard is as much based on a political decision promoting a certain ideology as altruistic standards.[85]

Secondly, the cultural element is restricted to the community aspect. Fairness always requires, as Thomas M. Franck has pointed out, a sense of community.[86] The relevant community for this project is the international business community. To discover the shared principles constituting "fair play" in this community is the endeavor to be undertaken. This is not illusory: In sports, trade or legal procedure communal standards are well-respected. Everyone would agree that in sports the

---

[82] For a critical assessment cf. Coleman, The Grounds of Welfare, 112 Yale L. J., 1511 ff. (2003); Stewart, Persons and Their Well-Being: A Critical Discussion of Kaplow and Shavell's Fairness versus Welfare, 30 Queen's L. J. 1 (2004).

[83] Cf. Coleman, The Grounds of Welfare, 112 Yale L. J. 1511, 1542 (2003).

[84] Cf. Dorff, Why Welfare Depends on Fairness: A Reply to Kaplow and Shavell, 75 S. Cal. L. Rev. 847, 897 (2002); *Stewart* points out that the efficiency approach reduces individuals to "things" if the aim of an aggregate amount of well-being is the ultimate goal, Stewart, Persons and Their Well-Being: A Critical Discussion of Kaplow and Shavell's Fairness versus Welfare, 30 Queen's L. J. 1, 27 (2004).

[85] Cf. Drexl, On the (a)political approach of the economic approach to competition law, in Drexl/Kerber/Podszun (eds.), Competition Policy and the Economic Approach, 2011, 312.

[86] Franck, Fairness in International Law and Institutions, 1998, 11.

fastest running man would deserve the winner's crown – everything else would be deemed unfair. The concept of fair trade means that all parties in the production chain are compensated according to the merits of their performance. The right to be heard is a common feature of "fair trial" all over the world. Why should it be impossible to find similar elements for a fairness-standard in international financial transactions?

Thirdly, the ambitious endeavor of defining communal standards of fairness for the business community finds support when surveying national legislation on rules in business.[87] It seems that legal rules on unfair practices can be found in most if not all jurisdictions to some extent. Of course, not all rules work with the notion of fairness, but they sanction similar practices as unlawful. Rules on misleading customers or an unfair behavior against competitors feature in many jurisdictions, e.g. under tort provisions in Common Law countries. The World Intellectual Property Organization (WIPO) came to the conclusion that most jurisdictions, including the U.S.A., have a body of law that governs the behavior of undertakings in a qualitative sense.[88] They sanction companies that do not respect the communal standards that ensure competition on the merits in business. Art. 10bis of the Paris Convention ratified by 173 countries stipulates the protection against unfair competition, defined as "act of competition contrary to honest practices in industrial or commercial matters". In the European Union, the 27 Member States implemented Directives on unfair commercial practices[89] and on misleading and comparative advertising[90], both regulating aspects of fairness in B2B- and B2C-relations. Apart from this harmonization, terminology differs within Europe and the norms are scattered across different fields of law in national jurisdictions. Some countries have developed specific laws, others deal with unfair commercial practices under general tort law provisions, some countries have administrative enforcement agencies, and others leave it to market participants and general courts.[91] In the U.S., many cases that would fall under these and similar provisions in Europe are covered by the jurisprudence on prima-facie-torts.[92] Asian jurisdictions offer an interesting example of economic legislation based on the fairness principle: Many competition laws in Asian countries combine the freedom and the fairness principle to a certain extent.[93]

---

[87] Cf. Henning-Bodewig, WRP 2010, 1094 ff.

[88] Cf. WIPO, Protection Against Unfair Competition, paras 19 ff.

[89] Directive 2005/29/EC.

[90] Directive 2006/114/EC.

[91] For an overview of the situation in Europe see Henning-Bodewig, Unfair competition law – European Union and Member State, 2006.

[92] See 1.4.5 above.

[93] Paas-Mohando, Fairness principle in the competition laws of some Asian countries, ECLR 2010, 466; Liu, In Fairness We Trust? – Why Fostering Competition Law and Policy Ain't Easy in Asia (19 October 2004) available at SSRN: http://ssrn.com/abstract=610822 or doi:10.2139/ssrn.610822.

2.3.5 Summary

Markets need fairness. Without a prominent role for the fairness principle the legitimacy of the market economy comes into question. To give a definition of the allegedly elusive term of "fairness" is not as hard as it seems – fairness as a concept has been discussed for centuries and all jurisdictions feature rules that may be classified as rules on fairness. The suggestion here is to define fairness in business transactions as the respect for the communal standards that ensure competition on the merits. To enforce this definition as a legal principle is a challenge since some critics do not see the systemic relevance of the fairness principle. Yet, in the long run markets fail that no longer keep the market participants in the boundaries of "fair play". In the next chapter it will be spelt out what this could mean for financial markets.

2.4 Unfair financial transactions

The disrespect for the standards that ensure competition on the merits constitutes a "qualitative market failure" that needs to be sanctioned to ensure the working of the market economy in the long run. The legal concept suggested here is a concept of fairness. It seems that in the buildup of the financial crisis fairness was not a high priority for financial institutions: Allegedly, Goldman Sachs aided Greece in brightening figures for the Euro; banks did not disclose their interests when advising private investors; in ever-more complex transactions banks talked small investors into subprime products; traders acted like gamblers with no respect for the possible consequences of their hazardous activities; and when the bubble burst the collection of boni was a priority while the taxpayer bailed out banks and bankers. This account is of course polemic, yet it reflects a common discomfort and points to the fact that respect for the community in which financial institutions operated was lacking. There was no control of systemic compatibility of transactions.

The current legal system has not provided many incentives to behave better: The fairness principle was rarely enforced in financial markets. It may help to introduce a general clause with certain examples of violations of the fairness principle in financial markets. Enforcement through private parties and in the international arena needs to be strengthened.

2.4.1 The enforcement lacuna

If fairness is a corner-stone of the market economy, this arrangement seems to be poorly founded: Fairness legislation exists in most countries, but it does not play a big role on an international level and often is not understood in its systemic relevance. Rules on fairness are often mistaken to be an aspect of consumer protection – while the opposite is true: consumer protection is based on the fairness principle. The financial crisis exposed the enforcement lacuna and in its aftermath showed a misconception of law-makers with regard to fairness provisions. It became evident that the existing rules on fairness were not tailored for financial markets. The proposals triggered by the financial crisis for a strengthening of fairness rely on enforcement mechanisms that proved inefficient before. The under-enforcement of fairness standards in business is the reason for the widespread discontent with the market economy. Rightly so: As pointed out earlier, fairness is a condition of legitimacy for an organizational principle in society. Adding such a principle in a meaningful way on an international basis would not just work as a regulatory remedy but it would also cure some of the affliction with capitalism.

2.4.1.1 Existing rules

Even in the aftermath of what Ben Bernanke, chairman of the Federal Reserve Bank, called the worst crisis since the 1930s there was very few litigation in courts relating to standards of fairness. Only few people who lost their assets and undertakings battered by the transactions of others tried to recover through fairness litigation. Fairness is not yet regarded as a standard for business transactions violation of which is sanctioned. This enforcement lacuna points to a problem: existing rules do not relate with what is going on in financial transactions although these are driving the economy.

The reason may lie in the historic circumstances when rules on unfair business practices were first developed. In Germany for instance, the modern rules on unfairness were introduced in the early 20th century and remained intact for decades. In that era modern retailing rose in Europe and so did aggressive marketing in a society that was on the one hand adapting to the progress coming with the new commercial rise, but on the other hand was still conservative and traditional. The results were rules against unfair commercial practices that had a strong moral sentiment, did not consider the freedom of markets a vital element and focused on the allegedly down-and-dirty practices of those days. For a long time, the terminology and the jurisprudence echoed the concerns of those days. In the past years, these norms were revised under European auspices, particularly through the directives on unfair business practices[94] and on comparative and misleading advertising[95]. These directives represent modern fairness legislation. Actually, in business-to-consumer-transactions the directive on unfair business practices even led to a substantial harmonization within the EU – with the exception of financial services (Art. 3 (9)).

The influential black list of practices that are in all circumstances considered unfair (Annex 1 of the Directive) reveals the spirit of this piece of legislation: it tackles modern forms of roguish behavior towards customers but it does not show an understanding of fairness that touches the foundations of the market economy. It singles out the shady characters and deals, those claiming quality marks they have not obtained, those coercing customers into contracts. The underlying image of transactions is of a private customer going into a shop on high street, discussing with the shop owner and buying a fridge. This is all worth fighting for, and fairness needs to govern such transactions, of course. Yet, the more systemic danger may stem from business strategies that are operated by players who were regarded as most serious: banks, financial institutions or big conglomerates with unclear struc-

[94] Directive 2005/29/EC.
[95] Directive 2006/114/EC.

tures. Not a single provision in Annex 1 of the Unfair Commercial Practices Directive is targeted at unfair financial transactions.

On an international level – and financial markets work internationally – the enforcement lacuna is evident: Rules and fora for enforcement are lacking. Unfair business practices neither feature in World Trade Law nor in international conventions very prominently (with exceptions noted below). In particular, there is no international institution or organization dealing with unfairness in the economic system with some rigor or power. While NGOs such as Consumers International or the International League of Competition Law (LIDC) present proposals for internationally valid criteria of fairness, international politics lags behind.

In short, the geographical reach of fairness rules confirms the subject-matter focus of existing rules: they are not designed as a systemic yardstick for important transactions in business but focus on rather traditional "roguish" high-street practices.

2.4.1.2 A wrong focus of reform

The financial crisis triggered a debate on how to strengthen regulation in financial markets.[96] Fairness, sometimes in the guise of consumer protection, plays an important role in many of the contributions. For instance, the OECD has published Draft G20 High-Level Principles on Financial Consumer Protection. As the third principle the OECD suggests: "Equitable and Fair Treatment of Consumers", or in detail:

> "Financial consumers should be treated equitably, honestly and fairly at all stages of their relationship with financial service providers. Treating consumers fairly should be an integral part of the day to day good governance and corporate culture of financial service providers. Consumers should benefit from comparable levels of financial consumer protection for similar products and services and for similar level of consumers sophistication. Special attention should be dedicated to the needs of vulnerable groups."[97]

The OECD Principles prove that there is a window of opportunity to strengthen the fairness principle in international business. Politicians understood that action needs to be taken and they are reminded by protesters doubting the legitimacy of the market economy. Now is the time for fairness as an enforceable legal tool.

Yet, the focus of most proposals for reform is on public authorities that should oversee financial markets with more power than before.[98] Essentially, the European governments and the U.S. administration propose to strengthen the financial markets watchdogs, to create new authorities and to provide for tougher sanctions. The OECD, as its second principle, deals with "oversight bodies".[99] The envisaged

96 Cf. Ramsay, Consumer Credit Regulation After the Fall: International Dimensions, euvr 2012, 24 ff.

97 OECD, Draft G20 High-Level Principles on Financial Consumer Protection, 1 August 2011.

98 In the overview by Ramsay, public enforcement plays the number one role while private enforcement only features on half a page; cf. Ramsay, Consumer Credit Regulation After the Fall: International Dimensions, euvr 2012, 24. Cf. the "Vickers Report", the Final Report of the Independent Commission on Banking in the UK, Sept. 2011, available at www.hm-treasury.gov. uk/d/ICB-Final-Report.pdf.

99 OECD, Draft G20 High-Level Principles on Financial Consumer Protection, 1 August 2011.

European Economic Government, an idea fostered by *Nicolas Sarkozy* and *Angela Merkel*,[100] heads into the same direction for economics in general: growing influence of public bodies, central overseeing, trust in governmental structures. This is disappointing, but need not trouble the advocates of freedom and fairness too much – failure is foreseeable. Such solutions lack creativity. They have at their bottom a fundamental belief that the existing control mechanisms were the right ones, but just not strong enough. One may legitimately doubt that public authorities will ever have the power and the means to tame the fast-moving financial actors with their possibilities to escape to regulatory havens. Enforcement authorities had the tools in their hands in the past, yet they failed to employ them in a meaningful way. Focusing on public law enforcement may prove not to be sufficient.

2.4.2 Starting Points

The endeavor to introduce an enforceable fairness obligation in financial markets builds on a general tendency to hand the law enforcement to private parties and on first international obligations regarding fair competition.

2.4.2.1 The turn to private law enforcement

An alternative to public regulation of financial markets is to strengthen the private enforcement of fairness obligations with damage claims. This idea of strengthening private enforcement instead of more public intervention is a cornerstone of Fair-Economy (cf. 3.3.2 and 4.2.4 below). The market participants themselves are best placed to remedy problematic constellations. They are directly concerned, they have the relevant information, they know the economic effects, they feel the points that prove worth litigating. Economic aims may be reached not just by exercising public competences, but also by enabling private individuals to do business in a certain way and to litigate. This is the regulatory function of private law, a neglected force in international business relations. As in other fields of law, e.g. antitrust law, legislators should entrust private parties with market regulation. Whether self-regulation, codes of conduct or corporate governance may play an important role in this regard remains to be seen. The turn to private may prove more efficient than the trust in public enforcement even though a certain oversight will remain necessary.

The freedom principle actually calls for such a more active role for private parties. As in business in general, a decentralized, "spontaneous order" (to use a Hayekian term) may also characterize law enforcement. In the fast-moving financial markets it is barely possibly to control in advance what happens. Markets are too complex and too creative to give specific norms of what constitutes a good financial product. A judge, i.e. a person entrusted by the democratic community to solve conflicts with the laws at hand, with the information of the case and with his common sense, is the right person to determine whether a practice was unfair.

---

[100] Cf. the Joint Press Statement of Sarkozy/Merkel, 14 June 2010, available at http://www.bundesregierung.de/Content/DE/Mitschrift/Pressekonferenzen/2010/06/2010-06-14-bkin-sarkozy.html.

Trusting judges and building on the private law enforcement mechanisms may, however, require reforms of some legal systems. The European Commission is already on the way to make private enforcement more effective.[101] Otherwise, if proceedings take too long, are too costly or offer too poor remedies, private enforcement may not take off.

2.4.2.2 The Paris Convention, TRIPS and the WIPO initiative

Regarding existing provisions for fairness on an international level, the prohibition of unfair competition in Art. 10bis of the Paris Convention for the Protection of Industrial Property serves as a starting point. It reads as follows:

> "(1) The countries of the Union are bound to assure to nationals of such countries effective protection against unfair competition.
> (2) Any act of competition contrary to honest practices in industrial or commercial matters constitutes an act of unfair competition.
> (3) The following in particular shall be prohibited:
> (i) all acts of such a nature as to create confusion by any means whatever with the establishment, the goods, or the industrial or commercial activities, of a competitor;
> (ii) false allegations in the course of trade of such a nature as to discredit the establishment, the goods, or the industrial or commercial activities, of a competitor;
> (iii) indications or allegations the use of which in the course of trade is liable to mislead the public as to the nature, the manufacturing process, the characteristics, the suitability for their purpose, or the quantity, of the goods."

The TRIPS agreement refers to the Paris Convention, particularly in Art. 2 para 1, incorporating Art. 10bis of the Paris Convention. It is unclear whether Art. 2 para 1 TRIPS may be read as referring only to aspects of intellectual property protection, not establishing an obligation to promote rules on unfair competition amongst members of the WTO, or whether it actually grants the possibility to enforce unfair competition law via the dispute mechanisms of the WTO.[102] The WTO Appellate Body seems to favor a wide understanding of Art. 2 TRIPS[103], but has not yet ruled on a case of classic unfair competition. Art. 39 TRIPS (on undisclosed information) and Art. 22(2) TRIPS (on geographical indications) also refer to Art. 10bis Paris Convention.

---

[101] Cf. the EU Commission initiative for new rules on collective redress, http://ec.europa.eu/consumers/redress_cons/collective_redress_en.htm.

[102] Cf. Drexl in Münchener Kommentar zum BGB, Vol. 11: Internationales Wirtschaftsrecht, 5th edition 2010, Internationales Recht gegen den Unlauteren Wettbewerb, 32; Henning-Bodewig, International Protection Against Unfair Competition – Art. 10bis Paris Convention, TRIPS and WIPO Model Provisions, IIC 1999, 166 (179).

[103] Cf. WTO Appellate Body, Report 2.1.2002 – United States – Section 211 Omnibus Appropriations Act 1998, WTO-Doc. WT/DS176/AB/R, 338; cf. Drexl, in Münchener Kommentar zum BGB, Vol. 11: Internationales Wirtschaftsrecht, 5th edition 2010, Internationales Recht gegen den Unlauteren Wettbewerb, 32.

Even if the examples and the context relate the provisions on unfair competition to the IP arena, the wording of these norms clearly opens the door for international standards of protection against unfairness in the WTO.[104] Cottier and Jevtic argue that Art. 10bis is actually precise enough to have a direct effect and may be relied upon directly in national courts.[105]

Now, in the wake of the financial crisis, a revitalization of these international starting points is worth the effort. This project also builds on the work of a group of scholars who proposed in the mid-nineties to include rules on fair competition in the framework of the World Intellectual Property Organization (WIPO).[106] They highlighted the relevance of unfair competition for the protection of IP rights and were inspired by the provision in Art. 10bis of the Paris Convention. The group of experts named six specific cases of unfairness: misrepresentation; misappropriation; misleading the public; discrediting others; violations of secrecy of information.

This proposal and the Paris Convention are excellent starting points for reflections on an international enforcement on unfair practices. In particular, they can easily relate to private law enforcement. Yet, the proposals are still very close to the context of IP protection and it may well be worth to include other specific cases of unfairness.

2.4.2.3 International private actions

Taking the turn to private and the first steps to an international fairness regime into account it is easy to spot the chance of establishing the fairness principle on an international scale: The WTO, establishing a first global economic order, but mainly addressing national states needs to open up for regulating business behavior. The WIPO, though focusing on IP issues only, may serve as an example: It has some routine with international civil law suits under the domain-grabbing regime.[107] Maybe this provides a model for private enforcement on an international scale in certain areas of unfair dealings. It is vital, nowadays, to address transactions of individuals. It is private parties that move the world economy. Nation-states and their trade relations have become less important as compared to the dealings of

---

[104] More cautious are Henning-Bodewig, International Protection Against Unfair Competition – Art. 10bis Paris Convention, TRIPS and WIPO Model Provisions, IIC 1999, 166, 181; Pflüger, Article 5 Paris Convention, in Cottier/Veron, Concise International and European IP law, 2nd edition 2011, 267; Reichmann, Universal Minimum Standards of Intellectual Property Protection, in Correa/Yusuf, Intellectual Property and International Trade: The TRIPS Agreement, 2nd edition 2008, 23, 62.

[105] Cottier/Jevtic, The protection against unfair competition in WTO law: Status, potential and prospects, in: Drexl a.o., Technology and Competition – Contributions in honour of Hanns Ullrich, 2009, 669, 681.

[106] WIPO, Model Provisions on Protection against Unfair Competition, WIPO Publication No. 832(E) (1996). Cf. Henning-Bodewig, International Protection Against Unfair Competition – Art. 10bis Paris Convention, TRIPS and WIPO Model Provisions, IIC 1999, 166, 181 ff.

[107] WIPO Uniform Domain Name Dispute Resolution Policy, cf. http://www.wipo.int/amc/en/domains/.

multinational corporations or simply an undertaking buying material from a company in another state or a consumer investing money in certificates of overseas companies. It is time for international institutions to manage this shift towards private initiative and private law.[108] To give momentum to this project, it is necessary to have an overseeing international body – be it with WIPO or WTO – to watch how the fairness principle is established in international finance.

For international law suits the rules of procedure would need a design that makes it realistic to win a case within a reasonable period of time and in an affordable manner.

In the long run an international regime of private enforcement of fairness would work preemptively: The regulatory power of civil law would unfold and business may become fairer and even more competitive.

2.4.3 The concept of general clauses

The core legal idea is to have a general clause on fairness on an international level (cf. 4.1.2 below). The enforcement of the general clause and its exemplary groups of cases should rest with private parties and an international coordinating body.

For high profile business transactions a fairness clause could read like this:

> "A behavior in business is considered unfair if it disrespects the communal standards of competition on the merits."

As seen above, fairness is a concept in many jurisdictions; the only question is how to transform it into a manageable legal provision that makes it clear that fairness is part of the *systemic* regulation of the economy. Such a transformation may be achieved with a blanket or general clause as in Art. 10bis Paris Convention or in the proposal of the WIPO group.

In a general clause definitions are open and need further specification by the judge dealing with the clause. The rationale for an openness of definition is the changing nature of the object of regulation: business practices and commercial strategies evolve over time, sometimes spring up in days, and the legal community needs to react. Regulation of financial markets will always lag behind if lawmakers try to capture specific activities. In the past, the lack of adequate rules may have contributed to the evolution of international financial markets into an area where the reach of the law was limited. The impression of many people was that some formal rules were observed but that the spirit of the legal order, in particular the fairness principle, were not respected at all. A blanket clause would give the possibility to sanction at least in part and *ex post* some of the violations of the fairness principle.

The trade-off with legal certainty seems acceptable: If some market participants act in such fast-moving fields as finance, they take the risk of changes in the business environment including the legal regimes. If they seek certainty and stability of external factors they should move into other commercial fields.

---

[108] E.g. through a "Financial Ombudsman", Ramsay, Consumer Credit Regulation After the Fall: International Dimensions, euvr 2012, 24.

In many fields of law, general clauses state the general aim and leave the concrete definition according to the specific circumstances up to the judge. She will determine whether in a case a violation of the principle has taken place. This concept is well-established. Open terms are standard in law enforcement, if you think of "abuse" in European antitrust law, for instance, or provisions of "good faith".[109] Many formulas dealing with fairness in national jurisdictions do not give specific guidance even if some examples are defined in precedent or in the law.[110] Lawyers have developed tools to reconcile the necessarily abstract level of definition in rules and the requirement to provide for legal certainty, in particular by identifying groups of cases that are exemplary and hit the core of the principle.

There is no general answer to what is unfair in a specific financial transaction. It depends on each individual case and on the circumstances of the transaction and the parties. This is all the more true for fairness, a principle that makes the individual circumstances part of the normative evaluation. This is why this proposal turns to private law enforcement and the wisdom of judges: they are called upon in society to take the specific circumstances into account that the law-maker cannot account for in detail. The decisions of judges in fairness matters require qualitative analyses, and therefore differ from the freedom approach set out above. While freedom clings to quantitative aspects that may be generalized and calculated in an easier way, fairness requires a value judgment.

2.4.4 Rules on fairness in financial transactions

What would such an international rule on fairness mean for financial transactions? This depends on the definition of the groups of cases that seem problematic. It is necessary to identify situations of unfairness that remained without a remedy and led to the loss of legitimacy of the economic order.

Apart from the well-established cases of unfairness that are laid down in the existing norms one may consider two other groups of cases that may be framed in legal terms as follows.

The first proposition would tackle the information asymmetries of financial institutions and their customers:

It is considered unfair if the legal or factual complexity of a financial product or service effectively deprives the customer of his choice or compensation.

The second proposition would address the imbalance of risks and merits:

It is considered unfair if the provider of a financial product or service bears no risk through a strategy of harming third parties and transferring the risk to the customer.

These two ideas, explained below, are perfectly in line with an economic system with a competitive market economy. They are, of course, only suggestions to spark

---

[109] Cf. WIPO, Protection Against Unfair Competition (1994), para. 28 ff.

[110] Cf. Cottier/Jevtic, The protection against unfair competition in WTO law: Status, potential and prospects, in: Drexl a.o., Technology and Competition – Contributions in honour of Hanns Ullrich, 2009, 669, 675.

a discussion on how to answer the challenges to fairness that were laid bare by the financial crisis.[111]

2.4.4.1 Complexity as unfairness

The first rule proposed here addresses problems of consumers who are confronted with overly complex products without having a choice. From a macro-economic standpoint it is welcome if private parties invest money and fuel the economic circle with their savings. Yet when meeting such an investment decision, private customers are confined to products that all carry hundreds of disclaimers and side terms. Regarding these terms of the contracts for multi-layered financial products, customers do not have a choice: There is no such thing as an "easy investment contract". Customers are left with the choice to invest or not to invest but they are not in the position to challenge the factual and legal complexity of the product or specific terms. This is partly due to a decision by the legislators regarding information obligations of the financial institutions, but it is also partly due to a strategy of risk-shifting by undertakings that invent ever more complex financial transactions combined with ever more complex legal provisions so as to minimize their risk. It is reported that advisors in banks do not understand all the products they sell to their clients. Sometimes, it is unclear who the contractual partners are or what institutions are involved in the transaction due to the complexity of the product and the intransparent structure of undertakings and their partners. Often, the real flow of money cannot be traced due to the complexity. Staff members who deal with the bank's client do not have authority or capacity to explain every detail nor to change products and ease the complexity burden. The result is that the customer needs to take it or leave it – there is no longer a competition for an informed decision by the customer.[112] The customer is no longer in the position to control the fairness of her counterpart, even more: sometimes she does not even get to know her counterpart. This makes it necessary for the law to step in: *It could be considered unfair if the legal or factual complexity of a financial product or service effectively deprives the customer of his choice or compensation.*

The WIPO group of expert had seen this problem already:

> "In theory consumers, in their role as referees of economic play, could deter dishonest entrepreneurs by disregarding their goods or services and favoring those of honest competitors. Reality, however, is different. As an economic situation becomes more complex, consumers become less able to act as referees."[113]

---

[111] To name one further suggestion, Ramsay proposes to introduce a norm on "responsible lending" in consumer credits where "the lender must take into account the other party's interests and needs throughout the relationship, and not act solely in her own interest", cf. Ramsay, Consumer Credit Regulation After the Fall: International Dimensions, euvr 2012, 24. For an overview of possible violations of fairness under existing rules, cf. Fikentscher, Finanzkrise, Wettbewerb und Regulierung, GRUR Int. 2009, 635 ff.

[112] Drexl, Die wirtschaftliche Selbstbestimmung des Verbrauchers, 1998, 328 ff.

[113] WIPO, Protection Against Unfair Competition, 1994, para 6.

If the staff of the undertaking selling the product is unable to understand the terms – how should the customer do that? A recent judgment from Austria illustrates this point: The Austrian High Court dealt with an investment and had to decide whether there was a misleading advertisement. The ads for the investment often referred to a lengthy prospectus which was giving all the right information. Yet, the Court stated that if the ads highlight certain aspects of the investment it is not sufficient to refer to the prospectus for potential disadvantages that go along with these aspects.[114] The complexity was not balanced.

Over-complexity reduces competition on the merits: The merits of a product are no longer discernible and competition becomes a mere gamble. The autonomous decision-making process that is the basis of competition is considerably hampered (cf. 3.7.2.3 below). Take the example of customers investing into subprime housing: Of course, one may say they have themselves to blame for not checking the credentials of their investment. Yet, considering the concrete situation it is no longer a clear-cut case of competition on the merits and an informed and autonomous decision. If the structural over-complexity of such deals plays out against the customer, the whole set may be considered unfair. Those profiting from the complexity or exploiting the complexity of products and contractual relations should bear a higher burden of liability. Their profit often stems from the inability of others to understand all details of the transactions without having substantial recourse to competitive products since all products come as similarly complex ones. The complexity often is a disguise for the transfer of risks to others or for the externalization of costs. This may be anti-competitive and unfair.

The critique of complexity is a critique of a model of regulation that relies heavily on transparency and customers' information[115]. In the legislators opinion a contract was seen as valid as long as a customer was informed about basically everything and gave his signature. Yet, in practice this information model did not provide a very high standard of consumer protection: few customers were ever able to digest the small print that came in overdoses. There was not information of customers (as was the original plan of law-makers and judges) but disinformation or information-overkill of customers. Since all competitors were exposed to the same obligations to inform there was no competition regarding the level and value of information. Liability was reduced to the question of correct information instead of a substantial standard that triggers liability. This system of informing customers of the risks they take has not reached the aim of enabling these customers to take good decisions. It has simply led to a zero-risk of financial institutions as long as their lawyers drafted the documents carefully enough. The information system has failed.[116]

---

[114] OGH, 20 January 2009, 4 Ob 188/08 p, ecolex 2009, 694 ff.

[115] Cf. Schön, Zwingendes Recht oder informierte Entscheidung – zu einer (neuen) Grundlage unserer Zivilrechtsordnung, in: Heldrich a.o. (eds), FS für C.-W. Canaris, Vol. I, 2007, 1191.

[116] Cf. Grundmann, Europa- und wirtschaftsrechtliche Grundlagen der Privatrechtsgesellschaft, in: Riesenhuber (ed.), Privatrechtsgesellschaft, 2007, 105, 125; Schön, Zwingendes Recht oder informierte Entscheidung – zu einer (neuen) Grundlage unserer Zivilrechtsordnung, in: Heldrich a.o. (eds), FS für C.-W. Canaris, Vol. I, 2007, 1191.

2.4.4.2 No-risk-strategies as unfairness

The second rule proposed here addresses unfair dealings through strategic risk avoidance. The financial crisis revealed the existence of products that effectively have as their object the speculation with harm for third parties. The intermediary selling the product bears no risk but only profits from his customer speculating against a third party. A systemic danger arises through the self-fulfilling forces in financial markets. *It could be considered unfair if the provider of a financial product or service bears no risk through a strategy of harming third parties and transferring the risk to the customer.*

It may be doubted already whether speculating with the loss or harm of others makes a fair product. Yet, this business model is particularly problematic if this speculation comes free from risks. It separates profits completely from liability, performance or productive work. Such investments look more like the exploitation of loopholes and remind of fraudulent tricks rather than financial foresight. The situation is similar to the behavior of Greece and its advisors when "designing" Greek figures so as to enter the Euro-Zone, and it is also similar to advisors in banks who seem to counsel in good faith but are induced by others to give specific advice into a certain direction. These groups of cases some of which have come up in the courts already have been classified as unfair for "inducement to neglect the interests of third parties"[117].

If fairness is an expression of a communal standard, of a spirit of meritocracy, such neglect endangers not just third parties, but the system as a whole. Customers can no longer place their trust on advisors or intermediaries but are induced to hope for the loss of others. If institutions that form an active part of such practices are "bailed out" for their "systemic relevance", it is obvious that the legitimacy of the whole system decreases. On a smaller scale, the incentives-regime within banks that hand out huge bonuses despite of gigantic losses provides another example of the possibility to take risks without being held liable. That is not fair: A competitive market economy lives on taking risks, but also on punishing those whose risks realize. This competitive paradigm was loosened before the financial crisis and led to an unfair distribution of losses.

2.4.5 Summary

The fairness principle is not enforced with any vigor in financial markets. This is due in part to the rather traditional framing of fairness rules. However, there is a momentum for reform. Yet, most proposals take a wrong focus: they wish to strengthen public enforcement bodies rather than turning to private law enforcement and they do not strengthen the fairness principle. This is striking since it seems barely possible to tame the financial markets with overseeing bodies acting *ex ante*. In the concept proposed here, fairness obligations would be enforced by judges in an *ex post*-control of transactions. In Chapter 3 the civil law obligation to avoid discrepancies of risk and liability is spelt out. In this chapter, the focal point

[117] Cf. Fritzsche, Annotation to BGH, 2 July 2009, I ZR 147/06, JZ 2010, 573, 575.

of tackling certain practices was fairness. The decisive point is to specify what constitutes an unfair transaction. The tool for a provision would be to work with a general clause giving a general definition of unfair business behavior. The disrespect for the communal standards ensuring competition on the merits would be deemed unfair. Specifying this for financial markets would work with the definition of subgroups of cases. Two constellations are proposed: Firstly, over-complexity of transactions to the detriment of the customer should be deemed unfair. Secondly, undertakings with a no-risk-strategy that speculate on the loss of third parties while the risk is borne by consumers act unfairly. These first ideas may trigger a debate on how to word fairness obligations that are up to the challenge of regulating fast-moving financial markets. For the enforcement of such rules the developments in international economic law provide excellent starting points: Ever more trust is placed on private law enforcement. In the Paris Convention, the WTO-Agreements and in the work of the WIPO group of experts there are many connections with enforcing fairness. The fairness principle, granting legitimacy to the market system, may be strengthened if private parties are encouraged to settle the situations in which they felt treated in an unfair manner.

3 A Matter of Risk and Balance – Discussing a System of Liability for Financial Products

3.1 Introduction

The Greek origin of the word "crisis" points to a situation in which decisions need to be taken, to a moment where a turning point has been reached and the contingent possibility of action has been condensed to a factual necessity. So far, the new millennium has witnessed a particularly obstinate string of economic, political and social crises. Hence, it is not surprising to see a multitude of proposals being forwarded to handle ongoing, prevent future, and reflect upon past crises. Supportive measures go hand in hand with possible sanctions to restore order to a world in not only but especially economically troubled waters. Thus, the sovereign debt crisis in the EU led to the creation of an emergency rescue fund for shaking states and faltering economies. But at the same time, accompanying mechanisms are sought in order to pre-emptively rein in and effectively sanction Member States lacking budgetary discipline. Proposals include measures that with a view to their radical character until lately would have required quite an unconventional exertion of visionary and idealistic imagination to be presented as feasible concepts, ranging from a European central economic government via a ban from voting in governing bodies of the EU for states breaching deficit rules to ultimately an exclusion of certain EU members. Rules are busily being drafted that aim at recalibrating incentives of states to restrict their spending and avoid state bankruptcy.

However, the sovereign debt crisis is hardly the first economic crisis since the turn of the millennium. And chances are it will not be the last. The subprime crisis, sparked by the insolvency of Lehman Brothers on September 18 2008, came before this current crisis. The rapid dawn of the sovereign debt crisis, among other things, however, eclipsed the appropriate dealing with the most fundamental misbalances in the global economic and financial sector which the subprime crisis had divulged. There is still pressing work to be done.

As much as the political focus has recently been absorbed by the financial turmoil of the EU and some of its Member States, this chapter aims to go back to track the origins of the financial subprime crisis, readjust the incentives of the agents and propose a new remedy: a financial product liability under which issuers of securities and derivatives, for example, would in certain cases be held liable for half of the losses their products inflict upon buyers. By refocusing the discussion on the incentives of the players already involved in the game, a counter-innovative complete ban of financial products as well as the creation of new authorities as in the American financial market reform may be avoided. It relies upon the power of decentralized private enforcement, not as the one and only measure to help preventing future crises, but as an efficient and essential tool alongside an array of further options being discussed and implemented at the moment.

Politicians are still trying to come up with an answer to the problems brought to daylight by the various economic crises of the last years. Their aftermath resembles an experimental laboratory in which all kinds of recipes are being tested. The space of public and scholarly discourse is an open discussion ground. This seems to be a good time for a strategic rethinking of the systematic workings of the financial sector, for a recalibration of the incentives inherent in its game and for the restoration of a balance between risk and liability in the commerce of financial products. This is what this chapter aims at.

The first section sets out the principles such a balanced system of financial product liability would have to abide by (3.2.1 and 3.2.7), and by drawing on empirical psychological research argues for its necessity and legitimacy in general (3.2.2 and 3.2.3) as well as for its applicability to issuing entities (3.2.4 and 3.2.5). This is followed by a survey of the incentives involved and an examination of the power of civil law in shaping behavior (3.3). Section 3.4 scrutinizes the concrete, detailed conditions for liability, before a summary on the conclusions closes the chapter (3.5).

3.2 Principles

3.2.1 Products without product liability

Reflecting upon the causes of the financial subprime crisis and the ensuing general economic downward spiral, one has to acknowledge that a major factor in the genesis of the crisis was the mismanagement of risk, both on the institutional level of the legal system and on the individual level of the agents in the financial sector. Legal prerogatives were missing as much as sufficient risk awareness on the part of the market participants. Complex securities were created whose issuer was deprived of specific legal liability for the post-issue development of the product.[1] This fostered the creation of risk asymmetries which would then erupt in cascade-like spirals of monetary damage. This chapter starts from the observation that the separation of risk and liability in the domain of complex financial products was a decisive causal factor of the crisis. It enabled the issuers to infuse risk into the market by the issue of toxic securities, to make profits independent of the realization of these risks, and to pass the risk of loss on to the buyers of the products, their subsequent buyers and finally, in case of default of a buyer, to the state who bailed the investor out. To put it sharply, in these cases, besides the end consumer, the taxpayer ended up paying the debt and not the issuing bank. This points to a flagrant problem: There simply is no specific set of legal rules which would provide for an efficient distribution of liability when it comes to the issue of financial products.

As of now, under general tort law of the capital markets an issuer may be liable on the grounds of liability for an erroneous or misleading prospectus, registration

[1] Hellwig, Finanzkrise und Reformbedarf, NJW-Beil. 2010, 94.

statements or consultation on the one hand, or on the other hand in the case of non-disclosure of relevant information after the issue.[2]

Both of these structurally similar approaches are based on the principle of liability not for a deficient product as such, but for a breach of information rules.[3] As will be shown using insights of behavioral economics in 3.2.6 of this section of the chapter, such liability striving to force the issuer to limit itself to the provision of sufficient information may in many cases not be enough to prevent the risk from getting into the wrong hands – and crises from evolving.

If one turns an eye to defective movable products, there are actually rules governing liability for them. In the EU, the Product Liability Directive[4] provides a legal frame of strict liability. However, it is not applicable to financial products. Similarly, although liability varies from state to state, courts in the United States have developed strict liability for defective products in most jurisdictions following Judge Taynor,[5] which again, however, does not comprise financial products. In theory the rulings may be extendable to the financial sector, but there is no sign that courts would be willing to do so and change their current position. And obviously, nobody can order them to do just that.

This brief survey leads to the thesis of this chapter: At this very moment liability in the sector of financial products is not adequately designed. Financial products are in a way products without product liability. Suggestions to close this gap of liability so far have been hard to find[6] and are not far-reaching enough. This chapter argues for a remedy of this paradoxical situation.

---

[2] Consequently, the discourse in court rulings and academia in Germany relating to the liability of financial institutions for emission or selling of derivatives focuses on the scope and limits of information obligations resulting from consultation contracts between bank and buyer, cf. BGH XI ZR 33/10 of March 22, 2011, NJW 2011, 1949, on a CMS Spread Ladder Swap; XI ZR 178/10 of 27 September 2011, BKR 2011, 508 and XI ZR 182/10 of the same date, BKR 2011, 514 – Lehman Brothers, on certificates issued by Lehman Brothers and sold by German banks to private investors; Bausch, Beratung und Beratungshaftung von Banken im Lichte der Pilotentscheidungen zu Lehman-Zertifikaten, NJW 2012, 354; Roberts, Beratungsbedarf bei Finanzderivaten im Lichte neuerer Rechtsprechungsentwicklungen, DStR 2011, 1231 (to quote only a few). For a broader perspective, see Hellwig, Finanzkrise und Reformbedarf, NJW-Beil. 2010, 94, 96. Zimmer proposes an incentive-driven regulation of banks by introducing fees on systemic risk in Finanzmarktregulierung – Welche Regelungen empfehlen sich für den deutschen und europäischen Finanzsektor?, NJW-Beil. 2010, 101, 103. Liability of issuing institutions beyond the breach of contractual or legal information duties is, however, not envisioned.

[3] An example from the U.S. is Sec. 11 and 12 of the Securities Act of 1933.

[4] Council Directive 85/374/EEC of 25 July 1985 on the approximation of the laws, regulations and administrative provisions of the Member States concerning liability for defective products, Official Journal Nr. L 210, 07/08/1985, 29 – 33.

[5] Escola v. Coca Cola Bottling Co., 24 Cal. 2d 453 (1944); Greenman v. Yuba Power Products, Inc., 59 Cal. 2d 57 (1963), and subsequent rulings.

[6] Schwarcz, Understanding the Subprime Financial Crisis, 60 South Carolina LR 549 (2009) suggests that the issuing banks have to retain a "risk of loss".

3.2.2 Benefits of securities, exemption from liabilities

But one needs to be cautious not to throw the baby out with the bath water: Economically speaking, high-risk credits may be very much desired in certain situations. Just think of credits for daring start-up businesses in new technology fields with unknown returns. Certainly, stifling development by avoidance of high-risk credits cannot generally be recommended. The transmission of risk to third parties in these cases can be utterly legitimate and make good economic sense.

Inching closer to the analysis of the subprime crisis, one can see that mortgage-backed credits also bear a number of risks due to the long time over the course of which they are to be paid back. Not the smallest among those risks is the development of credit interests on the market. There is no straight answer to the question of who should bear this risk of rising credit interest rates. Entrust the buyer of the real estate, i.e. the debtor, with it and rising interest rates will generate massive credit defaults and insolvency of debtors. If one endows the banks with holding the risk, they can get into dire straits, too: If soaring interest rates for the daily business of the bank happen to diverge heavily from lower fixed interest rates for the payback of the mortgage-backed credit, this opening rift can put enormous pressure on the bank, including up to its possible insolvency.[7] The logical exit from this dilemma of risk distribution is to pass the risk generated by long-term credits on to third parties who are better equipped to handle these risks due to their own long term investment models. This is where securities and their complex follow-on products come into the play. They were designed in the first place to achieve just this kind of necessary passing of risk into safer hands.

The transfer of risk by financial products is thus not a problem per se. The development of the financial subprime crisis, however, has shown that it can turn into one once the issuer is more or less completely exempted from liability for his product. This enticing situation enables him to introduce securities with a high margin of risk into the market regardless of any possible losses. The degree of risk a security bears oftentimes cannot be duly appreciated, neither by rating agencies nor by the buyers. If the underlying obligations prove to be worthless, the realization of the risk hits the final buyers right on.

The internalization of profit and benefits on the part of the issuers is paralleled by the externalization of costs and risk, creating fatal dynamics and incentive effects.

The crisis thus leaves us with the urgent task of recalibrating the risk distribution in the financial world in a more effective and fairer way. A reasonable balance will have to be struck between the freedom necessary to design and promote innovative financial products on the one hand, and the limiting function of a legal liability regime on the other one.

---

[7] Cf. Hellwig, The Causes of the Financial Crisis, CESifo Forum 12 (2008, Nr. 4) at 13; Schwarcz, Understanding the Subprime Financial Crisis, 60 South Carolina LR 568 (2009).

3.2.3 Two perspectives on risk: mathematics and behavior

The treatment and management of risk can be dealt with on two distinct levels, a mathematical and a behavioral one.

The first level is driven by mathematical standard models which were created to determine and optimize the exposure of an individual company, its value at risk. These models were in wide and habitual use before the crisis, but they obviously did not contribute much to prevent it. Their failure has received a number of critical research enquiries, focusing especially on the emblematic underrepresentation of highly unlikely events such as systemic crises.[8] This is certainly a fruitful and necessary field of critical work with a view on the prevention of future crises. It is, however, not within the scope of this chapter.

Rather, the focus is on a second level on which risk is not mathematically calculated but brought to the fore of consciousness of the agents in order to have an impact on their actions. In the last decades research into behavioral economics has shown that human behavior is not determined by purely rational, profit-maximizing choices as the neo-classical theory with its model of the homo economicus would have it. Very much to the contrary, individual actions are subjected to, and influenced by, a whole array of further factors other than rational decision making, leading to a model of a homo myopus.[9] This holds true also and especially for the treatment of risk.

Risk awareness is closely tied to factors such as dread and the possibility to gain profits, as new results in the field of decision psychology show. The higher the "dread factor" is, i.e. the more probable sufficiently disastrous consequences for oneself or the environment are to be expected, the more a risk is regarded relevant for and thus turned into a basis of the decision.[10] If on the other hand the consequences of risk taking are not viewed as being related to the person acting, the perception of risk wanes rapidly. Furthermore, studies have established that this perception is inversely correlated with the possibility to generate profits from the risk.[11] In other words: The expectation of profits stifles the awareness of risk.

Such patterns of behavior can be observed generally in human actions, independent of the social status and task of the individual agent, and thus apply not only

---

[8] Cf. the overview at Black, Empirical Legal Studies in Financial Markets: What have we learned?, LSE Law, Society and Economy Working Papers 4/2010, 35; Eichengreen, Origins and Responses to the Current Crisis, CESifo Forum 6 (2008, No. 4) at 9; For a proper mathematical approach on risk models, see Sheedy, Can Risk Modeling Work? Macquarie University Applied Finance Centre Research Paper No. 35, 2009 (available at: http://ssrn.com/abstract=1398486).

[9] For broader discussion of the matter, see the symposium "Homo Economicus, Homo Myopus", 73 University of Chicago Law Review 1 et pass. (2006).

[10] Slovic, Fischhoff, Lichtenstein, Facts and Fears – Understanding Perceived Risk, in: Slovic (ed.), The Perception of Risk, 2001, 137 et pass. at 143. On the necessity of incorporating these insights into competition law, cf. Stucke, Lessons from the Financial Crisis, 77 American Antitrust Law Journal 313 (2010) at 340 and 341, with further reference.

[11] Slovic a.o. (Fn. 10), 146.

to the investment decisions of inexperienced private consumers but also to professional traders.[12]

These observations can serve as a starting point for a new and differentiated system of liability. If the issuer of financial products has to face the imminent possibility of himself or his corporation, i.e. his immediate working environment, being held liable for his product, the existence and scope of this liability constitutes a significant dread factor and reduces the odds of generating profits independent of the development of the security after the issuing. Such a system of liability would therefore be a good candidate for an effective instrument to pre-emptively create and heighten risk awareness. It appears furthermore tempting to combine such an instrument with a realignment of the incentives of managerial compensation.[13] This topic, however, will be out of the focus of this paper, which limits its perspective on the liability of the securitizing entity as such.

The results of decision psychology thus show that only measuring risks mathematically and optimizing their distribution falls short of providing an effective tool for the management of risk: The mere fact of the existence of a quantitative analysis does not imply that a risk-relevant decision will be based on the mathematical insight. But exactly this would be crucial if risk is not only to be measured theoretically, but to be limited effectively.

3.2.4 Two types of agents: banks originating credits and entities issuing securities

This enhancement of awareness and limitative endeavor can generally target two types of agents: the banks handing out the credits to their final customers, or the issuers of securities who through processes of bundling and tranching turn these debts into products of structured finance (i.e. the securitizers).

With regard to the banks offering credits, the period leading up to the financial subprime crisis was marked by a practice which has come to be known as "originate-to-distribute".[14] Banks gave credits generating claims (originate) which were immediately sold to third parties (distribute), in many cases to the issuers of structured finance products. For the banks, this proved to be a lucrative and important mechanism to acquire liquidity.[15] But here again, a disjunction of risk and liability

---

[12] Klöhn: Kapitalmarkt, Spekulation und Behavioral Finance, 2006, at 146.

[13] For a closer look at the connection between managerial compensation and risky investment see Bhattacharyya/Purnanandam, Risk-Taking by Banks: What Did We Know and When Did We Know It?, 2011 (available at http://ssrn.com/abstract=1619472).

[14] Concerning the historical genesis of this phenomenon cf. Eichengreen, Origins and Responses to the Current Crisis, CESifo Forum 6 (2008, Nr. 4), 6, 7. Tarr looks at the political conditions leading to this business model in: The political, regulatory, and market failures that caused the US financial crisis: What are the lessons?, 2 Journal of Financial Economic Policy 163 – 186 (2010). An even broader historical perspective of the subprime crisis is offered in Reinhart/Rogoff, Is the 2007 U.S. Sub-prime Financial Crisis so different? An International Historical Comparison, 98 American Economic Review 339 – 344 (2008).

[15] For a short economic summary of the process of securitization, cf. Madhani, Bankruptcy of Lehman Brothers – A Pointer to the Subprime Crisis, 9 The Accounting World 33 (2009) at 34 f.

held sway: The banks could offer subprime credits, i.e. credits with drastically lowered standards as to the prerequisites a possible debtor had to fulfill in order to be awarded the credit, in a carefree manner as long as those credits were bought more or less immediately subsequent to their origination.[16] The risk of default was transferred away from the banks to the final buyers of the securities, leaving the former with relatively little incentives to hedge in risks. As described, the transfer of risk can be suitable and necessary in certain situations. If, however, the incentives for the banks to thoroughly examine the credit worthiness of the future debtors find themselves heavily minimized due to the de facto liability exemption, the very kinds of default risks will be easily fed into the market whose realization marked the beginning of the subprime crisis.

The logical consequence of this finding would be to scrutinize the banking practices for offering credits and then to either regulate these by means of binding standards for credit worthiness or to hold the banks themselves liable for the fate of their credits.

First impulses toward a liability of the banks were generated before the crisis by the autonomous interplay of the market forces.[17] The practices spanned from re-buy obligations of the banks in case of a default during the first repayment installments via the issuing of guarantees (which in case of emergency might not have been met by the banks, however) to a part of 10 % of the claims which banks were not allowed to sell but rather forced to keep.[18] Legal reforms could now strive to follow these market activities and to convert these models into binding legal obligations.

Even if an optimization of incentives on the part of the banks is certainly de rigueur, this chapter will defend the thesis that the problems will be more effectively dealt with if a new legal concept focuses on the issuers of financial products, i.e. the second type of agents. In a second step, liability of the issuers could be expanded to the credit offering banks. But their responsibility shall in a first approach be entrusted to the contractual practices between banks and professional buyers of claims, for a legal regulation should be subsidiary to a functioning system of checks and balances which the market participants develop autonomously. Fur-

---

16 For an empirical analysis of the increase in the issue of sub-prime credits, the lowering of lending standards and the role of securitization before the crisis cf. Purnanandam, Originate-to-distribute Model and the Subprime Mortgage Crisis, 24 Rev. Financ. Stud. 1881 – 1915 (2011); Mian/Sufi, The Consequences of Mortgage Credit Expansion: Evidence from the U.S. Mortgage Default Crisis, 124 The Quarterly Journal of Economics 1449-1496 (2009); Dell'Ariccia/Igan/Laeven, Credit Booms and Lending Standards: Evidence from the Subprime Mortgage Market, European Banking Center Discussion Paper No. 2009–14S, 2009 (available at: http://ssrn.com/abstract=1153728); Keys/Mukherjee/Seru/Vig, Did Securitization Lead to Lax Screening? Evidence from Subprime Loans, 125 The Quarterly Journal of Economics 307 –362 (2010).

17 Schwarcz, Protecting Financial Markets – Lessons from the Subprime Mortgage Meltdown, 93 Minn. L. Rev. 373 (2008) at 389, Fn. 82 quotes an unpublished essay by Van Gorp of 2007, according to which "early payment default protection" started to become common in the markets. This protection implied an obligation of the bank to re-buy the claim if the debtor failed to fulfill the first two or three repayment installments.

18 Schwarcz (Fn. 17), 389.

thermore, an immediate normative intervention on the part of the banks giving the credits seems to be less of a necessity for other reasons, too.

First, we may have to pay a high price for regulating strategies as well as liability rules applying directly to the credit-giving banks, notwithstanding their qualities of influencing behavior. They would render the offering of mortgage-backed credits a lot more arduous and potentially costly, thus raising the costs of acquiring property and generating administrative hurdles.[19] Certainly, all of this also holds true with respect to a possible liability system for financial products, where analogous consequences for the generation of these products may be foreseen. By comparison, however, a greater reluctance in the creation of financial products seems to be more acceptable than one in the offering of credits to final consumers. Only the latter ones have an immediate impact on the real economy and the concrete living situation of those asking for credit. As the first two chapters of this book have shown, it is primarily their interest and welfare which the economy is bound to serve. The incentives of the banks thus have to be realigned in a way so that by following them, the welfare of the citizens is being promoted, too. But tampering with their practices of credit offering should be deemed more dangerous and pernicious to welfare than readjusting the sector issuing derived products. Admittedly, one could disagree on this point.

But here comes a second argument: The level of complexity at the stage of offering a credit is much less pronounced than after bundling and tranching of big numbers and types of claims into a structured finance product. The buyer of a single mortgage-backed credit can judge the credit worthiness of the debtor and evaluate the circumstances of the credit offer itself rather conveniently. The buyer of a financial product may not be able to do so. This implies that risk awareness generated by the market participants endogenously will function much better and be rather conducive to developing effective strategies to hedge in these risks in the case of the first purchase of a claim than of a complex financial product. The quoted models creating liability of the banks by the sheer forces of the market effectively demonstrate this. If, however, the corrective forces of the market do work, a normative intrusion is not necessary.

Thirdly, the process of creating financial products does not simply pass on the risks of the underlying claims but modifies and, potentially, heightens these risks. While the absolute sum the originator of a credit may lose under the credit contract is limited by the value of the credit, the exposure of investors in financial products can, depending on the structure of the product, be theoretically unlimited. If it is the creation of risk that justifies liability, then financial products with their potential of massive losses should be in the focus.

3.2.5 A focus on the issuers

These three arguments show that it is wiser to target the issuers of financial products with a new system of liability. This would of course engender repercussions on

[19] Schwarcz (Fn. 17), 390.

the first level of the original selling of the claims to the issuers (distribute-component). For if the buyers of credits, who aim at integrating these primary claims into financial products and selling those products, have to reckon with being held liable under certain conditions for their own products, they can be expected to manifest a greater degree of caution when buying the claims in the first place and to install some regime of quality control for the bought claims. The banks themselves will expect such behavior and try to adapt their standards for the offering of credits. Chances are this would then thwart the part of the "originate-and-distribute" model operating on a subprime basis, just as an immediate regulation of this part of the game would do. A system of liability that tackles the issuers further downstream has the advantage to start off on a level where the potential impact on the real economy is smaller, whereas the potential failure of individual agents as well as of the market forces is greater.

3.2.6 A change of paradigms: rationales for a system of strict liability on the part of the issuers

A key thesis of this chapter is thus that a balanced system of liability of the issuers of financial products can achieve exactly the factual limitation of risk asked for: The perspective of concrete financial losses due to a system of strict liability constitutes a dread factor and limits chances of profit. These psychological consequences raise the awareness of risk thus – and this is crucial – entailing a pre-emptive estimation of risk already at the design of the specific financial product. The incentives at work unfold their potential when the risk is being created and not only at subsequent market stages when the product is being sold.

Pre-emptive action of this kind appears sensible. It goes hand in hand with a farewell to the traditional thinking that defends the mere publication of relevant information and the informed decision of rational actors as the one and only procedure to ensure systematic stability and self-regulation. Admittedly, information rules are valid tools to safeguard freedom of contract by fostering an informed decision. However, the workability of information rules rests on the implicit premises that (1) the party is endowed with the cognitive capabilities to understand the information and that (2) it will act according to its informed opinion. If one of the premises is shattered, information obligations cannot serve their purpose any more. There is growing empirical evidence that these cases of over-complexity and limited rationality are more common than one had thought, and that the time of the unfettered information or disclosure paradigm[20] has come to an end.[21]

Analyses of the investment behavior prior to the financial crisis have shed light on the peril of simply entrusting the informed buyers of financial products with the

---

[20] For more information, cf. Reich in: Reich/Micklitz, Europäisches Verbraucherrecht, 4th edition 2003, 9 ff.

[21] Regarding phenomena of limited rationality see for example Schön, Zwingendes Recht oder informierte Entscheidung – zu einer (neuen) Grundlage unserer Zivilrechtsordnung, in: Heldrich a.o. (eds.), FS für C.-W. Canaris zum 70. Geburtstag, Vol I, 2007, 1191 – 1211 at 1211.

task of risk limitation.[22] On the one hand, the product to be evaluated may be so complex that not even a rating agency, let alone a single investor, can carry the burden of thorough research on the components of the product and their respective default risk.[23] But even if complexity is limited and information available, a protective concept based only on the information paradigm is prone to quick failure. The financial crisis has demonstrated this powerfully, when cognitive deficits and unbridled trust formed an unholy alliance.

Publicity standards did force the issuers of financial products to produce prospectuses which also divulged the risks of the sold securities. Some buyers, well aware of the risks of the underlying obligations, indeed purchased the securities in order to bet against them. However, some putative investors unaware of the composition of the products seem not to have taken notice of the available information, or only in a deficient manner.[24] They trusted the working methods of the issuer who would as a "proof" of the quality of his products often acquire himself some tranches with the lowest priority, the equity tranche, which presumably is of the lowest quality.[25] Overly and unjustifiably benign ratings, in which the top tranches regardless of their origin often were branded as AAA (or equivalent top ratings), added to the fatal spiral of trust.[26] But there is more: Phenomena of bounded rationality impaired the very capacity of the investors to decide. Research in the field of behavioral economics shows that decisions are not being taken independently of those of other investors. Rather, individual investors display a group behavior, often called "herding", in which one follows the other more or less blindly and automatically.[27] Markets with high profit expectations and in which a pronounced mood for investment holds sway furthermore foster an overconfidence which puts warning signals aside.[28] These tendencies have already come to blur the image of the well-informed rational investor and cast more serious doubts on the possibility of ensuring good decision-making by promoting disclosure of information. One more distinguishing characteristic of human behavior is the penchant to take only recent events into account when it comes to measuring risk or profit.[29] This is exactly what happened before the crisis: Real estate prices went soaring apparently without lim-

---

[22] Andrews, The Clean Up: Investors Need Better Advice on Structured Finance Products, 26 Int'l Fin. L. Rev. 14 (2007); Schwarcz, Understanding the Subprime Financial Crisis, 60 South Carolina LR 549 (2009) at 381.

[23] Schwarcz, Understanding the Subprime Financial Crisis, 60 South Carolina LR 549 (2009), 383.

[24] Andrews, The Clean Up: Investors Need Better Advice on Structured Finance Products, 26 Int'l Fin. L. Rev. 14 (2007).

[25] Schwarcz, Understanding the Subprime Financial Crisis, 60 South Carolina LR 549 (2009), 381.

[26] Hellwig, The Causes of the Financial Crisis, CESifo Forum 12 (2008, Nr. 4), 12, 16. There is also a case for liability of the rating agencies. However, to address this intriguing issue falls beyond the scope of this chapter.

[27] Klöhn (Fn. 12).

[28] Klöhn (Fn. 12).

[29] Schwarcz, Understanding the Subprime Financial Crisis, 60 South Carolina LR 549 (2009) at 381; Avgouleas, The Global Financial Crisis and the Disclosure Paradigm, 4 ECFR 440 (2009), 444 ff.

its, and the general mood for investment in the market was more than cheerful. Researchers in behavioral economics like to call this phenomenon "disaster myopia" or "availability heuristic".[30] Together these human characteristics show that it does not suffice to require more disclosure of information and leave the determination of the risk to the informed buyer. He may not take notice of it at all, and if he does, not be able to process it, and even if he could, he would be generally driven by other, less rational forces.

It therefore appears more effective to tackle the problem at its roots and set incentives for the issuer himself so that he will act prudently and responsibly in designing a financial product. He is after all also the one with the best access to the information regarding underlying claims his product comprises.

3.2.7 The basic features of a liability system for financial products

We shall now summarily review the cornerstones of a law project realizing what may be called "Financial Product Liability" and then delve a bit deeper into the conditions under which such a legal system would trigger liability. Having outlined the basic components of the project, it is then time to discuss the pros and cons of such an endeavor.

3.2.7.1 The four pillars of the system

A system of liability for financial products should rest on four constitutive pillars:

(1) The basic idea of the system, based on the concept of FairEconomy, is a general principle of justice stating that whoever benefits from a risk he has created must also be liable for the realization of that risk and the damages this may cause.[31]
(2) In order to avoid an over-deterring effect of this liability stifling economic and financial invention, effective limits to liability have to be put in place. Furthermore, the triggering of liability needs to be put under the condition of certain quantitative thresholds in the devaluation of a security.
(3) A distribution of liability between the issuer on the one hand and the final buyer on the other one further reduces the risk of liability of the issuer and serves the principle that risk after all needs to be passed on in a sensible manner. It furthermore keeps the incentive for the buyer alive to control the quality of the product.
(4) Finally, it would be conducive to lay down international minimum standards for such liability rules on financial products. This could prevent an erosion of standards by the competition of different financial centers for the laxest rules and foreclose the development of local loopholes.

---

[30] Slovic, Fischhoff, Lichtenstein, Facts and Fears – Understanding Perceived Risk, in: Slovic (ed.), The Perception of Risk, 10, 105.

[31] Cf. Larenz/Canaris, Lehrbuch des Schuldrechts II, Vol. 2, 13th ed. 1994 at § 84 I 2. a), 605, calling the correspondence between benefit from risk and liability a "fundamental criterion of justice" (translation of the author). Additional references on the issue may be found there.

3.2.7.2 Scope and conditions of liability

In the concrete construction of such a system residing on the four pillars as outlined, one could propose a liability of the issuer of certain financial products in the field of tort law which is independent of any negligence on the part of the issuer, i.e. strict, but limited both in absolute terms and in the quota of a damage caused by its product which the issuer has to bear. This liability would encompass financial products which derive from primary claims and bundle, reallocate, or pass on these claims, and thus their risks. The legitimizing principle triggering liability, as in other cases of strict liability as well,[32] is the principle of liability in exchange for the benefit from a risk. In all of the cases in which this principle leads to a strict liability, i.e. independent of any negligence, the liable person is allowed to reap financial or other profit from a certain exercise which bears a higher degree of inherent risk. But he has to repair the damage caused by the materialization of that risk. This applies to common industrial products in particular. In its Art. 1 the European Product Liability Directive 85/374[33] provides for such strict liability in which the creator of a commonplace product is liable for flawed products and has to repair the damage caused to the final consumer, even if the product has been sold via many market stages. However, this directive does not apply to intangible financial products, as it defines a product in Art. 2 as "all movables, with the exception of primary agricultural products and game, even though incorporated into another movable or into an immovable." The same holds true for the *Greenman* doctrine in the United States.

The proposal would thus be that in a parallel manner, the issuer who in the creation of a financial product inappropriately raises the risk of devaluation of the product compared to the underlying obligations should be held liable. The rule would generally apply to all financial products which go beyond a mere ceding of a credit claim and which modify the original default risk of the underlying claim by bundling, tranching or otherwise processing the underlying claims. Therefore, all financial products should be within the scope of the regulation which are tradable and derived from one or more credit claims, be it in an immediate or intermediate way, and thus receive their value from them. This would especially apply to all kinds of securities. While it suffices to modify the risk of the underlying claims in order for the liability rule to apply, liability itself would be triggered only under further conditions. Therefore, this new "Financial Product Liability" would provide for an obligation to repair parts of the damage caused by a financial product within its scope which proves to be defective because it does not lessen, but rather heighten risks which then materialize in specific forms to be examined below.

The underlying principle of tort law triggering liability in exchange for the benefit from risk finds the legitimization of its application to the financial sector in its

---

[32] Cf. for example the German law on the liability for products (Produkthaftungsgesetz), liability for a qualified ownership of cars (§ 7 StVG) or animals held for pure pleasure (§ 833 phrase 1 German Civil Code).

[33] Council Directive 85/374/EEC of 25 July 1985 on the approximation of the laws, regulations and administrative provisions of the Member States concerning liability for defective products, Official Journal Nr. L 210, 07/08/1985, 29 – 33.

system stabilizing and risk reducing function. Its introduction can be seen as an attempt to rein in the systematic risk of such markets which are of crucial importance to the real economy and to channel this risk into tracks which set incentives for a sensible and balanced transmission of these risks to third parties. The market itself is not a corrective or normative instance in these cases, rather, it tends to fail: The systematic risk of the destabilization of a whole market does usually not form part of the reflections and calculations of the issuers of securities[34]. This is why the law should step in.

3.2.7.3 Weighing the arguments: discussion of the need of "Financial Product Liability"

Several objections may be raised against the relevance and usefulness of the above described project.

First, there is a marked difference to the provisions of the cited general product liability both in the EU and the United States: In that field, just as in tort law generally, liability presupposes the violation of a concrete right or object of legal protection, such as the human body or health or property. A simple financial damage does not normally trigger legal consequences because this may engender an unforeseeable explosion of liability.

This principle will obviously have to be discarded if a liability for financial products is to be introduced since the securities dealt with have only their financial value. Thus, the damage is always limited to a mere financial one. So the aim of the discarded principle, avoiding an undue wave of liability, will need to be fulfilled by other means. This is exactly where pillars two and three of the system come into play. Limits, thresholds and a division of damages between the buyer and the issuer can effectively prevent an over-deterring and unforeseeable scope of liability.

Second, one should briefly consider the specific nature of deals involving the transmission of risk for the purpose of a legitimization of the regulation. It could easily be argued that he who enters a risky game as a buyer of a product encompassing possibly unrealizable claims knows what he does and thus must bear the (financial) consequences of his actions. This should especially hold true if the buyer happens to be, as in most of the relevant transactions, a professional financial investor who is not buying a painting of unknown origin at a flea market for his personal pleasure, but striking a deal worth hundreds of millions of dollars on highly complex collateralized debt obligations.

There are normative arguments supporting this view. In German law, for instance, a party of a contract is not able to challenge the contract on the basis of an error concerning essential features of the bought product, § 119 (2) German Civil Code, if the risk inherent in the contract or product actualizes. Also, the materialization of risk would not constitute a material defect of the product with respect to the law of sales contracts, § 434 German Civil Code. And other claims could be

---

[34] Nor of the considerations of the National Antitrust Authorities when clearing a merger, cf. Stucke, Lessons from the Financial Crisis, 77 American Antitrust Law Journal 313 (2010), 322.

foreclosed by the thought that the buyer himself is, at least partly, responsible for the damage (§ 254 (1) German Civil Code).

If one transfers these arguments onto the purchase of risky financial products, one might jump to the conclusion that liability of the issuer is unjustified if simply the inherent risk of the underlying obligations materializes and if this risk has influenced the price of the product. If compensation is high enough to cover those risks, why oppose the deal? After all, professional buyers of obligations of a value of several million dollars should know what they are doing.

Two arguments may be advanced against this kind of reasoning.

First, an asymmetrical distribution of information concerning the underlying claims regularly entails that a buyer will not be able to sufficiently gauge the factual risk load of the product. The issuer designing the security on the basis of certain defined parameters has a structural information advantage over the buyer. If this is not the case and the buyer does have the possibility to judge the risk level of the product, perhaps due to the fact that he proposed certain claims to the issuer to be included in the package, this could certainly rule out any obligation of the issuer to repair damages in application of the above cited legal arguments. One may, however, consider the case in which the buyer has not ordered specific claims to be part of the package he purchases. In this case, the financial product can be compared to a "lemon good" in which due to informational deficits and asymmetries the risk is only deficiently reflected in the price.[35] Just as a used car, it may look good to the buyer on the outside, but is defective on the inside. The risk of a multi-layered financial product becomes so abstract from the underlying obligations that the buyer is not able to make a conscious, informed decision on the concrete risk the product is associated with. The development of the financial crisis has demonstrated that rating agencies could not bridge that gap. They were not able to provide transparent and reliable estimations of the risk of the securities.

Admittedly nobody forces the buyer to jump onto opaque deals and expose himself to the abstract risk of a financial product. However, as discussed under 3.2.5 of this section, psychological effects of risk perception can push the buyer into making irrational deals. Thus if one does not want to globally forbid the commerce with such products, which would imply a denial of the positive effects such trade can have as shown before, the informational asymmetry that can be generally assumed speaks in favor of setting legal incentives to discipline the issuer in the choice and design of his products.

Secondly, the striking argument is that the principle of non-liability in the case of risky deals must recede exceptionally for reasons of systematic stabilization. The modification of the behavior of the market participants in the direction of risk awareness and responsible risk management through the proposed system of strict

[35] Avgouleas, The Global Financial Crisis and the Disclosure Paradigm, 4 ECFR 440 (2009), 449. Cf. also Duffie/Gârleanu, Risk and Valuation of Collateralized Debt Obligations, 57 Financial Analysts Journal 41 (2001), 42 who describe "lemon premiums" for certain types of securities (CDOs); on the original "lemon" market Akerloff: The Market for "Lemons". Quality Uncertainty and the Market Mechanism, 84 The Quarterly Journal of Economics 488-500 (1970).

liability justifies such an exception. Lack of liability in a system as volatile and capricious as the financial one can easily impact upon and wreak havoc in the domain of the whole global economic system, as the financial crisis has strikingly demonstrated. The consequences may easily go well beyond the financial loss of the individual investor making a bad investment decision and destabilize the entire system, inflicting damage on non-involved third parties. This is why one cannot simply say: "Well, tough luck for the investor."

This reasoning does not imply that a liability system would have to be introduced in every domain with a certain relevance to global problems and a pronounced degree of interconnectedness with other processes deemed vital for the progress of humankind. This chapter does not generally call for an "ordre public liability" in all of these cases, such as global warming or harm to the environment. The argument of systematic stability only overcomes the doubts cast by the possible objection to liability in the context of deals involving risk. The triggering principle of liability is another context and can range from the reproach of negligence to the principle of trust to the benefit from risk, as is the case here. There are, thus, two levels of risk which in their combination make a strong case for financial product liability: The limitation of *systemic* risk generally posed by financial products is the main justifying element for the entire liability system here envisaged, while the increase of "*default* risk" by the individual product is the trigger for concrete liability of specific issuers.

This does not mean that a regime of strict liability may not be an option in other contexts where a need to form and influence individual behavior exists. To be explained in the next section, civil law is not the worst method of achieving just that.

3.3 Setting incentives and shaping behavior

Legal measures must have an effect on human behavior lest they become mere "law in the books". Generally, this can be achieved in two different ways: on the one hand, by direct regulation or prohibition enforced by the power of the state, as happens in public or penal law; and on the other hand, by the indirect laying down of consequences of actions, which are entrusted to private enforcement, as in civil law. The first method relies on power and force, the second sets more subtle economic incentives so that the individual agents autonomously adapt their actions to the desired effect. Responding to the subprime financial crisis, both approaches can be pursued. The necessary revision of the supervision of the banking sector[36] and a possible inclusion of other financial entities under the controlling authority of a regulating body could be called the external side of a reform. Steps are being taken in different countries to advance this. To maximize the impact on actual behavior, a balanced system of liability should join this process as the inner side of reform which tackles the motivation of the market participants directly. In this context, it

---

36 Cf. Schwarcz, Understanding the Subprime Financial Crisis, 60 South Carolina LR 566 (2009): "[T]he solution to systemic risk is to impose regulation that internalizes [...] externalities."

would be a desideratum to pass on liability inside the issuing enterprise so that it does not only hit the company but also, to a certain degree, the trader who designed the security himself. This may be achieved through an adaptation of bonuses or other measures. However, working out exact patterns of the internal distribution of liability within companies remains beyond the scope of this chapter and should be dealt with individually by each company. Here, the possible effects and incentives set by a liability approach based on civil rather than public law shall be considered.

3.3.1 Incentives on both sides

On the side of the generation of the product, the issuer must be induced to a responsible estimation of risk. He should be bound to issue only such securities whose validity he has stress-tested, including scenarios of extreme economic constellations. That he is potentially liable for damage resulting from his products reverses the comfortable situation in which profits can be internalized and losses externalized. This might very well engender a market discipline that may in the long run purge the market of a good part of overrated securities created without adherence to any standards and sold under an informational asymmetry. Whoever has to assume legal responsibility for his product will care for its quality much more than anyone exempted from it.

The fact that part of the damage will remain with the buyer has the purpose of encouraging an independent risk assessment by the buyer, as far as that is possible, so that he does not blindly buy into the votes of the rating agencies but reflects upon the validity of their categorizations.

3.3.2 Advantages of private enforcement

The question whether private or public enforcement better serves the purpose of a normative venture is under constant debate among scholars. The decentralized mechanism of private enforcement seems to better suit the objectives the current proposal aims at. It may be supported by regulative endeavors,[37] but seems an indispensable part of the reaction to the financial crises, for the following three reasons:

(1) Private enforcement is independent of the discretion of a regulatory authority whether or not to pursue a specific case. The motivation of the damaged parties to bring financial product liability cases to court can be considered to be quite high since liability is strict and negligence therefore needs not to be proven. The rate of prosecution will probably be higher than in a model with an authority charged with the enforcement.

---

[37] Proposals for enhanced regulation abound. Pertaining to banks issuing mortgage-backed credits, cf. only Dagher/Fu, What Fuels the Boom Drives the Bust: Regulation and the Mortgage Crisis, 2011, 29 – 35 (available at http://ssrn.com/abstract=1728260); Awrey, Regulating Financial Innovation: A More Principles-Based Alternative?, 5 Brooklyn Journal of Corporate, Financial and Commercial Law 273 (2011).

(2) Especially in complex and extreme economic situations, private enforcement has the great advantage of being decentralized. This ensures that even in scenarios in which a single body would be overwhelmed by the task of acting on different frontiers simultaneously, enforcement can still be guaranteed through autonomous and independent private litigation.

(3) It may be argued that due to this widespread potential of action, the actual trader deciding on the part of the issuers finds himself more impressed by the imminent danger of a number of tort law processes than by the very vague possibility of being sanctioned by a supervision authority unable to double-check on every sold financial product, anyway.[38] But buyers will follow the development of their purchased products very carefully. The chances of passing through the net unheeded are much smaller for the issuers. This should translate into a higher rate of adaption of behavior in the desired direction.

3.4 Concrete contents

Following an outline of the basic features and arguments in favor of the model, the content of a possible law on financial product liability shall now be covered in detail.

3.4.1 Applicability

3.4.1.1 The Financial Products

Schwarcz states that "[a]ny regulation of credit derivatives will have to grapple with the problem of defining what is being regulated [...]."[39] The subprime financial crisis started from the market of mortgages and securities derived from it. But no crisis is like the one before it, as the current sovereign debt crisis shows, and it is quite impossible to predict which area will be the starting point of the next crisis. One could think of "subprime" student and credit card credits, but concrete estimations cannot be made. This in turn implies that the range of products the new liability system applies to must be drawn rather wide if it is not only meant to retrace the ways of the last crisis but also to help to stifle the germs of future crises.

The purpose of the present legal initiative is to foster transparency, risk awareness and risk limiting standards in the creation of securities. Thus, as mentioned before, it seems fit to apply the regulation to all financial products that go beyond a mere ceding of a credit claim and that by bundling, tranching, betting on or otherwise structuring the underlying claims or assets manifest a risk profile that is different from the simple original default risk of the underlying claim(s) (What is said about the default risk of underlying claims analogously applies to the devaluation of underlying assets in general). Risk may be modified vis-à-vis the original default

[38] An equally pessimistiv stance on regulatory bodies's power to prevent future crises is found in: Shachmurove, The Next Financial Crisis, PIER Working Paper No. 10-027, 2010 (available at: http://ssrn.com/abstract=1654361).

[39] Schwarcz, Understanding the Subprime Financial Crisis, 60 South Carolina LR 567 (2009).

risk in absolute terms: a sum higher than the value of the underlying claims may be lost through the instrument, or in relative terms: the probability of losing money by investing on the financial product is higher than the original aggregate default risk of the underlying claims. Therefore, all such financial products should be within the scope of the regulation that are tradable and derived from one or more credit claims or assets, either in an immediate or intermediate way, and thus receive their value from their development or performance. This would especially apply to all kinds of securities who receive their value from the anticipated cash flow of claims.[40]

3.4.1.2 The entities capable to sue and to be sued

As regards the entities able to be sued, not only must commercial or investment banks fall under the scope of the law, but every legal entity issuing the above mentioned financial products. This comprises conduits, SPV/SIPs, hedge funds and private equity firms.

It will be made clear below that the one able to sue is only the entity holding the security at the moment in which all conditions of the law triggering liability are being met for the first time.

3.4.1.3 Time and space

This rule should apply to all products being traded within the jurisdiction of a state that has passed the law. To determine whether products are being traded in a certain state, one could rely on the methods used in private international law in order to determine the applicable national tort law. Regarding time, it might be worth considering letting the law take effect only once a qualitatively and quantitatively sufficient selection of WTO Member States has passed a law fulfilling a minimum standard in the matter.

3.4.2 Conditions for liability

3.4.2.1 The general framework

The issuer is liable according to a general clause regulating financial products and must cover half of the damages of the buyer able to sue in the above sense independent of his position in the sale chain if two basic conditions are met:

(1) The product must have increased the default risk in an inappropriate way by comparison to the underlying claims. The increase of risk may be absolute, where there is the possibility of a loss for the investor which is higher than the

[40] For a very informative definition of "derivatives", and their difference from securities, see Lynch, Derivatives: A Twenty-First Century Understanding, 43 Loyola University Chicago Law Journal 1 (2011), especially at 29. His definition of derivatives comprises, however, contracts depending generally on the outcome of external events (such as the outcome of the Super Bowl or of elections, see op. cit., 3 and 25 under Fn. 90), an approach which is, however, overinclusive for the purpose of this paper. The liability system envisaged focuses less on bets on external events in general but more on products deriving from concrete claims or assets and their development. Only in this case, an original risk is modified.

original value of the credit (or than the sum of the multitude of bundled credit tranches); or it may be relative if the probability of devaluation of the financial product is higher than the (mean) probability of default of the underlying.

For the absolute risk, one has to look at the value at risk in the original contracts and in the product, and compare the two amounts. If claims were split up into tranches, only the amount proportionate to the part of the claim that entered into the product counts. An example of a product with increased absolute risk is a credit default swap[41] in which the amount to be paid by the buyer in case of default of the credit is higher than the value of the credit itself.

To measure the relative increase, a comparison between two levels of risk is necessary. On the one hand, there is the risk of the underlying claims defaulting, i.e. of the original debtors, the house buyers, students or other credit seekers, being unable to pay back the credit. On the other hand, there is the risk that the new financial product, designed out of these underlying claims, "defaults", i.e. that its value dramatically decreases, possibly diving down to a value of 0. An increase of relative risk then supposes that the default risk of the product is higher than the mean default risk of the underlying claims.

An example of the increase of relative risk is the equity tranche of a collateralized debt obligation.[42] Generally, the risk of devaluation of this tranche is higher than the average risk of the underlying pool of mortgage-backed claims or securities.

Details on the proof of the increase are given below.

The increase may be considered inappropriate, for example, if none of the parties hedges against a pre-existing risk (because the seller of the mentioned credit swap is not the holder of the original credit) or if the increase is particularly high or otherwise not justified by the circumstances or if adverse selection,[43] i.e. selection of bad components, is practiced in the creation of the product.

---

[41] A credit default swap (CDS) is a derivative under which one party commits to paying fixed premiums to the other party who, in turn, has to make a payment only in case a specified "credit event" takes place. This event may be the default of a credit loan, or the downgrading of an entity by rating agencies, for example. By this mechanism, the CDS functions as a sort of insurance to the seller who can pass on credit risks. Cf. Lynch, Derivatives: A Twenty-First Century Understanding, 43 Loyola University Chicago Law Journal 1 (2011), 22 under Fn. 81.

[42] A collateralized debt obligation (CDO) is a product of structured finance whose underlying mostly is a pool of claims, for example bank loans. These loans, after being pooled, are split up into different tranches which differ in terms of the priority of cash flows. The "senior" tranche, of presumably highest quality, receives payments of the debtors of the original claims with priority. The next payments go to the "mezzanine" tranche, while only the very last payments are awarded to the "equity" tranche. Since most of the "junk loans" fall into the equity tranche, the risk of devaluation of this tranche is higher than the average risk of devaluation of the whole pool of claims, i.e. the underlying. However, depending on the structure and composition of the other tranches, these tranches may also expose the investor to higher risk than the average risk of the pool. For more insight on the construction and risk structure of CDOs, cf. Duffie/Gârleanu, Risk and Valuation of Collateralized Debt Obligations, 57 Financial Analysts Journal, 2001, 41 f.

[43] For adverse selection in the construction of CDOs cf. equally Duffie/Gârleanu, Risk and Valuation of Collateralized Debt Obligations, 57 Financial Analysts Journal 41, 2001, 42.

(2) The "default risk" of the financial product has materialized in a sufficiently clear way. Depending on the type of the product, the realization of the risk can generally take three forms:
   (a) The inner value of a product is its "real", objective value, which may be approximated by the market value, but which is, especially in times of market bubbles, not congruent with the latter. If it can be determined – which it rarely can –, the risk is assumed to have realized itself once the inner value drops below a threshold that could be placed at 50 % of the issuing price. Thus, liability would commence at an absolute devaluation of 50 % measured from the issuing price.
   (b) If the inner value of the product cannot be determined with sufficient accuracy, but a market value of the product can, this market value can be used to measure whether the product has fallen below the threshold.
   (c) If neither an inner value nor a market value can be calculated, the realization of the risk will depend on a range of qualitative criteria. Among those are the repayment and default rate of the underlying claims, the general development of the market and as a first approximation the evaluation of the product by rating agencies.

On the one hand the threshold and the qualitative criteria prevent every minute oscillation of the market value from leading to a liability of the issuer; on the other hand they guarantee that liability is only triggered if there is a high probability that the underlying claims have been wrongly valued and the risk thus been increased instead of mitigated.

3.4.2.2 The general clause principle

Why should a general clause be apt to tackle the highlighted problems of risk awareness, and what justifies the margin of interpretative indetermination a general clause necessarily brings with it?

(1) Anticipation of avoidance strategies

Empirical research scrutinizing the interaction of market and law has found that legal provisions do not easily translate into the kind of market behavior aimed at by the regulation.[44] Direct influence on actions is difficult to achieve. Rather, a common reaction of market participants is not compliance, but the creation of avoidance strategies. Much thought is then being given to maneuver around new provisions in order to keep things running as they are. If this is to be taken seriously into account, one should not buy into the illusion that a new legal provision will be accepted by the market and its participants as an inevitable fact. This implies that if in spite of the complex, non-linear transmission of law into actual behavior, the regulation aims to exert influence on behavior of the agents, it has to anticipate avoidance strategies. This is exactly the role a general clause can play. Any regula-

[44] Black, Empirical Legal Studies in Financial Markets: What have we learned?, LSE Law, Society and Economy Working Papers 4/2010, 21ff.

tion striving to depart from specific types of products or clearly defined unlawful behavior would be doomed to be surpassed by the development of the markets on the day of its promulgation. The types and possibilities of combinations of financial products are too varied and unclassifiable to permit such an undertaking. The wide range of applicability of the liability provisions and the general condition of "inappropriate increase of risk" are conceived to counter this phenomenon.

(2) Necessity of concrete scrutiny

A general clause has the additional advantage of calling for a thorough analysis of each particular case as a counterweight against its wide scope and general terms. This would ensure that the law is not just being applied in a swift and carefree way, but that a detailed evaluation of the specific circumstances of the individual case, similar to the application of a "rule of reason" in common law, be observed. The role of reason could also be the legal mechanism translating a general clause into legal systems based on common law.

As shown in Chapter 1 of this book, even Anglo-Saxon law traditions have a mechanism, in their concept of prima-facie-tort liability, that operates with an applicability which in its broadness surpasses even a classical "continental" general clause.

3.4.2.3 Increase of risk and strict liability

The crucial condition triggering liability in the context of the general clause is the inappropriate increase of the risk of the financial product compared to risk of the underlying claims. The increased risk of the financial product adds, as experienced throughout the financial crisis, to the systemic risk of the economy, which in turn justifies liability of the issuer, as explained earlier.

Risk may be heightened in absolute terms, when the buyer due to the design of the financial instrument may lose more money on it than the value of the underlying claim or, in case of a multitude of claims, more money than the sum of the underlying claims proportionately contained in the instrument. If for example the claim is split up into 10 tranches, then each financial product deriving from it would contain one tenth of the value of the original claim. Furthermore, risk may be increased in relative terms if the probability of a loss of value of the product is higher than that of the claim or of the claims on average. Four points need to be discussed here on this difficult issue:

(1) Unnoticeable increase of risk

The increase of risk vis-à-vis the risk of the underlying claims is, as expounded above, the central justifying point of departure for a system of liability based on the idea of benefit from risk. In order to hold the issuer liable for a part of the realization of that risk, it is not even necessary that he was aware of the increase in risk at the time of the issuing, or that he at least ought to have been aware of it.

One could object to this by saying that what is impossible to detect cannot be sanctioned. However, the criterion for liability is not negligent behavior, in which case any liability would indeed have to be ruled out if the increase was undetectable, but the abstract phenomenon of dealing with possibly (financially) harmful products. Liability in this concept is just the flip side of being allowed to trade in these products and, by offering services in their issuing, to generate profit and to benefit from the general risk of such behavior. However, the risk has to have been increased relative to the risk of the underlying claims at the moment of the issue. If only circumstances after this benchmark lead to an elevation of default risk of the product, this risk cannot be attributed to the issuer since the deterioration of a product by arbitrary effects is part of the general risk of life, and not one inherent to the financial product. Also, the risk must have been increased by factors whose impact on the product is generally under the control of the issuer, such as the selection of the underlying claims or the specificity of the mechanism of bundling and tranching. Completely exogenous factors increasing risk may not lead to liability.

(2) Reversal of the burden of proof

Under normal circumstances, however, it will be fairly difficult for the damaged party to prove that the purchased financial product has in fact inappropriately increased the default risk since derivative securities generally have a tendency to distribute and thus decrease (especially relative) risk. An example is the bundling of mortgage-backed securities originating from a wide range of areas the mortgaged compounds come from. Information about the value and correlation of the underlying claims is usually available to the issuer, but not to the buyer. The latter will thus encounter much greater difficulty than the issuer in answering the question whether, for example, the concrete structure of a mezzanine tranche still has risk diminishing effects. This structural misallocation of information could in its interplay with the burden of proof residing usually on the damaged party seriously decrease its incentives to sue the issuer. This in turn would thwart the decentralized self-regulation described above.

The fact that liability is strict and that negligence needs not be proven does not help the plaintiff in his difficulties to prove an increase in risk, either. Therefore, much is to be said for a reversal of the burden of proof on that condition, parallel to such an inversion in traditional product liability concerning the deficiency of the product. Once the plaintiff proves that a risk has materialized in a specific way expounded below, it is incumbent on the defendant to prove that he has not inappropriately increased the risk of default. The application of general quality standards in the choice of the claims and the configuration of the product should, however, suffice to exonerate the defendant.

(3) The competence of the judges

This reversal of the burden of proof also helps the judge viewing the case to get the job done. After all, it may legitimately be asked how a judge who is not an expert in financial products should be able to assess whether risk has been inappropriately increased by the product. There are four possible counterarguments to this presumption:

First, a judge can take more time to view the case than both the issuer and the buyer may have taken. Although modern judges have a fair workload, they are not part of the (financial) economic world where time is money to a degree that everything ought to have been done yesterday. So an assessment of a judge may be more thorough than the time-pressured approach by the parties of the deal.

Second, judges are democratically entrusted to deal with basically all features of complex modern life, and economic affairs should by no means be exempted from that. Specialization of judges sitting in chambers of commerce also heightens economic competence. And wherever needed, the judge may take recourse to the help of expert opinions.

Third, the reversal of the burden of proof forces the issuer to divulge – if necessary in a non-public hearing – his basis of the construction of the product. This in turn provides the judge with the necessary information he needs to evaluate whether risk has been increased or not.

Finally, numbers and economic prowess will not have the last word. A qualitative, normative judgment is required to ascertain the inappropriateness of the increase. A judge will value whether reasonable security and quality standards have been observed in the construction of the product. This is, after all, very much the daily work of a civil judge.

As in all fields of law, it remains true that the functioning of the system of liability depends on the quality of the judiciary. If the most demanding criteria in this respect are not met in all countries at all times, this does, however, not speak against the implementation of the above described system of liability, or the rule of law as such. Rather, it calls for measures to enhance the quality of the formation of judges, primarily at the university level, and of their selection. Generally, however, especially in those Western countries which are and were rocked by the financial crises of past and present, judges seem well equipped to master the difficulties a general clause imposes on them. They are certainly more up to the job than any other body of a legally bound society.

(4) Strict liability vs. negligence

On an even more abstract level one could object to the general principle of strict liability devoid of any necessity for the plaintiff to prove negligent behavior on the defendant's side. The mere fact of an inappropriate increase of risk substitutes this otherwise rampant concept of "culpa", or fault. An argument could be that strict liability does not set any incentives to a rational issuer to enhance his product. His liability is independent of his observation of standards of behavior, which would in turn exclude negligence, because liability follows directly from objective events, such as the necessary passage of a threshold. Marginal costs for higher standards of behavior would always exceed the marginal profits of the escape from liability, since such profits do not exist due to the independence of liability from negligence.[45] Such an argumentation, however, does not apply to the cases considered here.

---

[45] Cf. Hellgardt, Kapitalmarktdeliktsrecht, 2008, 463, who deduces from this a liability for gross negligence only as a principle of capital market tort law; critically Köndgen, Die Ad hoc-Publizität als Prüfstein informationsrechlicher Prinzipien, in: Schweizer/Burkert/Gasser (eds.), FS für Druey, 2002, 791 – 809, who argues in favor of ordinary negligence.

First, the issuer may actually reap profit from a heightened level of behavioral standards by making them public and thus increasing the attractiveness of his product.

But second and more importantly, he will not strive to escape liability by fulfilling behavioral standards, but by preventing the conditions that trigger liability from materializing. This implies – on the side of risk realization – not to sell products at excessive prices, in order to minimize the probability of market values dropping below the threshold, and – on the side of increase of risk – to thoroughly select the underlying being introduced in complex derivatives. The issuer will prefer such claims whose value can best be granted, for example through the observation of qualitative, "prime" standards in the generation of the claims vis-à-vis the consumers. The positive selection of such claims by the agents of the financial sector itself, instead of government bodies or regulation agencies, matches exactly the approach chosen in this book focusing on self-control and decentralized enforcement of market discipline. This inherently auto-selective practice seems to be the only one to ensure an efficient control of the enormous amounts of different financial products. Any central state body overseeing financial products would be doomed to fail at the moment of its creation.

3.4.2.4 Realization of risk

As briefly mentioned above, the realization of risk will have to be measured differently with respect to the character of the sold product. The relevant risk, triggering liability, is that due to the configuration of the product, it may lose value drastically. Thus, it seems reasonable to measure the realization of risk by the concrete devaluation of the product. However, many of the complex products are very hard to evaluate[46] and in many cases, secondary markets on which these products would be sold at certain market values do not exist.

The basic idea for proof of the realization of risk is that certain thresholds, to be determined quantitatively or qualitatively, need to be exceeded. If a quantitative determination of value is possible, the risk is deemed to have materialized if the value has dropped below the threshold of half of the price the product has been sold at the moment of its issue. If such an evaluation should prove impossible, the analysis has to be based on qualitative criteria.

(1) Inner value

If the more or less exact inner, i.e. "real" and objective value of the financial product is indeed determinable, the following rule applies, as noted above: If the value has dropped under the threshold of 50 % of the price at issue, the risk has realized itself.

---

[46] Cf. Fender/Kiff, CDO rating methodology: Some thoughts on model risk and its implications, 1 Journal of Credit Risk, 2005, 37 – 58, who find that the mere categorization of the rating agencies can heavily depend upon the used mathematical model.

Three arguments justify this threshold approach:

(1) An objective threshold of liability conduces to the certainty of the fulfillment of the condition of risk realization and thereby creates incentives for the damaged party to defend its rights by private enforcement.
(2) On the other hand, the threshold protects the issuer from having to fear to be held liable for every devaluation of his product. Only a massive absolute devaluation by 50 % justifies liability to commence. Risk realization is the structural counterpart of the violation of a right or a protected legal object in the domain of traditional product liability. In transferring this feature to liability for financial damage, one has to make sure that its limiting function remains intact so as to prevent an over-deterring liability.
(3) The devaluation of 50 % is measured by comparison with the price of the product at the moment of the issue, i.e. the price on a primary, not secondary market. This is based on the assumption that the moment of the issue is the relevant moment for strict liability. At this moment the risk has had to be increased and at this moment, the product leaves the domain controlled by the issuer. He may have report and information duties after the issue, but they unleash their own sanctions in a regime of capital markets tort law. The strict liability, however, is deeply entwined with the benefit the issuer may reap. Therefore, in this context he can only be held responsible for the price at issue, not the further development of prices in the market.

(2) Market value

If the inner value of the product is not determinable, as might be the case with many of the financial devices, one can make use of the market value to prove the passing of the threshold. The market value may, as in general capital market tort law,[47] be understood as an approximation of the inner value. In case this model is chosen to calculate the concrete damage, too, this has consequences that will be shown later in the context of general aspects of damage regulation.

(3) Qualitative criteria

In a balanced perspective on the details of the case, the realization of risk has to be deduced from an array of qualitative criteria if neither an inner nor a market value can be determined. It is difficult to make general proposals for such criteria given the wide range of products considered. However, the repayment and default rate of the underlying claim, the general development of trade in the specific securities backed by the same collaterals and, if only with restrictions due to the unreliability of the categorizations, the evaluation of the products by the rating agencies can be pieces of circumstantial evidence for the realization of risk.

---

[47] Hellgardt, Kapitalmarktdeliktsrecht, 2008, 505 f.

3.2.4.5 Loss and ability to sue: limiting liability

The term of "loss" is key to the legal consequences of liability. It is the amount of money half of which the damaged party may claim from the issuer. The ability to sue is deeply interwoven with the question of loss, in the following way: Only that person is able to sue who holds the product in the moment in which all of the conditions for liability are fulfilled for the first time, i.e. when the threshold is passed. The relevant loss is in principle to be calculated by the difference of the actual price paid for the product by the holder able to sue, or the price at issue respectively, from the inner or market value of the product. If the latter values are not determinable, however, an alternative solution is to be enacted. These mechanisms shall be explained and justified in detail below. The restriction of liability to losses occurring below the price at issue and only once a threshold lying even further below has been passed needs to be especially argued for. The same holds true for the limitation of the ability to sue to the person holding the product at the moment of passage of the threshold.

As in cases of damage being passed on to the respective buyer of cartelized products in antitrust law, it would theoretically be imaginable that every former and future buyer of a product who suffers some sort of damage through purchase and sale of the product should be able to sue the issuer, once the value of the product has dropped below the threshold. This would, for example, yield claims to holders who sold the product in the far past if after a steep soar the value of the product was dropping, but still far away from the threshold and way above the price of issue. Also, holders buying the product after it dropped below the threshold but who still suffered financial damage would be able to sue the issuer. It should be clear that from a pragmatic perspective, such a model would generate a wave of liability that neither the issuer nor his insurance would be able to bear. This seems both unfair and practically unworkable. Thus, a limitation of the ability to sue as well as of the relevant losses to be claimed are inevitable, both for pragmatic and teleological reasons.

This limitation has to start with the objective of liability for complex financial products. If its aim is to urge the issuer to responsibly evaluate the risks of the products, two types of behavior can be reproached to the issuer: First, that he issued the product at all despite the lacking value of the underlying claims or despite an increase of risk in the derived product, or second, that he issued it at an excessive price. Until the moment of the issue, the fate of the product lies within the hands of the issuer, with respect both to its existence and to its price at issue being largely calculated on the basis of the information the issuer, who is in the best condition to do so, discloses. In dealing with his liability in civil law, this price at issue becomes therefore a decisive factor.

(1) Losses above the price at issue

Trade in the product on a secondary market is not the primary responsibility of the issuer as long as the value of the product does not drop below the price at issue. Of course, if the issuer receives information on his product after the issue, he may be liable in case of non-disclosure according to the general rules of capital market tort law. Strict liability, however, does not provide for this eventuality. Rather, it needs to be ruled out for any losses occurring above the price at issue since the justifying moment for the strict liability is the increase of risk *before* the issue. One may object that if the risk was increased at the moment of issue, it should not matter whether the risk materializes above or below the price at issue or a threshold. After all, it is still the same risk.

There is a truth to that. However, on a pragmatic level, this would generate a massive and potentially stifling wave of claims unbearable to the issuer. More importantly, however, it seems unfair if the issuer is facing more costly claims only because his product has once soared and fared well in the market. If the issuer fuelled this rise by erroneous information – he will be subject to capital market tort law. But if he didn't, it seems unjust to hold the one whose product had fared well, and then dropped a lot more, liable on a much greater scale than the one whose product lost value directly without a value spike. There is no ground to justify this, if the rise was independent of misleading influence of the issuer.

Thus, for reasons of pragmatic enforcement and "horizontal" justice among the issuers themselves, as well as a limited "zone of responsibility" of the issuer, holders incurring losses above the price at issue are not capable to sue the issuer, even if the value later on drops below the threshold. In the zone above the price of issue, they act on their own risk.

(2) Losses between the price at issue and the threshold

Once the value of the product drops below the price at issue, it enters the pre-legal margin of responsibility of the issuer. The question arises whether such holders suffering losses by selling in the zone between the price at issue and the threshold should be granted the ability to sue if the value drops below the threshold in the end. After all, at least that part of the loss lying below the price at issue forms part of the zone for which the issuer is responsible, according to the aim of the law.

However, pragmatic and structural arguments have to be forwarded against such an ability.

First, imagine that the value of the product, after the sale of the holder considered, starts to oscillate between the price at issue and the threshold (50 % of the price at issue), without passing any one of these, and ends up passing the threshold after many oscillations. Imagine further that the respective holders buy and sell the product near the local maxima and minima of the value. This implies a whole cascade of profits of those selling at the maxima and of losses of those selling at the minima. The scenario leads to redistribution of wealth through damages on the part of the losers and profits on the part of the winners without any social damage on aggregate. The profits are just the flipside of the losses. If one were to grant an ability to sue to all of the losers of the oscillatory movement who have made losses below the price at issue, the issuer would be faced with an avalanche of claims comprising to a great degree such individual losses which have not generated social losses and thus no systematic instability. This, however, runs contrary to the very motivation of the law, which is to foster systematic stability. These thoughts therefore speak against an ability to sue of the holders considered.

Second, it is impossible to select any of the holders of the scenario, such as the first one suffering damages, or the last or the middle one, and grant him and only him the ability to sue. This may alleviate the danger of a wave of claims against the issuer. But any selection of any single holder would be close to arbitrary, and the argument of lacking social damage would not be refuted.

(3) Losses at first passage of the threshold

Rather, he and only he is able to sue who holds the product at the moment of the first passage of the threshold.

This selection may seem arbitrary at first sight, too. Why just this one person? We will deal with the persons holding the product below the threshold in part d), and will find good reasons not to grant them the ability to sue.

But what about the person selling at a price that lies just one dollar above the threshold, and who has suffered millions in losses? He should be excluded?

First, a general rule allowing him to claim his losses would provoke scenarios such as the one described supra under (2). Furthermore, the person selling one dollar before passage is an extreme case: Every threshold generates such borderline cases. So does the instrument of the limitation of claims, which may restrict action to three years, and not three years and one day. These borderline cases do produce a margin of felt injustice, but are justified by the general necessity of the threshold as such. Its raison d'être stems from the pragmatically limitative effect, and the teleologically deduced zone of responsibility of the issuer.

Finally, the exclusive ability to sue by the person holding the product at the first moment of passage prevents the subsequent generation of a multitude of claims in case of a multiple passage of the threshold if the value oscillates around the threshold. Again, what seems arbitrary is an indispensable measure of protection of the issuer.

Why the first and not the last or the middle man who holds the product in a series of passages? Whereas only the first holder had bought the product before the final drop under the threshold, all the later ones should have been more intensely warned than the first holder that the product in question may sink dangerously towards the bottom. Therefore, the first holder is best fit to receive the ability to sue even in the extreme and rare case of an oscillation around the threshold.

(i) Calculating losses in a concrete manner

The question now arises how a concrete loss is to be calculated, half of which the issuer will have to bear. As a model, one can fall back upon strategies for the calculation of damage in case of violation of disclosure rules in the German general capital market tort law. The rules would only have to be slightly modified for the purposes here. Furthermore, a parallel can be drawn to the techniques for the determination of the passage of the threshold.

Compensation of damages in Germany is generally based on the principle of restitution in kind. In capital market tort law, this leads to two possible ways of compensation if, for example, an investor has paid too much for an investment or sold it at too low a price as a consequence of erroneous disclosure of the enterprise offering the investment: In principle, the damage consists of the difference between the price actually paid and the "real" price of the investment at the moment of the transaction that would have developed in the case of lawful behavior of the issuer.[48] As an exception to that rule, it is sometimes necessary to enact the tool of "restitution" in which the issuer has to take back the financial instrument while paying the investor the price actually paid.[49] This is of particular relevance in the situation of a market crash which makes the calculation of a real value impossible.

This model can be adapted and used for the calculation of the relevant loss in the system of strict liability. In a first approach, the loss of the holder is made up of the difference between the actual price paid for the financial product and the real, inner value of this product at the time of the purchase.

Upon closer scrutiny, minuend and subtrahend of this difference, however, prove to be terms in need of some revision. Regarding the minuend, since the issuer is not supposed to be held liable for losses occurring in the zone above the price at issue, this value represents an upper limit for the minuend, for any losses above it fall under the investment responsibility of each and every buyer. So if the actual price paid is higher than the price at issue, it is only the latter that will form the minuend of the difference. Parallels to this calculation method limiting the compensable damage again can be found in capital markets tort law. In general, the relevant differential damage of the investor, in the case of prospectus liability, is determined by the difference between the actual price paid and the real value, as stated. But scholars suggest that the upper limit must be the difference between the actual price paid and the hypothetical value of the product it would have if the erroneous information triggering liability was correct. The idea is not to hold the issuer liable for damages that occur independent of his misinformation and that must thus be ascribed to a bad investment decision of the damaged party. He has simply paid more than even the misinformation would suggest the investment would be worth.[50] The case of that part of the damage incurred above the price at issue is very similar. It has to be ascribed not to the issuer, but to the holder of the financial product who in this zone acts at his own risk. Any further responsibility of the issuer due to mis- or non-information falls under capital market tort law.

The corrective limit of the minuend also acts as an effective restriction of the strict liability as such and adds to a balanced structure of incentives.

There are alternative ways of determining the subtrahend of the difference, as discussed below.

---

48 Hellgardt, Kapitalmarktdeliktsrecht, 2008, 494.

49 Hellgardt, Kapitalmarktdeliktsrecht, 2008, 494 ff.

50 Zimmer/Cloppenburg, Haftung für falsche Information des Sekundärmarktes auch bei Kapitalanlagen des nicht geregelten Kapitalmarktes? ZHR 171 (2007), 519 – 542; agreeing Hellgardt, Kapitalmarktdeliktsrecht, 2008, 508.

(ii) Facilitating the loss calculation: market value and restitution

An alternative mode of compensation needs to be provided to the creditor of the claim in case the determination of the subtrahend, the inner value, proves to be mathematically impossible or at least economically unjustified. The method employed in this case derives from a parallel to restitution in capital market tort law.

To this end, the right to alter the legal relationship with the issuer is to be granted to the creditor. This right enables him to freely choose any moment after the passage of the threshold as relevant for liability. The loss can then be calculated as the difference between the actual price paid and the market value, if it exists, at the moment of the exercise of the right, i.e. at the time the issuer receives the declaration. If the trade in the concerned product has been suspended, the market value would be zero.

Unfortunately, this gives rise to a subsequent problem: The holder could choose to bear, i.e. to speculate on a temporary slump. For if he exercises his right at the local minimum of the market value but continues to hold the financial product, he would claim a loss that possibly has materialized in his balance sheets, but had never been converted into an actual loss. This would run counter to the principle of damage law which forbids the enrichment of the damaged party by means of damage law. This problem does not arise in the case of the calculation of the loss according to the inner value, since there, the real value of the financial product is to be brought into play. This in turn means that the holder did suffer an actual damage at the moment of the transaction. This cannot be contrary to the prohibition of enrichment. There is only need for a correction in the case of the exercise of the right to calculate loss by the market value.

Here, the parallel to restitution emerges. At the moment of the exercise of the right by the holder, the issuer has to take back the product from the buyer. This prevents the holder from benefitting from a rise in market value after having exercised his right and thus gained a claim of half of the losses which have never actually materialized. The issuer therefore is granted a right to claim the assignment of the product, from the holder onto him. If the issuer takes back the product, he does not only have to pay half of the losses of the holder. He also has to pay a certain sum to the holder in exchange for the assignment of the product. Contrary to capital market tort law, however, the issuer does not have to pay the full amount of the actual price paid to the holder, but, in addition to half of the losses, has to pay the market value at the time of the exercise of the right of the holder. The payment of the latter amount, which can be claimed by the holder following the exercise of his right, is necessary to prevent the issuer from making a bargain by receiving the product for less than its market value (by paying, for example, only half of the loss calculated by the difference between the price at issue and the market value).

The creditor of the claim of strict liability can thus decide whether he would prefer to calculate the loss using the inner value and keep the product, or exercise his right and receive, in addition to half of the losses, the market value in exchange for handing the product back to the issuer.

(iii) Qualitative criteria and restitution

The last scenario to be dealt with in this context is one in which neither an inner nor a market value can be determined. Since the calculation of loss is bound to fail in the absence of quantitative approximations of value, only the mechanism of restitution provides a feasible option. The price the issuer has to pay for taking back the products should lie between half and 75 % of the price at issue and strive to equally distribute the loss between the parties according to the qualitative criteria that have been applied to prove the realization of risk. If the parties cannot agree on a price, it has to be determined by estimation of the court.

(4) Losses of subsequent holders below the threshold

Finally, the losses of those holders who buy the product at a price below the threshold are considered. One could now argue that these would have to be granted a fortiori a claim against the issuer since the risk of the financial product has further materialized by yet another decline of its value. This scenario is usually only relevant if the holder passing the threshold chooses the calculation of the inner value, for otherwise, the product would return to the issuer via restitution. If the loss is calculated in this concrete manner, the issuer, however, will already have been held liable for the total difference between the actual price paid and the inner value. Any further liability based on the same difference would be unjustified and unreasonable. The protection of the issuer has priority over the above mentioned a fortiori-inferment since the aim of the strict liability lies in the preventive shaping of behavior and less in a sanction or compensation a posteriori for damage inflicted owing to the trade in financial products. This is why also in the presumably rare case of the issuer reselling the product after restitution and the buyer suffering damage, liability needs to be declined. Whoever buys a financial product that has already suffered the whole process of restitution and has not been improved thereafter cannot legitimately trust in the quality of the product. The information that the product has already been restituted must be provided by the seller, in default of which he will be liable under the terms of *culpa in contrahendo* or general capital market tort law as a result of the violation of disclosure obligations. This information given to the potential buyer, by the way, adds to the improbability of a constellation of further resale.

3.4.3 Limits to liability

Approaches based on incentives must not only lead to a, potentially lop-sided, tightening of liability rules, but also need to be taken into account in connection with the necessary restraints of this liability. These are crucial to prevent over-deterrence on the side of the issuers and to strike a balance between liability for risk and freedom of innovation. Considering the potentially massive costs of liability to the issuers, effective precautions need to be taken so that the system of liability does not end up as a mechanism stifling financial innovation. This subject is the focus of the paragraphs 3.4.3.1 and 3.4.3.2.

3.4.3.1 An upper limit to the amount of liability

The maximum amount of liability is limited by the narrow definition of relevant losses and, in close connection to that, the ability to sue. Imagining devaluation down to a value of 0, the issuer would in case of concrete damage calculation have to bear no more than 50 % of the price at issue. If the path of restitution is chosen, a maximum of 75 % of the price at issue would have to be paid by the issuer who in return would become owner of the product. Granted, this may amount to a heavy financial burden for the issuer, which will be dealt with below. Generally, however, this sets a strong incentive for preventing such liability through responsible product development.[51] Moreover, it is not unlikely that ownership of the products in this case proves to be profitable in the long run: Market values tend to drop below the inner values of the products once much trust in their value has been lost and mark-to-market accounting has led to deleveraging by the selling of further securities. This may lead to actual benefits of the issuers from the take-over of the products if the markets later rise again and draw closer to the inner value of the products, in a phenomenon very much parallel to the buy-out of toxic, but undervalued, securities by the governments at the time of the subprime financial crisis.[52] The incentive structure, however, is not undermined by these possible profit options in the far future, since in times of limited liquidity the imminent payment obligations weigh much heavier.

However, an absolute limit of the total amount of liability for one issued product may be worth for considering. This would prevent claims from rising so high that, especially in times of crises and scarce liquidity resources, their fulfillment would be rendered highly unlikely. Another positive side effect of such an absolute maximum is that this makes the risk of liability much more calculable and thus insurable.

3.4.3.2 Limits to the time of relevant losses

(1) Relative to threshold passage

In order to promote foreseeability and legal pacification, it appears sensible to exclude those originally relevant losses from the loss calculation which have not occurred within a certain time frame before the passage of the threshold. The aim of the system, to limit risk a priori rather than to compensate losses a posteriori, also speaks in favor of a short limitation period.

The period of one year, calculated backwards from the moment of the passage of the threshold, may be a convenient choice here as it equals the usual accounting time frame. Thus, if the value of the paper had already dropped below the price at issue over one year before the passage of the actual threshold and has not risen above the price at issue since, then the subtrahend for the calculation of losses must

---

[51] Hellgardt, Kapitalmarktdeliktsrecht, 2008, 510.

[52] The hope would be that an ensuing rise in the value of the products will reimburse part of the investments the governments have made, cf. Schwarcz, Understanding the Subprime Financial Crisis, 60 South Carolina LR 549 (2009), 557.

not be the price at issue, but rather the market value one year before the threshold passage.

(2) Absolute limitation

In times of unclear market development, it will further legal security to introduce an absolute limitation period of two years from the time of the issuing. This, again, adds to the insurability of the products. Depending on the nature of the backed risk, however, longer periods may be appropriate, as mortgages, for instance, run longer than two years.

3.4.4 Distribution of risk

Insurability has come up twice as an argument above. Every system of strict liability is bound to spur the generation of a system that insures against such liability. This is not to argue for an interference with the autonomous self-regulation of the sector for the moment, as long as it functions in such a way that issuers cannot simply pass on all liability to the insurance companies. This would run counter to the incentives set by the whole project, but is a rather unlikely scenario given the market and negotiation power of the insurance companies. But a few remarks may be useful as to the distribution of risk once insurance companies come into play because the efficiency of this distribution is the raison d'être of the entire initiative.

The crisis has shown just how far the financial reality had drifted away from its theoretical background: Not pension funds, that calculate in the long run and are able to absorb market fluctuations to greater degrees, or other apt entities were holding risky securities, as the theory of risk passage we examined above would have it, but financial investors looking for short term profits and thus exhibiting a fairly low tolerance to loss.[53] This entailed that the realization of risk could not be countered by long term investment strategies, as in the model. Rather, the immediate reaction was a massive sale of toxic securities leading to a further loss of value at the very moment when it would have been crucial to prevent risk from materializing and being dragged onto the markets. Obviously, risk had not ended up in the right hands, economically speaking.

The system of liability expounded tries to reverse this trend. A good deal of the losses stays with the investors, which is necessary to keep risk awareness up. But another part may, via the issuers, be ultimately passed on to private insurance companies. One would expect them to be better equipped to digest turbulent markets and losses than hedge funds calculating on a short term basis. A part of the risk thus returns into safer hands.

[53] Compare Schwarcz, Protecting Financial Markets – Lessons from the Subprime Mortgage Meltdown, 93 Minn. L. Rev. 373 (2008), 391, Fn. 88.

3.5 Summarizing conclusions

A regime introducing financial product liability as a form of strict liability is a completely new frontier. Not every detail has been fully developed yet. The main ideas, however, can now be outlined as they rest on two basic premises:

(1) Whoever benefits from a risk should be held liable for at least part of the damage when things go wrong and the risk materializes. Internalization of profits paralleling externalization of costs is inacceptable.
(2) Research in behavioral economics points to the need for a revision of the rational homo economicus model. Especially in heated markets investors are prone to discard relevant information and to over-optimistic decisions, blindly following other investors who take the lead. Therefore, a reform tackling the roots of the crisis needs to set the incentives of the issuers straight and prevent toxic securities from even being designed and thrown onto the market. A liability system for issuers would do just that.

Two conditions have to be met for liability derived from these two premises to be set off at all: First, the product under consideration must at the time of its issue have inappropriately increased the default risk of the product compared to the underlying claims. Second, a quantitative or qualitative threshold of devaluation must have been passed by the product. Once these criteria are met, strict liability, independent of any charges of negligence, sets in.

Furthermore, if the threshold is proven to have passed, the burden of proof as to the inappropriate risk increase is reversed. Judges should be in a good position to decide those cases, with recourse to expert opinions where necessary.

The ability to sue shall only be conferred upon him who holds the deficient financial product at the very moment of its passage over the relevant threshold. He may choose between a concrete and an approximating way of loss calculation by means of a restitution regime.

3.5.1 General consequences for the buyer

The effects of the regime on the buyer's side may be outlined as follows: The holder having the ability to sue has to bear half of the relevant losses himself. If he chooses a facilitated method of loss calculation, he does not have to prove his concrete losses, but he also loses the possibility to reap profits from a later rise of the value of the product by having to hand it back to the issuer. The issuer in this case, in addition to half of the losses, has to pay the market value for the product. By these procedures, the function to set incentives for risk awareness on the buyer side is upheld just as the possibility to pass risks on in an economically efficient way. The investing parties have to bear at least half of the risk they have taken.

3.5.2 The general clause

The need of a general clause arises from the infinite variety of constellations the rule has to apply to, and is thus immanent to a system of liability itself, if it does not want to be outdated at the very moment of its promulgation. Due to the inherent indetermination of the general clause, the standards an issuer has to fulfill in order to escape liability are less foreseeable than in cases of clear cut rules. However, it lies still within the faculties of the issuer to create risk minimizing products if he wants to be sure to be liability-exempt.

3.5.3 Strict liability of the issuer

The issuer is strictly liable, i.e. regardless of any negligent behavior, for the other half of the relevant losses or is obliged to take back the product against a due fee in case of loss calculation by the market value as well as restitution. Just as in classic product liability, the deficient product is therefore being returned to the "producer" who then has to bear the consequences of the market development of his creation. This follows from a just distribution of liability based on the principle that benefit from risk entails liability if things go awry. On the other hand, it sets strong incentives for the issuer to thoroughly weigh risks in the creation of the product.

3.5.4 Lessons from and for the crisis

Only history may show whether policy makers and economists have learned the right lessons from the consequences of the financial and economic crises of the last years. The system of liability here expounded does, of course, not pretend to prevent such crises by itself. But it can make an effective contribution to this objective. It joins the efforts to restructure the financial sector and the economy as such in a fairer way. An amalgamation of economic incentives for a conscious, responsible risk management on the one hand and for a decentralized sanction by a facilitated private enforcement on the other closes gaps the financial crisis has brought to the fore. And by putting losses back into the hands of those who set risks, it pursues the path of a FairEconomy which adheres to the principles of free yet risk-conscious economic action. In accordance with its original meaning, this crisis may prove to be not only an uncontrollable catastrophe, but also a stimulating opportunity: for good decisions.

4 Sanctions and Procedure

4.1 The normative framework

In the fifties and sixties of the last century, a remark made the rounds in the American business world: "If you are in business, you are wrong". The quip indicated a general discontent at the time with U.S. economic policy and law, in particular, antitrust, not so much as to the letter of the law but all the more how it was administered. This was the climate in which Robert H. Bork's "Antitrust Paradox" emerged,[1] along with the Chicago School time-indifferent (but in reality: short term) efficiency understood as consumer welfare. Chicago School time-indifference also favored deregulation without equilibration by stricter antitrust (since deregulated public utilities will almost immediately be reregulated by private restraints of competition). The same time indifference caused crisis proclivity of "bubble" economies characterized by eating tomorrow's bread.

In the first line, Bork's critique was not directed at antitrust as such but against what he thought to be wrong antitrust implementation. According to Bork, in antitrust short-term welfare-economic goals prevail. As long as big business is able to provide for consumer welfare better than medium and small businesses, big business should be aided to follow its welfare economics goals, while medium and small businesses may be disfavored even at the price of monopolization and Robinson-Patman Act types of discriminations. At this point, Bork notices antitrust's "war against itself". Weighting antitrust's policy goals against one another, Robert Bork prefers welfare economic positions and thus joins, in this publication (not in all of his later works), the main tenets of the Chicago School of economics: Antitrust sanctions should favor consumer welfare ideals rather than an abstract ideal of competition.[2] Should antitrust sanction market power and its abuse or violations of welfare goals? Could either one of them be called unfair?

In this context, therefore, it is time to ask for appropriate sanctions of offenses against FairEconomy, the latter understood as a combination of a crisis-safe and possibly paradox-free combination of antitrust and the safe-guarding of competitive fairness. Can FairEconomy do better than the antitrust provisions of the sixties, seventies and eighties of the twentieth century, better than Robert Bork and the Chicago School?

The purpose of Chapter 4 is not to present a full picture of possible legal sanctions of violations of FairEconomy. Rather, the aim is to discuss the general trend in which direction consequences of violations of the rules of FairEconomy in different

---

1 Bork, The Antitrust Paradox: A Policy at War with Itself, 1978 (2nd edition 1993).

2 See, on the Bork and Chicago School debate, Greaves (ed.), Competition Law, Burlington, 2003: Ashgate's International Library of Essays in Law and Legal Theory Series, vol. 14 No. 1 (2004), and the review by Schultz, http://www.bsos.umd.edu/gvpt/lpbr(subpages/reviews/greaves104.htm (visited 24 October 2011).

kinds of economies in this globalized economic world might go and, inversely, which consequences might prove counterproductive. The discussion is not one *de lege lata*. Describing the actual legal situation is not the task to be performed here. Rather, those sanctions that might be in line with the concept of FairEconomy, as developed before, are to be discussed *de lege ferenda*, by way of proposals. Here, completeness of recommendations cannot be sought, nor guaranteed. Trying to give advice is one matter, pointing to possible outcomes when such advice is followed or rejected is another. The latter is more ambiguous than the former – and certainly more perilous.

4.1.1 International Treaties

National law and the law of regional conventions and unions with corporate personality such as the European Union are subject to the law of global international treaties. Two main instruments of concern for the control by such treaties are the Paris Convention for the Protection of Industrial Property of 1883 (Paris Convention) and the Agreement on Trade-related Aspects of Intellectual Property Rights (TRIPS) of 1994. The Paris Convention has 173 member states, the WTO/TRIPS Agreement 148. Art. 2 TRIPS refers to Art. 10bis and 10ter Paris Convention and binds TRIPS members and their citizens to the law of Paris Convention. Art. 10bis and Art. 10ter Paris Convention say: By adhering to the Paris Convention, member states are subject to its rules. This covers the national laws of France (1884), Great Britain (1884), U.S.A (1901) and Germany (1907), to name just a few. The norms of the Paris Convention include Art. 10bis and 10ter. Art. 2 (1) TRIPs reconfirms this validity of obligations in favor of, and against, the members of TRIPS. Art. 41 ff. TRIPS give details of how the rights flowing from intellectual property including from Art.10bis and Art. 10ter Paris Convention combined with Art 2 TRIPS regarding the inhibition of unfair competition are to be implemented. Furthermore, Art 2 III a) Directive 2004/48EG repeats the validity of the foregoing norms providing for the protection of fair competition for EU members and their nationals. Since the EU is a member of Paris Convention and TRIPS, the direct effect of EU norms for and against all nationals, natural or corporate, of EU member states applies as well. The EU's changing treaty history running from the "Rome" European Economic Treaty (EEC), ratified in 1958, the Single European Act (SEA, 1986), the Maastricht Treaty on the European Union (TEU of 1994), the Amsterdam Treaty on the relations among the Treaty's three supranational institutions – the Commission of the European Communities, the European Court of Justice, and the European Parliament – and between these actors and the Intergovernmental Council of Ministers (Amsterdam Treaty of 1999) to the Lisbon Treaty on the Functioning of the European Union (TFEU)[3] did not change this direct applicability.

[3] Of December 13, 2007, OJ of 9 May 2008 (115/47).

To illustrate the foregoing, few excerpts from the texts may be quoted:

Art. 10*bis* Paris Convention (concerning unfair competition)

(1) The countries of the Union are bound to assure to nationals of such countries effective protection against unfair competition.

(2) Any act of competition contrary to honest practices in industrial or commercial matters constitutes an act of unfair competition.

(3) The following in particular shall be prohibited:

(i) all acts of such a nature as to create confusion by any means whatever with the establishment, the goods, or the industrial or commercial activities, of a competitor;

(ii) false allegations in the course of trade of such a nature as to discredit the establishment, the goods, or the industrial or commercial activities, of a competitor;

(iii) indications or allegations the use of which in the course of trade is liable to mislead the public as to the nature, the manufacturing process, the characteristics, the suitability for their purpose, or the quantity, of the goods.

Art. 10*ter* Paris Convention (concerning trademarks, trade names, false indications, unfair competition: remedies, ability to sue)

(1) The countries of the Union undertake to assure to nationals of the other countries of the Union appropriate legal remedies effectively to repress all the acts referred to in Articles 9, 10, and 10*bis*.

(2) They undertake, further, to provide measures to permit federations and associations representing interested industrialists, producers, or merchants, provided that the existence of such federations and associations is not contrary to the laws of their countries, to take action in the courts or before the administrative authorities, with a view to the repression of the acts referred to in Articles 9, 10, and 10bis, in so far as the law of the country in which protection is claimed allows such action by federations and associations of that country.

Art. 2 and Art. 41 (1), (2) phrase 1 **TRIPS Agreement** read:

Art. 2 (concerning intellectual property conventions)

1. In respect of Parts II, III and IV of this Agreement, Members shall comply with Articles 1 through 12, and Art. 19, of the Paris Convention (1967).
2. Nothing in Parts I to IV of this Agreement shall derogate from existing obligations that Members may have to each other under the Paris Convention, the Berne Convention, the Rome Convention and the Treaty on Intellectual Property in Respect of Integrated Circuits.

Art. 41 (concerning effective action)

1. Members shall ensure that enforcement procedures as specified in this Part are available under their law so as to permit effective action against any act of infringement of intellectual property rights covered by this Agreement,

including expeditious remedies to prevent infringements and remedies which constitute a deterrent to further infringements. These procedures shall be applied in such manner as to avoid the creation of barriers to legitimate trade and to provide for safeguards against their abuse.

2. Procedures concerning the enforcement of intellectual property rights shall be fair and equitable. […].

4.1.2 Self-executing general clauses. Direct application

As to sanctions, the conventions of intellectual property protection are "self-executing" in the sense that their most important sections establish individual rights and duties between the citizens and firms of their member states regardless of their national origin.[4] From the structure of the Paris Convention in relation to TRIPs there follows the embodiment of the protection of free and fair competition – also in the sense of FairCompetition – in Paris Convention and TRIPS Agreement and thus in valid law. Art. 41 ff. TRIPS regulate details of the direct applicability. For TRIPS members, such as U.S.A. and U.K., and their nationals therefore self-executingness as such of relevant treaty obligations is no longer an issue, as far as Art. 41 ff. TRIPS go (their scope, however, may be an issue).

For many a legal system, this may mean a polite – whether subtle or considerable – correction of home-grown law by international standards. For example, Germany never legislatively accepted injunctive relief or damages in unfair competition cases to be claimed by individual plaintiffs. Consequently, when the EU Directive 2005/29/EC on business to consumer ("B2C") unfair practices providing for individual consumer claims against "traders" was transformed into German law, little prior preparatory theoretical work had been done so that the analysis of the new law today remains difficult. Modern Anglo-American common law has always been slow to develop a workable legal concept of "unfairness" in competition law. Doctrine thus played down the international legal duty contained in Art. 10bis Paris Convention and Art. 2 (1) TRIPs to introduce an unfair competition law.[5] Therefore, British competition lawmakers are now confronted with brushing up older stories told by Justices Bowen and Holmes as well as by Professors Prosser and Oppenheim to cope with one of the true "general clauses" of the common law, the

---

4 For details see Fikentscher, Was bedeutet "self-executing"? Überlegungen zur Rechtsnatur des GATT im Blick auf einen GATT-Immaterialgüterschutz, in: FS für E. Steindorff, 1990, 1185 – 1192, with references, also concerning the common-law adage "the international law is the law of the land"; the issue of self-executingness of the conventions of intellectual property protection is a matter of debate, see, e.g., Baumbach, Kommentar zum Wettbewerbsrecht, 1st edn. 1929, 539 – 550. Baumbach's view is representative of the older stricter theory of the non, or at best limited, self-executing nature of the conventions. Art. 2 (1) and (2) TRIPS correctly acknowledges the difference between rights and duties in general – including citizens and firms – on the one hand and among the member states on the other. See also Fikentscher, Führt der Weg zu einem Wettbewerbsrecht der Welthandelsorganisation –WTO – über Souveränitätseinbußen?, FS für A. Shoda zum 70. Geburtstag, 1999, 468 – 477.

5 See supra, Subchapter 2.4.2.

prima facie tort theory of liability, and its intricacies of burden of proof.[6] However, the recent U.S. suit against Goldman Sachs for damages is a practical example of a civil claim.[7] An equally recent German Federal High Court case stating the liability of a foreign broker as joint actor in an options and trading in futures scheme is a German example of a successful suit for damages, based on the general clause of § 826 Civil Code (violation of good mores).[8]

Lawyers from common law countries like to make the point that common law does not recognize general clauses in the meaning this term has in the law of the civil code countries.[9] However, Anglo-American common law abounds in general clauses in the sense of Continental civil law. Examples include contributory negligence, comparative negligence, reasonable care, rule of reason (a concept used in the English common law of monopoly control since 1624, in U.S. antitrust law since

---

6 On prima facie tort theory of liability see supra, 1.4.5. A stern refusal by legal experts from the common law tradition to deal with "unfair competition" in WIPO and the ensuing blocking effect of this resistance is part of the history of the discussions in the WIPO Standing Committee on the Law of Trademarks towards the end of the years 1990s. No WIPO committee seems to have dared raise this issue ever since (until August 2010), and there seem to be no plans for that, with the exception of a small scale study in the International Committee of WIPO. Therefore, Henning-Bodewig calls the present state of affairs "the unsolved problem of the general clauses and the definition of (un)fairness". Henning-Bodewig, Nationale Eigenständigkeit und europäische Vorgaben im Lauterkeitsrecht, GRUR Int 2010, 549 – 563, 561 f. Since around 1960, prima-facie-tort liability as an early theme in common law unfair competition theory seems to have been lost in the depths of legal history; cf., e.g. Gerber's criticism of the unfairness concept, Gerber, Anthropology, History, and the "More Economic Approach" in European Competition Law, IIC 2010, 441 – 449. Gerber thinks holding unfair competition as legally unjust to be demodé, and the proposition of scientific value judgments in law (that is, philosophically, Kant's synthetic a priori of practical reason) to be a donquichotery. A thorough analysis of this "hegemonial" claim of Angloamerican socio-economical-legal culture vis-à-vis Continental European traditions of private autonomy and free and fair competition – helpful as comparative-civilizational background to the present study of an international culture of Fair-Economy – is provided by Stürner, Privatautonomie und Wettbewerb unter der Hegemonie der angloamerikanischen Rechtskultur?, AcP 210 (2010) 105 n- 155; in a similar vein (slightly less legal-politically, but more anthropologically accentuated) Fikentscher, Staat vs. Government – eine Beobachtung zum Thema Kulturpersönlichkeit – , in: Ziemske et al. (eds), FS für M., Kriele, 1997, 1407 – 1416; idem, Ein juristisches Jahrhundert, Rechtshistorisches Journal 19,2000, 560 – 567.

7 Media of 16 April 2010, for example Google news <Goldman Sachs 4-16-10>: Goldman Sachs Group Inc. was sued by U.S. regulators [SEC] for fraud tied to collateralized debt obligations that contributed to the worst financial crisis since the Great Depression [Commentator Mr. Adams is quoted saying:] "There haven't been many investor lawsuits on these kinds of deals. [...] This opens the door to civil claims across a number of transactions.[...]" – A survey on sanctions in other EU member states: De Cristofaro, Die zivilrechtlichen Folgen des Verstoßes gegen das Verbot unlauterer Geschäftspraktiken: eine vergleichende Analyse der Lösungen der EU-Mitgliedstaaten, GRUR-Int 2010, 1 – 18. See also note 339, below.

8 BGH XI ZR 93/09 of 9 March 2010, Der Betrieb 2010, 894 –- 898 – foreign options broker; the case is interesting also because of its jurisdictional aspects.

9 For material see, Henning-Bodewig, Nationale Eigenständigkeit und europäische Vorgaben im Lauterkeitsrecht, GRUR Int 2010, 549.

1911, in the Allied Occupation (Control Council) law of the post-war years 1945 – 1955, and in the largely identical (West) German antitrust law of 1955 - 1958), reasonable man, due care, due diligence, full faith and credit, fair trade (in U.S. laws, both federal and state), less than fair value (LTFV, a concept in U.S. international trade law), fairness in the sense of the Class Action Fairness Act of 2005, 28 U.S.C.A. 1712(d), due risk assessment, privity of contract, the *Palsgraf* doctrine of negligence as an act covering a limited territory or extent,[10] prima facie tort theory of liability, due process, estoppel, clean hands, strict interpretation, legitimate trade,[11] give and take of life, and others. Art. 41 (2) TRIPS requires member states to enact legislation that provides for "fair" and "just" procedures of implementing the rights granted under the Paris Convention of 1883 and the TRIPS Agreement of 1994 aiming at the protection of intellectual property and fair competition.[12] It would be incongruous to agree, in international treaty law, to a legislative duty to enact *fair* laws to inhibit a behavior that may not be called what in the eyes of the rest of the world is the opposite, *unfair*.

4.1.3 Possible sanctions

Following the line of thought developed above under 2., possible sanctions related to admissible forms of property and other sanctions include the following:

4.1.3.1 Protection of property under EU law

Pursuant to Art. 345 TFEU, the EU has limited jurisdiction in matters of property laws of member states. Art 345 TFEU says that this "Treaty shall in no way prejudice the rules in Member states governing the system of property ownership". However, research conducted over the last decades shows that neither the scope of application nor the exact meaning of Art. 345 TFEU (ex-Art. 295 EC, formerly Art 222 EEC) is clear from its wording.[13] Akkermans and Raemakers state: "Most importantly, the Article does not concern the content of the right of ownership, nor the objects of a right of ownership. It does therefore not form an obstacle to the development of a European property law".[14] A European property law, as unitary law, so Akkermans and Raemekers, may be created in addition to property laws of the Member states; so that, as far as Community law admits, European Member states possess the definitorial power of what under *their* legal systems may be understood by "property." Akkermans' and Raemakers' line of reasoning is fol-

---

[10] Palsgraf v. Long Island Railroad Co., 248 N.Y. 339 (1928); through B.N. Cardozo, Ch.J.; Andrews, J, dissenting.

[11] Art. 41 (1) phrase 2 TRIPS Agreement

[12] See supra, Subchapter 1.

[13] Akkermans & Raemakers, Article 345 TFEU (ex Article 295 EC), Its Meanings and Interpretations, http://unimaas.academia.edu/BramAkkermans/Papers/169797/Article_345_TFEU_ex (visited 27 January 2011): Article 345 TFEU relates only to ownership from which the Community is barred to concern itself with.

[14] Akkermans & Raemekers (Fn. 13).

lowed here because it convincingly follows from the plain wording of the provisions mentioned above in this paragraph.

Property need not be tangible. Usufruct and other servitudes are intangibles, as are intellectual property rights. The property rights under national law – in the sense of the civil property law that includes the law of movables and immovables – follow a *numerus clausus*, that is, a limitation of admissible types. The reason for this *numerus clausus* is the opposability of property rights against third persons. If A and B could by mutual agreement invent a new type of property right opposable against everybody in the world, they would be able to stifle the ordinary exchange of goods between persons as the gist of economy at will.

Among the many ideas how to construct safeguards against a repetition of the crises of 2006 – 2010 there is the proposal to limit the number of admissible types of negotiable instruments, at least of high-risk nature, and tradable like a chattel. This suggestion is reminiscent of the former § 764 German Civil Code, repealed in 2002 as a step towards market liberalization, to use a provision of German law for illustration.[15] Before the year 2002, this section did illegalize the contractually binding force of a "difference deal" by reference to the legal treatment of a game and of a bet. Under law still in force a game and a bet are not straightforwardly prohibited (§ 762 German Civil Code). Yet, these two types of contract are stripped of legal enforceability. Doctrine calls this – somehow confusingly – a "natural obligation" which means that the loser may not reclaim once he has paid, for instance for unjust enrichment.

Instead of abolishing § 764, the legislator could have raised the degree of unlawfulness of a "difference deal" or at least some high-risk types of it to invalidity. For example, applied to the experiences of the aforementioned crises, both the European and the national legislators could permit low-risk papers and exclude high-risk ones from the number of admitted papers, in line with the principles of risk and liability, as discussed in Chapter 3 above. EU legislature and national parliaments could decide this, either independently or even better in a joint effort, in order to settle on similar standards of low and high risks. Absent international agreements, out-of-EU trade in high-risk papers would remain possible, but a discouragement to engage in the issuance and trading of high-risk "products" would work as a warning and could enhance general trust. Under EU law and its consumer-friendly attitude this reduction of high-risk instruments could be dressed in the form of consumer legislation.

The restriction of tradable typically high-risk negotiable instruments could be based on contract law. Within the EU, this would require harmonization (of EU

[15] § 764 phrase 1 German Civil Code reads: "A contract that is directed at a delivery of a merchandize or negotiable instrument with the intent that the difference between the agreed price and the bourse or market price at the time of delivery shall be paid by the loosing partner to the winning partner, will be regarded as a game". A game in the sense of the German Civil Code does not create an obligation, § 762 (1) phrase 1 German Civil Code (still in force). But what has been paid on the basis of a game cannot be reclaimed on the ground that the nature of the deal was a game, § 762 (1) phrase 2 German Civil Code (also still in force).

type) because such regulation would affect the market of more than one EU member. However, since these instruments are traded like chattels, and since the member states own the definitorial power of what under *their* legal systems may be understood by property, also under the civil law of chattel dealing every member state has the jurisdiction of limiting the issuance of and the dealing in high-risk papers of that sort. Then, the underlying legal policy would not primarily concern market issues, but the *numerus clausus* of property, assignable to persons, in the general sense as discussed already. The advantage of this approach would be that one member state of the EU (possibly less exposed to lobbyism than others) or a number of like-minded member states, could take the initiative.

4.2 Sanctions under contracts and torts law, including rules of equity

More conspicuous are sanctions derived from the laws of contracts and torts. Torts have civil and criminal sides. In common law countries, sanctions may be taken from law proper or consist in equitable relief. The field is broad, and from the legal cultures underlying the many systems of law in the world's countries numerous kinds of sanctions covering a great variety of relief may be deducted. Only general remarks can be presented here, and they may be categorized fourfold: the basic idea of compensation of damages inflicted upon another (4.); the condensation of such relief in a type of tort known in every legal system of the globe (5.); and the more refined division of such relief in torts, contract, and criminal law (6.). However, the question who may sue for a violation of FairEconomy touches the theoretical foundations of democracy. Whether a single plaintiff is entitled to question the wisdom of public administration or not and so potentially leave correction to agents allegedly acting in the public interest bears upon the build-up of the *Rechtsstaat* and a question of participation and rule of law (7). One consequence of this concerns public law interventions into private law creations such as corporations (8.). Another is the question whether class actions are a way out of the democratic dilemma (9.).

4.2.1 The universal meaning of prima facie tort theory of liability

It may be a principle of law in all legal systems of the world that damage done to another should be repaired. Art. 1382 French Civil Code of 1804 expresses this legal principle with the following words: "Tout fait quelconque de l'homme qui a causé à autrui un dommage, oblige par la faute duquel il est arrivé à le réparer." This article became the model for many legal systems of the Roman legal family of law.[16] The same principle is enunicated by the prima facie tort theory of liability of Anglo-American common law. In this context, Justice Oliver W. Holmes, Jr., and Professor Prosser have been quoted before.[17] German law starts from the same general premise. When law-makers began to draft the German civil code in 1874, only

[16] Zweigert/ Kötz, Einführung in die Rechtsvergleichung auf dem Gebiete des Privatrechts, 3rd ed. 1996, 73-129.

[17] Cf. supra 1.4.5 and 4.1.2.

certain parts drawn from the French model were accepted. Issues of burden of proof and other difficulties had become apparent in French case law experience since 1804, especially as to the concepts of illegality and personal blame.[18]

Following the distinction between objective illegality and reproachable blame discovered by Rudolf von Ihering in his studies of *culpa*,[19] German torts law treats the objective breach of the law differently from the personal blame to be attached to that breach. Both have to be present, of course, otherwise no tort would exist. But having to allege and in case of contestation having to prove the breach of the law and having to allege and in case of contestation having to prove the personal blame are not the same. The first, the breach of the objective law, is easier to be established for the plaintiff in court than the second, personal blame. The tool for making allegation and proof easier for the plaintiff to establish is a list, included in the wording of § 823 (1) German Civil Code, the central tort norm, of certain particularly valuable goods. Whenever the tortfeasor violates such a good, illegality (but not *culpa*) is rebuttably presumed. This means, the tortfeasor may offer an excuse by claiming a right to inflict the damage, e.g. acting in self-defense. But alleging and proving such an excuse is his burden. The list of goods includes life, body, health, liberty to leave a place, property and "other rights" (scil., of absolutely protected nature, such as intellectual property rights and the right to one's family name[20]).

French code law neither enumerates specially protected values nor differentiates burdens of proof of tortfeasor and victim with the result that, in theory and by verbal interpretation of Art. 1382 CC, damage done to others for instance in ordinary course of competitive business or in labor disputes, would have to be fully compensated. *Faute* – the Roman law *culpa* – includes both, the illegal breach of law that binds everyone, and the reproach against a certain person that there is blame involved.

Anglo-American law of torts, starting from the same ideas as the French conceptions of *neminem laedere* and *faute* (the latter either intentional or negligent), resorts to the prima facie tort theory of liability. Yet, there remains the task of avoiding the undesirable result of having to compensate damages caused in the ordinary course of business or labor relations. According to Holmes, Prosser and their followers, this result is reached by granting a privilege to inflict damage upon the competitor, and master or servant respectively, if acting in ordinary course of business or labor, in what Art. 41 (1) phrase 2 calls in the English version "legitimate trade", in German "*rechtmäßiger Handel*" and in Art 10bis Paris Convention "honest practices in industrial commercial matters", that is, in what in most legal

---

[18] Ferid, Das französische Zivilrecht, Band 1, Allgemeine Lehren, Recht der Schuldverhältnisse, 1971; Fikentscher/Heinemann, Schuldrecht, 10th ed. 2006, § 101.

[19] See v. Ihering, Das Schuldmoment im römischen Recht, 1867.

[20] Judge-made law adds two "frame rights" (*Rahmenrechte*), the right to one's enterprise and the right of privacy, for which the shift of burden of allegation and proof from plaintiff to defendant does not apply.

systems of the world would be called free and fair competition and market relations.

Therefore, damage done *in violation of* the rules of free and fair competition is damage in the categories of prima facie tort theory of liability, a principle to be conceived of as a legal universal. The damage has to be repaired, or not repaired, according to the outcome of the prima facie test. This is no Anglo-American "hegemony" in Stürner's sense.[21] Rather as valid law in most legal systems it takes the shape of a general clause, including Anglo-American common law and its daughter laws. It is, therefore, of global importance.[22]

4.2.2 Breach of statutory duty – the tort action of avail

The principle upon which prima facie tort liability and Art. 1382 French CC are founded is a valid *principle* of law of the kind Justice Benjamin Cardozo has discussed in his "Nature of the Judicial Process."[23] As such it is valid law and may be refined to more concrete rules of law.[24] This process of concretization may lead to various types of torts, including innominate ones.[25]

When it comes to violations of the rules governing free and fair competition the tort action that is closest at hand is the tort of breach of statutory duty.[26] Statutes in this sense are, for example, statutes prohibiting trade boycotts, dumping, or the sale of stolen goods.

Two others – also rather general ones – out of the number of statutes that may be referred to in the context of legal protection of free and fair competition are:

---

[21] Stürner, Privatautonomie und Wettbewerb unter der Hegemonie der angloamerikanischen Rechtskultur?, AcP 210 (2010) 105.

[22] To its full extent (that is, including consumers' rights to sue for injunction or damages, see the remarks on private abilities to sue in Ch. 3 above) it is according to dominant opinion not part of German unfair competition law outside the impact of EU law, but it should of course be *de lege ferenda*.

[23] Cardozo, The Nature of the Judicial Process, 1921. On the influence of Cardozo on Continental theory of law, see for example Esser, Grundsatz und Norm in der richterlichen Fortbildung des Privatrechts, 1956 (3rd ed. 1974); Fikentscher (Fn. 41), Vol. 2, 1975, 240-254.

[24] A discussion: Fikentscher, Methoden, (Fn. 41), 241 ff., 251 f.

[25] Cf. supra 1.4.5.

[26] Often regarded as a subcategory of the tort of negligence *per se*; see, for example, Osborne v. McMasters, 40 Minn. 103 (1899); Evers v. Davis, Court of Errors and Appeals, New Jersey, 86 N.J.L. 196 (1914) where Garrisin states that for this tort the plaintiff "be one of the class for whose protection it was enacted and the breach of such statute was the cause of the injury..."; Racine v. Morris, New York Court of Appeals, 201 N.Y. 240 (1911); Denton v. Missouri, Supreme Court of Kansas, 90 Kansas 51 (1913); Schell v. DuBois, Supreme Court of Ohio, 94 Ohio St. 93 (1916); Ross v. Hartman, 78 App. D.C. 217 (1943); from the literature, cf. Winfield/Jolowicz on Torts, 18th ed. 2010, 265 – 267 with references. – The German counterpart of negligence per se committed by breach of statutory duty and causal for plaintiff's harm is § 823 (2) German Civil Code, the intentious or negligent violation of a protective law (*Schutzgesetz*); for this, see also Ch. 1, above, Fn. 27.

a. in the realm of *free* competition rules, the Restrictive Business Practices Code, created by the United Nations General Assembly of 1980 with the help of UNCTAD. The RBP Code is a global "soft" law which as such has no binding force in the UN member states. Still, it can be interpreted as a "statute" in the sense of the tort of breach of statutory duty under national law.[27] Here valid torts law is applicable in all UN member states for the protection of free and fair competition, with an accent on antitrust issues (which in Asian UN member states often are called "fair trade" issues).
b. in the precinct of *fair* competition rules, Art. 10bis and 10ter Paris Convention in their character as valid national law ("law of the land" or otherwise transformed into national law under the nationally different transformation rules).[28] In Asian (and other) national legal systems that use "fair competition" to cover both antitrust and unfair trade practices offenses, the protection granted under Art. 10bis and ter Paris Convention to individual plaintiffs relates to both free and fair competition.

In a contemporary interpretation, Art. 10bis and ter Paris Convention in the sense of the Asian (and other) "fair competition" legislations, and also in correct interpretation of the term "distortion" in Art. 101 TFEU, Art. 10bis and 10ter would also cover antitrust. A traditionalist reading of international competition law would deny this. Art. 10bis and 10ter were introduced into the uniform law of the Paris Convention in 1909. In 1909, the U.S. Sherman Act of 1890 was too young and, for another example, the German Reichstag enquete hearings of 1903-1905 in preparation of a law controlling restraints of competition were too little advanced to expressly or by interpretation add antitrust to the scope of the Paris Convention agenda. A few years later, World War I interrupted any progress. But even without this updated interpretation of the Paris Convention, the interpretation of the United Nations Restrictive Business Practices (RBP-) Code of 1980 that contains norms in the meaning of the tort of breach of statutory duty under national tort law, valid national tort law rules for the protection of fair competition are available.[29] A clarification of the interpretation of Art. 10bis and 10ter Paris Convention in an agreement among the member states (perhaps merely plurilateral and thus comparable to the DIAC) is desirable but not necessary to make these provisions directly applicable.

---

[27] For details, especially on the character of directives as protective rules, see Fikentscher/Straub, Der RBP-Kodex der Vereinten Nationen: Weltkartellrichtlinien, GRUR Int 1982, 637 – 646, and 727 – 739; Fikentscher, United Nations Codes of Conduct: New Paths in International Law, 30 American Journal of Comparative Law, 1982, 577 – 604.

[28] On the „self-executing" and "direct effect" characters of Art. 10bis and ter Paris Convention, see part 4.1.2 above.

[29] Fikentscher/Straub, Der RBP-Kodex der Vereinten Nationen: Weltkartellrichtlinien, GRUR Int. 1982, 637 – 646 und 727 – 739. – The debate of whether fair competition law includes antitrust, or whether antitrust includes rules against unfair competition concerns a legal-systematic aspect that is not identical with the subject matter of norm extension as discussed in the text above.

4.2.3 Torts, contracts, and criminal law (and equity)

As shown above, the point of gravity in the field of sanctions against violations of rules protecting free and fair competition is on torts law (and equity).[30] It grants damages (of various kinds), restitutions, injunctions such as cease and desist orders, orders on keeping a case pending to allow for consideration of future developments, among others.

Contract law becomes applicable once violations of rules to protect free and fair competition lead to invalidity of contracts, or to compulsory contracting.[31] For the validity of contracts with banks, for instance, it is of importance that the bank is obliged to apply a fair risk assessment in view of itself and in relation to its clients.[32]

Criminal law may be relevant, too. Both antitrust and unfair practices laws of UN and Paris Convention members' legal systems provide for criminal sanctions.[33]

4.2.4 Recent developments in democratic theory and politics and their impact on private litigation in legal-economic affairs

The question who may sue for a violation of FairEconomy principles touches upon the theoretical foundations of democracy. The issue of the role and the standing of the individual within a democratically organized group of people have accompanied the theory of democracy since its earliest times.[34] The gist of democracy is thus not that 51% wins and 49% loses but the attention to the role and protection of

---

[30] A survey: Hellgardt, Kapitalmarktdeliktsrecht, 2008; for surveys on the English background in equity (not in law) and its influence on the present mechanism of antitrust enforcement – including consent decrees – see Oppenheim, Cases in Federal Antitrust Laws, Trade Regulation, 1948, 826 – 961. In European law the Court of Justice has considerably strengthened private enforcement by obliging the Member States to provide for effective remedies, cf. ECJ, 20.09.2009, Case C-453/99 – *Courage*; ECJ, 13.07.2004, Case C-295/04 – *Manfredi*. The details, however, are matters of national law, cf. ECJ, 14.06. 2011, Case C-360/09 – *Pfleiderer*.

[31] For example: Hellgardt, Kapitalmarktsdeliktsrecht, 2008, 340 ff; De Cristofaro, Die zivilrechtlichen Folgen des Verstoßes gegen das Verbot unlauterer Geschäftspraktiken: eine vergleichende Analyse der Lösungen der EU-Mitgliedstaaten, GRUR Int 2010, 1; Nipperdey, Kontrahierungszwang und diktierter Vertrag, 1920; Busche, Privatautonomie und Kontrahierungszwang, 1999.

[32] See Chapter 3, above.

[33] See Hellgardt, Kapitalmarktdeliktsrecht, 2008, 71 ff., 77, 177, 415; Schünemann, Bavarian Academy of Sciences, Report (forthcoming).

[34] For example in Thukydides' renditions of Pericles' orations to the Athenian citizens, Thukydides, Historiae 2 vols.; revised by J.E. Powell, etc., 1900; comments by Fikentscher, Oikos and Polis und die Moral der Bienen, FS Arthur Kaufmann, 1993, 71 – 80; and idem, Law and Anthropology, 2009, 368, at note 845; Fiske, The Beginning of New-England or the Puritane Theocracy in its Relation to Civil and Religious Liberty, 1898, reprinted 1930; Fiske relates the roots of the discrepancy between direct and representative democracy to the different organizations of the (in modern terms) Congregational and the Presbyterian churches.

the minority, the "opposition", which one day may become the majority.[35] It is a frequent misunderstanding of democracy that the numerically strongest nation, tribe, clan or other group of the population exercises dictatorial power over numerical minorities, families or single persons. However, the understanding of the minority as an essential constituent of democracy hinges upon the conception of a unit that embraces majority and minority.

The technical term for such a unit is superaddition (in German: *Übersumme*), meaning that majority and minority need to be considered as a whole that, expressed in numbers, is one more than the addition of the members of majority plus minority. Studies in cultural and historical anthropology show that an internalization of that consideration is rarely to be found throughout cultures.[36] Without the internalization of that unit and its inside and outside requirements democracy is not conceivable. Consequently, under the conditions to be found in many countries, the single person has a rare chance to claim its rights. This is the main reason why here attention is paid to the single, politically unaided plaintiff who desires to be respected as a partner of a free and fair economy.

Another problematic development in recent dealings with democratic institutions is lobbyism. On the one hand lobbies are welcome or even needed because bodies and institutions often lack the detailed knowledge necessary for making decisions. On the other hand, lobbies open a gate for taking substantive influence being exerted upon the decisions to be made and thus disturb a desirable impartiality in preparing a decision. Any single citizen who is confronted with alliances of parliaments and experts who are interested in specific results may be in a poor position. Even worse are situations where governments steer and abuse science to disguise political decisions as scientific achievements.

These and other malformations of democracy are conceivable and need to be heeded. The theory of the separation of powers, usually attributed to legislature, administration, and judiciary, should not overlook the single person as the fourth pillar because the three others might fail. However, the single citizen tends to be helpless if not equipped by the law. When it comes to FairEconomy, a field where lobby-informed legislature, an ambitious administration and a misinformed (if not corrupt) judicature may join forces to form a cartel against the underprivileged, the

[35] Waldron, Democracy and Conflict, in: El Fadl, Islam and the Challenge of Democracy, ed. by Cohen and Chasman, 2004, 55 – 58; Fikentscher, Demokratie – eine Einführung, 1993; idem, Law and Anthropology, 2009, Chap. 9, on the principle of superaddition.

[36] Examples may be limited to the Ancient Greek polis (600 – 350 B.C.E.), the synagogue of the exile (550(?) B.C.E.) and thereafter, the pledge-of-faith system establishing the confederation of the Franks (*Franconia*, 250 – 1806 A.D.), the League of Iroquois (1.300 – 1.400 A.D.?) , the Tewa speaking Pueblos (after the neolithic revolution, 3.000 B.C.E.?), and maybe the Otoe Indians; for details see Fikentscher, Law and Anthropology, Chap. 9. The only Slavic nation inside and outside of the EU with a superadditive tradition are the Slowenians (today members of the EU) who received the Frankish pledge-of-faith system, imposed by or borrowed from the Franks via the Bavarians, before 743 A.D. The EU itself follows the Frankish model.

unswerving plaintiff and the independent imaginative lawyer ought to be able to look out for justice.[37]

4.2.5 Public law interventions aiming at preventing, mitigating and curing crises into private law creations such as corporations and contracts

The main goal of the present study is to define the position of the private citizen, undertaking or consumer involved in economic activities vis-a-vis those who violate her or his economic engagement by disregarding rules of free and fair competition. Therefore, public law interventions into creations of private law such as corporations are not of prime interest here. However, a short view may be permitted.

Of course, such interventions may considerably support an individual's market position by forbidding and abolishing discriminatory arrangements, by permitting mergers or ordering corporate divestitures or dissolutions, or by regulating corporate behavior. But these are legal matters less fit for private litigation. Reference may thus be made to this field of investigation, without going into details here.[38]

Public law interventions in private law are frequently contained in proposals how to prevent future financial and economic crises similar to the present one. For example, a bill drafted in the U.S. Senate on May, 21 2010, upon suggestion of U.S. President Barack Obama, and presently pending in the House of Representatives, provides for a public law prohibition of highly speculative business transactions, deconcentration of banks which are "too big to fail", a new consumer protection agency in charge of inhibiting the issuance of bank products likely to become "toxic papers", and the control of CEO bonuses. Another example of the numerous proposals is the idea by EU Commissioner Michel Barnier to establish an EU fund for

[37] Some recent cases of this sort have enjoyed considerable publicity. In the European Court of Justice (ECJ) at Luxemburg, a Suebian bee-keeper won a case in which the safety distances around fields with gene-manipulated crops were decisive. The bee-keeper's evidence proved that his bees fly farther than experts of corporations specializing in producing and selling gene-manipulated plants had alleged, Karl Heinz Bablok and others v. Freistaat Bayern, ECJ of Sept. 6, 2011 – C442/09, BeckRS 2011, 81290 – bee-keeper –The decision may influence international trade with gene-manipulated products. – In the decisions Football Association Premier League Ltd. v. QC Leisure, David Richardson and others, and Karen Murphy v. Media Protection Services Ltd., ECJ of Oct. 4, 2011 – C 403/08, C – 429/08, C – 429/08, BeckRS 2011, 81423 – football games –, the plaintiff, Mrs. Murphy, owner of a restaurant, won her antrust case against football commercializing firms. She was permitted to show her guests premier league games by use of decoders acquired in third countries in violation of territorial exclusive arrangements of the football games rights holders. The presentation of the games on television was for her more favorable than it had been under those arrangements. For other David v. Goliath cases see, e.g., Weinstein, Recent Decisions from the European Court of Human Rights, http://www.asil.org/insight45.cfm, visited 30 October 2011.

[38] On "industrial policy" French style Fikentscher, Recht und wirtschaftliche Freiheit, Vol. 2, Transnationales Marktrecht, 1993, IX – XIX.

the devolution of bankrupt banks, to be pre-financed by the banking sector. The Bank for International Settlements (BIS) in Basel/Switzerland, convened a commission on a new international regulatory framework for banks ("Basel III" in September 2010). The goal was a proposed revision of the Basel Accords on financial regulation. The Basel III regulations include an increase of common equity (banks must hold 4.5% by January 2015, from then on a further 2.5%, totaling 7%); the introduction of a leverage ratio (risk weighing, to begin with 3%); countercyclical capital buffers; measures to limit counterparty credit risk; and improved short and medium-term liquidity ratios.[39] A proposal for public law intervention into private law submitted by the side of private business is the introduction of a safety standards authority ("MOT"; in German "TÜV") for bank papers to be issued. Among others, the German entrepreneur Michael Otto floated this idea.[40] A problem of these and other regulative attempts to cure and prevent crises is transborder trade affecting more than one national legal system.

Issues of this kind arose when the Draft International Antitrust Code of 1993 was prepared for GATT/WTO by the Munich Group's members at the time. Safeguarding national legal sovereignty in view of cross-national needs of public economic policy then called and still calls for a balanced approach.[41]

---

[39] E.g., Report: Strengere Regeln in der Schublade, iwd No. 49 of 9 December 2010; critical surveys: Cassidy, The Basel III Proposals' Flaws, 175 American Banker, 5/13/2010, Issue 74, 8, 1/2p; Milleker/Sauerschell, Ein Korsett für alle Finanzakteure, Financial Times Deutschland of 4 September 2010. The „Brussels Summit" of 16 October 2011 raised common equity to 9%.

[40] Theodor-Heuss-Stiftung (ed.), Soziale Marktwirtschaft in der Globalisierung, 2010, 38.

[41] Cf. Art. 19 (2) DIAC and related literature on DIAC: International Antitrust Working Group, Draft International Antitrust Code – as a GATT/WTO – Plurilateral Agreement, Munich/Germany (mimeogr.) 10 July 1993: Max-Planck-Institut für Gewerblichen Rechtsschutz und Urheberrecht (Wolfgang Fikentscher, Josef Drexl, Eleanor M. Fox, Andreas Fuchs, Andreas Heinemann, Ulrich Immenga, Hans Peter Kunz-Hallstein, Ernst-Ulrich Petersmann, Walther R. Schluep, Stanislaw J. Soltisinski and Lawrence A. Sullivan); eight reprints and translations: (Monograph) Special Supplement, The Bureau of National Affairs, Antitrust and Trade Regulation report, Vol. 64 No. 1628, August 19, 1993, Washington, D.C., 20037; in: World Trade Materials Vol. 5 No. 5 (Sept. 1993), 126 – 196; and in the following journals and publications: Jurist (Japanese law journal) No. 1036 of Dec. 15, 1993, translation by Shoda and Shibata; WuW 1994, 128 – 139 (without comments); 49 Aussenwirtschaft – Schweizerische Zeitschrift für internationale Wirtschaftsbeziehungen, Heft II/III, 1994, 310 – 325 (without comments); Fikentscher & Immenga, Draft International Antitrust Code. Kommentierter Entwurf eines internationalen Wettbewerbsrechts mit ergänzenden Beiträgen, 1995, 53 – 110; Fikentscher & Kuhn, Internationales Kartellrecht und Lauterkeitsrecht: Dokumente, Entwürfe und Abkommen, International Antitrust and Unfair Trade Law: Documents, Drafts and Agreements 1990-1996, Max-Planck-Institut für ausländischen und internationales Patent-, Urheber- und Wettbewerbsrecht, 1996, 212 – 299; Multilaterale Regeln für den internationalen Wettbewerb? in: Kantzenbach & Mayer (eds.), Von der internationalen Handels- zur Wettbewerbsordnung, 1996, 159 – 170 (with a draft of an international agreement on competition as plurilateral GATT/MTO Trade Agreement, 171 – 219.

4.2.6 Single or class actions. Blocking laws. Ordre public

Regarding the situations addressed in this book individual law suits can be expected to be the rule. Recent consumer legislation has attempted to pave the way to court for disappointed customers.[42] Collective damage actions may help as well.[43] Nation states need to be aware of unfriendly blocking laws and may be advised to seek the assistance of WTO.[44] In private litigation, the application of public policy (*ordre public*) rules of written or customary law may be helpful.[45]

4.3 Summary

The Chapters above start from the observation that one of the major characteristics in today's economic-political world is the desire to turn to rule-of-law conforming individual participation in daily political and economic life. The sanctions discussed in Chapter 4 focus on that aspect. Private litigation in economic matters exists in the EU and in some of its member states, albeit to a somewhat limited degree. It has been stated that younger antitrust and unfair trade practices systems tend to prefer an administrative approach instead of private claims to be raised by individuals, and that it depends on the social and economic culture whether a legislator may take the one or the other approach. The authors of this book assume the EU legal system to have become one of the more mature laws, no longer in need of being almost exclusively guided by administrative input and activities. More

---

42 On Directive 2005/29/EC see 2.3.2 and 4.1.2 above; De Cristofaro, Die zivilrechtlichen Folgen des Verstoßes gegen das Verbot unlauterer Geschäftspraktiken: eine vergleichende Analyse der Lösungen der EU-Mitgliedstaaten, GRUR Int 2010, 1; see also the case BGH XI ZR 93/09 of 9 March 2010, Der Betrieb 2010, 894 – 898 and LG Berlin, 12 O 587/09 of 17 February 2011, BKR 2011, 254 – Kapitalanlagevermittlungsvertrag –; BGH, XI ZR 33/10 of 22 March 2011, to be published in BGHZ and BGHR – Swap Aufklärungspflicht –. On legislative plans see Federal Ministry of Justice, http://www.bmj.bund.de/media/archive/1056.pdf.

43 Cf. Ebbing, Class Action – Die Gruppenklage: Ein Vorbild für das deutsche Recht? 103 ZvglR-Wiss 31 – 56 (1994); Mattil & Dessoutter, Die europäische Sammelklage, 12 WM 521 – 525 (2008); Parker, EU Considers Consumer Class Action, Financial Times of 4 March 2007; http://europeansclassactions.eu;/"THE; Beisner & Borden, On the Road to Litigation Abuse: The Continuing Export of U.S. Class Action and Antitrust Law, U.S. Chamber Institute for Legal Reform, October 2006; Halfmeier, Trippelschritte auf dem Weg zum kollektiven Rechtsschutz: Der Referentenentwurf zur Entfristung des KapMuG, ZIP 2011, 1900.

44 Blocking laws are laws that attempt at frustrating or at least neutralizing transborder effects of trade regulation such as antitrust, fair trade, tariff or capital market laws. Cf. Harris, American Bar Association, Section of Antitrust Law, Competition Laws Outside the United States, Chicago 2001, Overview-99; McNew, Blocking Laws and Secrecy Provisions: Do International Negotiations Concerning Insider Trading Provide a Solution to Conflicts in Discovery Rules?, 26 Cal. W.L. Rev. 103 (1989/90).

45 A circumspect and comparative introduction: Regen, Prozessbetrug als Anerkennungshindernis: Ein Beitrag zur Konkretisierung des ordre-public-Vorbehaltes, 2008; on public policy resp ordre public, e.g., see Kegel, Internationales Privatrecht, 6th edition 1987, 323 – 337; Zweigert & Kötz, Einführung in die Rechtsvergleichung auf dem Gebiete des Privatrechts, 3rd ed. 1996, 374 – 382; Fikentscher (Fn. 1), Chapter 13 (for examples from legal-ethnological practice).

important than an EU "Economic Government" as intended by some European protagonists - and having one day become reality in one form or the other as its most important constituent - EU conforming national legal systems that establish and improve the rights and standings of private plaintiffs are what is needed next. They are in demand because they serve to heal, prevent and cure economic crises, by providing for the establishment, maintenance, protection, and if need be as-if-imposition of free and fair competitive market relations. FairEconomy might contribute the required contents.

5 Conclusion: the Concept of FairEconomy

After the real estate, banking, currency, credit, and general business crises of the years 2006 to 2011, the global economy needs a new legal framework. With this book, we suggest principles for the design of such a new framework that we call "FairEconomy". The free market remains at the core of our concept. Yet, we see a need to tame the self-destructive powers of freedom – the freedom to abolish freedom (called the freedom paradox) –, to re-establish fairness as a fundamental pillar of a market economy, and to reconcile freedom and liability. For the enforcement of the rules that we propose we rely on individual claims and civil courts rather than on new bureaucracies (indispensable as they may be as public controllers of private misbehavior and as clearing houses of public policies).

Rules for a general framework of the economy need to take account of the purpose of the economy. This is an anthropological issue. Engaging in economic activities is not an end in itself, but serves the fundamental need to allay human hunger. Once this need is taken care of, the economy caters to our further wants. Since there is usually a scarcity of resources the exercise of human freedom leads to rivalry and competition. This is the basic concept of a free market. The framework we propose aims at governing this rivalry. Unrestrained rivalry would lead to a collapse of the whole system by calling for the powers of monopolies (again, the freedom paradox).

The rivalry in free markets does not work if certain prerequisites are not in place and guaranteed. In particular, the market economy needs a functioning legal system, free communication, and trust into the general legitimacy of the economic activities of other market participants. To grant these prerequisites and to impede the self-destruction of freedom is the task of the organized society, in our culture: the state, and in a globalized business world the international community of free states. In a democracy, and under the rule of law, it is society that defines economics, not vice versa. A driving insight of the FairEconomy is that free and state-planned economy are not the true opposites. True opposites are the legally organized sustainable freedom on the one hand and private or state constraints on the other hand.

The rules for rivalry in the marketplace have become deficient in three regards and we propose principles to overcome these deficits:

Many rules do no longer fit today's organization of the economy. The finance- and technology-driven world of business today has little in common with the economy of the early 20th century. Yet, many rules are modeled according to the ideas of how business was done in those days. Our first set of suggestions aims at transferring the basic ideas of competition law into our time. The idea of competition laws – including antitrust and rules of fairness – is to enable everyone to engage in a rivalry for economic success on the merits of their contribution. The limits of what markets can achieve will be expressed by an optimum curve drawn from property rights and freedom of trading them, and from a new theory of market elasticity (instead of a neoclassical approach to so-called market failures).

Today's rules lack a central normative element. It was a mistake to believe that a free-market economy can be stripped of all values and be turned into a culture-blind money-machine. Our second set of proposals introduces the standard of fairness (as in fair competition) as a yardstick for transactions. The standard we develop is aligned with the governing principle of markets, competition. This principle is universally accepted in the market economy. Looking at its normative elements – autonomous decision-making, performance on the merits, taking risks with liability – provides for guidance how to deal with transactions in financial markets. The system we have in mind calls upon the judges to rule on the fairness of complex transactions since more specific laws and supervisory authorities will fail to get to grips with fast-moving financial markets. Lawyers in common law jurisdictions dislike concepts such as "fair competition". Still, judge-made prima-facie-tort liability has been introduced as "innominate torts" instead and works very similarly compared to the fairness standards developed in other, for instance civil code, countries. As a substantial standard for fairness one may rely on the communal standards that ensure competition on the merits. Over-complexity or inducement to harm third parties may be relevant examples.

The rules currently in place partly ignore the twin sister of freedom: responsibility. While the benefits of engaging in economic activities, particularly in finance, were kept private, costs were often externalized. Our third set of proposals restores the relationship of freedom and liability, instead of allowing some to take risks at the expense of others. This inspires a system of financial product liability in which the issuer of, for example, a complex security would be held liable for part of the damage this product causes to a buyer if in the creation of the product the former has inappropriately increased risk. Under certain conditions, the issuer can no more walk away with the profits independent of the fate of his product.

Regarding the enforcement of rules, there is a tendency at present to call for new authorities with wider ranging powers to prevent another crisis. But there is little justification in pinning hopes on ever-new bureaucracies. Our approach differs. We favor a system that relies on individual claims to be dealt with by judges and courts of civil jurisdiction. A judiciary, bound by the submissions of private parties involved, is best-equipped to deal with new cases. This requires, however, to foster the economic understanding of judges and to grant fast and easy access to a politically independent court system.

FairEconomy is a concept for a free and fair market economy that is rule-oriented, aware of the freedom paradox, attentive to what a market can achieve and what not, availing itself of the initiatives of private parties, their associations, ombudsmen, judges, amici curiae, attorneys, non-governmental organizations and other caretakers of primarily private interests. FairEconomy is a concept for a law-based governance of markets: If rules guarantee freedom and innovation, fairness and responsibility, markets will unfold their magic in performing their task: enabling humans to meet their needs.

Index

MIX
Papier aus verantwortungsvollen Quellen
Paper from responsible sources
FSC® C105338

If you have any concerns about our products,
you can contact us on
ProductSafety@springernature.com

In case Publisher is established outside the EU,
the EU authorized representative is:
Springer Nature Customer Service Center GmbH
Europaplatz 3, 69115 Heidelberg, Germany

Printed by Libri Plureos GmbH
in Hamburg, Germany